Cultural Values and Entrepreneurship

Cultural Values and Entrepreneurship aims to broaden and deepen our understanding of which elements of 'culture' influence, or are influenced by, entrepreneurial activity. Differences in entrepreneurial activity among countries, and regions within those countries, are persistent and cannot be fully explained by institutional and economic variables. A substantial number of these differences have been attributed to culture, and it is clear that some socio-cultural practices, values and norms are more conducive to driving or inhibiting entrepreneurial intentions and activity. However, we need to dig deeper into 'how' and 'why' cultural practices and underlying values and norms matter in entrepreneurial action, in order to more fully understand the complexities of the processes, without making cross-cultural or cross-national generalizations. Unique cultural, national, and institutional contexts present different practices in terms of opportunities and challenges for driving entrepreneurial action. The contributions to this book consider some of the many different facets of the culture-entrepreneurship relationship, and offer valuable insights to our understanding of the field.

This book was originally published as a special issue of the *Journal of Entrepreneurship & Regional Development.*

Francisco Liñán is an Associate Professor at the University of Seville, Spain. He has several publications in the areas of entrepreneurial culture, cognitive entrepreneurship, entrepreneurial intentions and entrepreneurship education. He is Head of the Masters in Entrepreneurship Development, and has participated in projects funded by the Spanish national government, the EU, and the OECD.

Ghulam Nabi is a Senior Lecturer at Manchester Metropolitan University, UK. He has publications in the areas of entrepreneurial intentions, student-to-entrepreneur transition, graduate entrepreneurship, entrepreneurship education and entrepreneurial culture. He has been guest editor for Special Issues of several journals, and has led projects funded by the UK NCGE, UFHRD and IGEN.

Norris Krueger has a wide range of consulting and high tech entrepreneurial experience and is very active in all the major entrepreneurship academic organizations. He sits on the Executive Committee of the Academy of Management's Entrepreneurship Division. His work has ranged from public policy analysis to cutting-edge research to designing entrepreneurial education and training programs that have won multiple national best practice awards.

Cultural Values and Entrepreneurship

Edited by
Francisco Liñán, Ghulam Nabi and
Norris Krueger

Routledge
Taylor & Francis Group

LONDON AND NEW YORK

First published 2016
by Routledge
2 Park Square, Milton Park, Abingdon, Oxon, OX14 4RN, UK

and by Routledge
711 Third Avenue, New York, NY 10017, USA

Routledge is an imprint of the Taylor & Francis Group, an informa business

British Library Cataloguing in Publication Data
A catalogue record for this book is available from the British Library

ISBN 13: 978-1-138-93930-1

Typeset in Times New Roman
by RefineCatch Limited, Bungay, Suffolk

Publisher's Note
The publisher accepts responsibility for any inconsistencies that may have
arisen during the conversion of this book from journal articles to book chapters,
namely the possible inclusion of journal terminology.

Disclaimer
Every effort has been made to contact copyright holders for their permission to
reprint material in this book. The publishers would be grateful to hear from any
copyright holder who is not here acknowledged and will undertake to rectify
any errors or omissions in future editions of this book.

Contents

Citation Information

The following chapters were originally published in the *Journal of Entrepreneurship & Regional Development*, volume 25, issues 9–10 (December 2013). When citing this material, please use the original page numbering for each article, as follows:

Chapter 5
Bourdieuian approaches to the geography of entrepreneurial cultures
Ben Spigel
Journal of Entrepreneurship & Regional Development, volume 25, issues 9–10
(December 2013) pp. 804–818

For any permission-related enquiries please visit:
http://www.tandfonline.com/page/help/permissions

Notes on Contributors

Alaistair R. Anderson is Professor of Entrepreneurship and Director of the Centre for Entrepreneurship at Robert Gordon University, Aberdeen, UK. His research interests include entrepreneurship and small businesses, and the social aspects of entrepreneurship and SMEs. He is the editor of the *Journal of Entrepreneurship & Regional Development*.

Erkko Autio is Chair in Technology Transfer and Entrepreneurship in the Imperial College London Business School, London, UK. He is also based in the Department of Industrial Engineering and Engineering Management at Aalto University, Helsinki, Finland.

Gabriella Cacciotti is a PhD student in the Warwick Business School at the University of Warwick, UK.

Selin Metin Camgöz is based in the Department of Business Administration at Hacettepe University, Ankara, Turkey.

Michael Frese is a Professor in the Department of Management and Organization at the National University of Singapore Business School, Singapore.

James C. Hayton is a Professor in the Warwick Business School at the University of Warwick, UK. His research focuses on how human resource management practices foster organizations' capacity for entrepreneurship and strategic renewal.

Pinar Bayhan Karapinar is based in the Department of Business Administration at Hacettepe University, Ankara, Turkey.

Norris Krueger has a wide range of consulting and high tech entrepreneurial experience and is very active in all the major entrepreneurship academic organizations. He sits on the Executive Committee of the Academy of Management's Entrepreneurship Division. His work has ranged from public policy analysis to cutting-edge research to designing entrepreneurial education and training programs that have won multiple national best practice awards.

Vita Kupcha was based in the Department of Work and Organizational Psychology at the University of Gießen, Germany.

Francisco Liñán is an Associate Professor at the University of Seville, Spain. He has several publications in the areas of entrepreneurial culture, cognitive entrepreneurship, entrepreneurial intentions and entrepreneurship education. He is Head of the Masters in Entrepreneurship Development, and has participated in projects funded by the Spanish national government, the EU and the OECD.

Maria Lozada was based in the Department of Work and Organizational Psychology at the University of Gießen, Germany.

Ghulam Nabi is a Senior Lecturer at Manchester Metropolitan University, UK. He has publications in the areas of entrepreneurial intentions, student-to-entrepreneur transition, graduate entrepreneurship, entrepreneurship education and entrepreneurial culture. He has been guest editor for Special Issues of several journals, and has led projects funded by the UK NCGE, UFHRD and IGEN.

Saurav Pathak is Assistant Professor of Entrepreneurship and Innovation in the School of Business and Economics at Michigan Technological University, Houghton, Michigan, USA.

Andreas Rauch is Professor in the Innovation Incubator, Leuphana University, Lüneberg, Germany.

Rotem Shneor is an Associate Professor in the Institute of Economics at the University of Agder, Kristiansand, Norway.

Ben Spigel is a Chancellor's Fellow in the Business School at the University of Edinburgh, UK.

Tanja Spirina was based in the Department of Work and Organizational Psychology at the University of Gießen, Germany.

Jens Unger was based in the Department of Work and Organizational Psychology at the University of Gießen, Germany.

Zhong-Ming Wang is Professor of Business Administration in the School of Management at Zhejiang University, Hangzhou, China.

Karl Wennberg is a Professor in the Department of Management and Organization at the Stockholm School of Economics, Sweden. He is also based at the Ratio Institute, Stockholm, Sweden.

Preface

Alistair R. Anderson

Culture is sometimes neglected, yet it seems to explain a great deal about entrepreneurship. Culture is pervasive and surrounds what entrepreneurs do; culture penetrates actions and may even persuade people to be entrepreneurial. But the width of the concept means that when we try to determine precisely what culture does (Spigel 2013), we may find the concept of *culture* is like *trust*. Paradoxically, it accounts for a great deal, but may provide little detailed explanation. Moreover, the sheer utility of the concept contentiously confers it with a universalist explanatory power-culture explains 'how we do things around here.' Indeed, Williams (1981), described culture as one of the two or three most complicated words in the English language (Dodd and Anderson 2001).

However, in my view, if we treat culture in, or as, a social perspective of entrepreneurship it can provide us with a powerful alternative to a functionalist view of entrepreneurship. Culture can thus help us to *understand* entrepreneurship (Anderson 2015). We can begin to see why people choose entrepreneurship and how they become entrepreneurial. Culture can explicate the social context of, and for, enterprise (McKeever et al. 2014). We can discern why some societies place a high value on enterprise as a mechanism for growth and why some individuals are seen as entrepreneurial heroes. The notion of an enterprise culture allows us to see differences between societies. Nonetheless, this view carries an important caveat; we must acknowledge that entrepreneurship itself is a cultural construct. As a social construction, what we think of as entrepreneurship is unavoidably bound up in what our society, and our own world views, deems to be entrepreneurial. Indeed the GEM (Global Entrepreneurship Monitor) offers us evidence of how a functionalist perspective can gloss over cultural but nonetheless fundamental differences in the nature and value of entrepreneurship in its social and cultural settings. Culture, as much as motivational variables, may shape what is seen as opportunity and what is necessity enterprise (Harbi and Anderson 2010). In this way any study of cultural implications for entrepreneurship is caught up in the hermeneutic problem; that in examining enterprising culture we inevitably and inescapably apply our own culturally shaped version!

That caveat aside, culture offers some answers to the overarching academic questions about entrepreneurship; what, how and why? Of course the individual must remain central in all accounts and explanations of entrepreneurship. However the relationships between that individual and her society can be better understood by an appreciation of culture. At the broadest level, culture explains how societies work. Thus an enterprise culture is one that supports and sustains entrepreneurial actions. Culture may delineate the moral space for entrepreneurship (Anderson and Smith 2007) offering legitimacy or vilification (Dodd et al. 2013). Moreover, at a lower level of analysis in the firm, entrepreneurial orientation is actually a cultural construct. Similarly we can usefully describe the cultures which support innovation at firm level (Harbi et al. 2009). More grounded still, culture can help us understand an individual's entrepreneurial aspirations, and how what they wish for is shaped by the prevailing cultural norms and values. Thus seen in this way, culture becomes the factor that relates entrepreneurship to society and offers explanatory relational links for individuals and firms to prevailing norms and values. Hence culture has considerable explanatory potential.

Krueger, Liñán and Nabi (2013) recognize these qualities in their introduction to the papers. They show us how entrepreneurship literature has grappled with a satisfactory definition of culture. They illustrate how culture can be conceived as patterns of thinking, believing and acting, yet they also describe how culture shapes what we do and how we feel. Moreover, they acknowledge the multiple facets of culture and its manifestations at different levels to propose how culture is a fertile ground for exploring interesting entrepreneurial questions.

The papers themselves take up this challenge and offer culturally informed insights on entrepreneurship. Reflecting the range of aspects of culture and the diversity of cultural manifestations, the papers provide a critical and informed appreciation of this fascinating topic but each makes a different contribution. Hayton and Cacciotti (2013) review what we already know about the extent and pervasion of enterprise cultures. Rauch et al., (2013) demonstrate the importance of culture for innovation and growth. In contrast, Wennberg et al., (2013) examine the international relationships between individuals' self-efficacy, fear of failure and culture. Shneor et al., (2013) also make international cultural comparisons and show how culture differently effects male and female entrepreneurial intention. Spigel's paper (2013) offers a conceptual framework to help understand the implications of culture at different levels and contexts. Taken together the papers show us the importance of culture in our understanding of entrepreneurship.

References

Anderson, A. R. (2015). "Conceptualising Entrepreneurship as Economic 'Explanation' and the Consequent Loss of 'Understanding'." *International Journal of Business and Globalisation* 14 (2): 145–157.

Anderson, A. R., and R. Smith. (2007). "The Moral Space in Entrepreneurship: An Exploration of Ethical Imperatives and the Moral Legitimacy of being Enterprising." *Entrepreneurship & Regional Development* 19 (6): 479–497.

Dodd, S. D., and A. R. Anderson. (2001). "Understanding the Enterprise Culture Paradigm, Paradox and Policy." *The International Journal of Entrepreneurship and Innovation* 2 (1): 13–26.

Dodd, S. D., S. Jack, and A. R. Anderson. (2013). "From Admiration to Repugnance: The Contentious Appeal of Entrepreneurship across Europe." *Entrepreneurship & Regional Development* 25 (1–2): 69–89.

Harbi, S., M. Amamou, and A. R. Anderson. (2009). "Establishing High-tech Industry: The Tunisian ICT experience." *Technovation* 29 (6–7): 465–480.

Harbi, S., and A. R. Anderson. (2010). "Institutions and the Shaping of Different Forms of Entrepreneurship." *The Journal of Socio-Economics* 39 (3): 436–444.

Hayton, J. C., and G. Cacciotti. (2013). "Is there an Entrepreneurial Culture? A Review of Empirical Research." *Entrepreneurship & Regional Development* 25 (9–10): 708–731.

Krueger, N., F. Liñán, and G. Nabi. (2013). "Cultural Values and Entrepreneurship." *Entrepreneurship & Regional Development* 25 (9–10): 703–707.

McKeever, E., A. R. Anderson, and S. Jack. (2014). "Entrepreneurship and Mutuality: Social Capital in Processes and Practices." *Entrepreneurship & Regional Development* 26 (5–6): 453–477.

Rauch, A., M. Frese, Z.-M. Wang, J. Unger, M. Lozada, V. Kupcha, and T. Sprina. (2013). "Natural Culture and Cultural Orientation affecting the Innovation-Growth Relationship in Five Countries." *Entrepreneurship & Regional Development* 25 (9–10): 732–755.

Shneor, R., S. M. Camgöz, and P. B. Karapinar. (2013). "The Interaction between Culture and Sex in the Formation of Entrepreneurial Intentions." *Entrepreneurship & Regional Development* 25 (9–10): 781–803.

Spigel, B. (2013). "Bourdieuian Approaches to the Geography of Entrepreneurial Cultures." *Entre-preneurship & Regional Development* 25 (9–10): 804–818.

Wennberg, K., S. Pathak, and E. Autio. (2013). "How Culture Moulds the Effects of Self-efficacy and Fear of Failure on Entrepreneurship." *Entrepreneurship & Regional Development* 25 (9–10): 756–780.

Williams R. (1981). *Culture*. London: Fontana.

INTRODUCTION

Cultural values and entrepreneurship

Norris Krueger[a,b], Francisco Liñán[c] and Ghulam Nabi[d]

[a]Entrepreneurship Northwest, Boise, ID, USA; [b]Max Planck Institute for Economics, Jena, Germany; [c]University of Seville, Seville, Spain; [d]Manchester Metropolitan University, Manchester, UK

A greater understanding of the relationship between cultural issues and entrepreneurial activity is important because of its implication for national and regional development and growth. Yet, many questions remain unanswered. For example, what is an 'entrepreneurial culture'? What does it look like, what influences its presence or absence? How do we know, how do we measure it? Furthermore, the central question is: How do cultural values influence entrepreneurial activity? Conversely, how does entrepreneurial activity influence cultural values? Entrepreneurship scholars do not need experts like Granovetter (1983) to persuade us that entrepreneurial activity is irretrievably embedded in social and cultural norms and values. However, we have found rather quickly that understanding this co-embeddedness beyond a superficial level is challenging. Accepting these challenges will move the field forward in important and likely in unexpected directions.

Even though the definition of culture is still controversial (Boggs 2004), Inglehart (1997) defines it as the set of basic common values which contributes to shaping people's behaviour in a society. The notion of culture also includes patterns of thinking, feeling and acting, which are learned and shared by people living within the same social environment (Hofstede 1991, 2003). However, we recognize that 'culture' has many facets, just as each of us live in multiple groups with differing norms and values. Thus, 'culture' cannot be equated to nation anymore. Multiculturalism and immigration are widespread characteristics of present-day societies, and different sub-cultures do exist within any given country (Davidsson and Wiklund 1997; Garcia-Cabrera and Garcia-Soto 2008; Levie 2007), interacting at different levels, such as industry or organizational levels (Fayolle, Basso, and Bouchard 2010). Again, the objective is to broaden and deepen our understanding of what elements of 'culture' influence (or are influenced) by entrepreneurial activity.

What we do know is that differences in entrepreneurial activity among countries, and regions within those countries, are persistent and cannot be fully explained by institutional and economic variables (Davidsson and Wiklund 1997; Frederking 2004). A substantial part of these differences has been attributed to culture, which may influence entrepreneurship through two main mechanisms (Davidsson 1995). First, a supportive culture would lead to *social legitimation*, making the entrepreneurial career more valued and socially recognized in that culture, thus creating a favourable institutional environment. Therefore, more people will try to start their ventures, irrespective of their personal beliefs and attitudes (Etzioni 1987). Second, a culture sharing more pro-entrepreneurial values and patterns of thinking would lead to more individuals showing *psychological traits and attitudes* consistent with entrepreneurship (Krueger 2000, 2003). Thus, more people will try to become entrepreneurs (McGrath et al. 1992; Mueller and Thomas 2001). In this sense, it has been suggested that a high-perceived valuation of entrepreneurship in a society will lead to more positive attitudes and intentions by individuals (Krueger and Carsrud 1993; Liñán, Urbano, and Guerrero 2011). Alternatively, it has also been argued that it is 'misfit' individuals who attempt to start a venture. That is, irrespective of the specific cultural characteristics of a country, people not sharing dominant cultural values – *dissatisfied individuals* – will attempt the entrepreneurial path (Hofstede et al. 2004). Either way, we ignore cultural and social influences at our peril. That also suggests fertile ground for exploring important research questions about entrepreneurs and entrepreneurship.

It is clear that some socio-cultural practices, values and norms are more conducive to driving or inhibiting entrepreneurship. For example, historically in countries such as the former Soviet Union or Singapore, socialist practices or low tolerance of failure or risk taking was not conducive to entrepreneurship (c.f., Henry, Hill, and Leitch 2003). However, we need to dig deeper into 'how' and 'why' cultural practices, and underlying values and norms, matter in entrepreneurial action to more fully understand the complexities of the processes, without making cross-cultural or cross-national generalizations. Unique cultural, national and institutional contexts present different practices in terms of opportunities and challenges for driving entrepreneurial action (Nabi and Liñán 2011).

This Special Issue provides us with a vehicle to advance our understanding of value-driven behaviours. Many unanswered questions remain, due to the difficulties in understanding, defining and measuring culture in its different forms. Ethnic minorities have often been found to present high entrepreneurial rates (Vinogradov and Kolvereid 2007). The interplay between wider societal culture, group-level and individual-level values is, however, far from clear (Basu and Altinay 2002). Therefore, in this Special Issue we sought to select high-quality papers that may contribute to a broader understanding of the many different roles culture plays in shaping entrepreneurial activity.

The contributions that follow have addressed some of these very interesting gaps, though so many others remain. The additional complexity of multi-level concepts of culture has been well reflected in Spigel's theoretical paper. This author contemplates the need for a framework to link each local, regional or national culture because they emerge in each territory in a unique way and influence the local entrepreneurship process. In contrast, the remaining empirical papers have all stuck to the country-level notion of culture. As Hayton and Cacciotti explain in their review of the literature, Hofstede's cultural dimensions are still the predominant (almost single) approach used in this field. This is reflected in our Special Issue, in which only Spigel's work is based on an alternative approach.

Culture may exert its influence at different steps of the entrepreneurial activity. In this sense, the paper by Rauch, Frese, Wang, Unger, Lozada, Kupcha and Spirina analyses the relationship between innovation and business growth in different countries. Very interestingly, though, they find that this innovation–growth relationship is moderated by both the national culture and the owner's personal-level values. What is more, the process of venture creation seems to develop differently in each cultural setting. In this sense, Wennberg, Pathak and Autio find that self-efficacy is positively related to new venture creation, but this relationship is moderated by the cultural practices of institutional collectivism, uncertainty avoidance and performance orientation. Finally, the interaction between culture and person is also confirmed by Shneor, Metin Camgöz, and Bayhan Karapinar, who find that sex differences in entrepreneurial intentions are contingent on the national culture.

The papers included in this Special Issue open very interesting avenues for further research. For instance, the influence of specific cultural values seems to be contingent on the institutional and economic characteristics of a country or region. In this sense, some recent research suggests evidence of nonlinear and interaction effects between cultural dimensions and income level (Pinillos and Reyes 2011). That is, in developing countries, embeddedness or hierarchy values – following Schwartz's (2004) classification – are associated with higher entrepreneurial activity. In developed countries, in turn, the opposite values of autonomy and egalitarianism promote entrepreneurship (Liñán, Fernández, and Romero 2013). Even within developed countries, culture is related to the relative strength of the relationship between personal attitudes and self-efficacy on the one hand and entrepreneurial intention on the other (Liñán, Nabi, and Krueger 2013).

Similarly, as pointed out by Rauch et al., the interplay between cultural level and personal level variables is another fascinating area for future research. Two identical people (same experiences, perceptions and preferences) are likely to behave differently if they are under different cultural pressures. Thus, being individualistic may not be so important per se; rather it is the emphasis on *more individualistic* (or *less individualistic*) values *compared to the rest* of the society that is important in entrepreneurial activity (Moriano, Jaén, and Liñán 2013).

The papers published in this Special Issue are intended to be of value to relevant entrepreneurial stakeholders. We all benefit from a clearer understanding of the ways in which culture shapes entrepreneurial activity, but we hope it will contribute meaningfully to devising newer and improved measures and approaches by policy-makers and government officials to promote a higher entrepreneurial culture in their country/region. Similarly, entrepreneurship education and training programmes could benefit from this new knowledge by making explicit the values associated with entrepreneurship. At the same time, specific value-transmission and value-transformation activities may be designed and incorporated into training programmes. Overall, the entrepreneurship and regional science research communities would benefit from advancement in the knowledge frontier within these fields.

The Guest Editors hope that this Special Issue inspires further researchers in this fascinating and valuable field. They are open to hear from researchers working in these areas, with a view to discussing *collaborative research projects* with them in the future. Finally, the Guest Editors would like to thank all the reviewers involved in this Special Issue (in alphabetical order): Amal Abbas (Cairo University), Sue Baines (Manchester Metropolitan University), Zuleika Beaven (Manchester Metropolitan University), Robert Blackburn (University of Kingston), Yi-Wen Chen (National Chengchi University), Naima Cherchem (HEC Montréal), Alain Fayolle (EM Lyon), Maribel Guerrero (Instituto Vasco de Competitividad), James Hayton (Newcastle University), Esther Hormiga (University of Barcelona), Teemu Kautonen (Anglia Ruskin University), Rita Klapper (Rouen Business School), Lars Kolvereid (University of Norland), Jason Lortie (Florida Atlantic Universtiy), Juan A. Moriano (UNED Madrid), Erik Noyes (Babson College), Saurav Pathak (Michigan Technological University), Andreas Rauch (Leuphana University), Rotem Shneor (University of Agder), Piers Thompson (Nottingham Trent University), David Urbano (Autonomous University of Barcelona), Andreas Walmsley (York St John University), Karl Wennberg (Stockholm School of Economics) and Robert Whapshott (University of Sheffield). We also thank the Editor (Prof Alistair Anderson) and the publishers for their advice and guidance.

References

Basu, A., and E. Altinay. 2002. "The Interaction Between Culture and Entrepreneurship in London's Immigrant Business." *International Small Business Journal* 20 (4): 371–393.

Boggs, J. P. 2004. "The Culture Concept as Theory, in Context." *Current Anthropology* 45 (2): 187–209.

Davidsson, P. 1995. "Culture, Structure and Regional Levels of Entrepreneurship." *Entrepreneurship and Regional Development* 7 (1): 41–62.

Davidsson, P., and J. Wiklund. 1997. "Values, Beliefs and Regional Variations in New Firm Formation Rates." *Journal of Economic Psychology* 18 (2–3): 179–199.

Etzioni, A. 1987. "Entrepreneurship, Adaptation and Legitimation: A Macro-Behavioral Perspective." *Journal of Economic Behavior & Organization* 8 (2): 175–189.

Fayolle, A., O. Basso, and V. Bouchard. 2010. "Three Levels of Culture and Firms' Entrepreneurial Orientation: A Research Agenda." *Entrepreneurship and Regional Development* 22 (7–8): 707–730.

Frederking, L. C. 2004. "A Cross-National Study of Culture, Organization and Entrepreneurship in Three Neighbourhoods." *Entrepreneurship and Regional Development* 16 (3): 197–215.

Garcia-Cabrera, A. M., and M. G. Garcia-Soto. 2008. "Cultural Differences and Entrepreneurial Behaviour: An Intra-Country Cross-Cultural Analysis in Cape Verde." *Entrepreneurship and Regional Development* 20 (5): 451–483.

Granovetter, M. 1983. "The Strength of Weak Ties: A Network Theory Revisited." *Sociological Theory* 1: 201–233.

Henry, C., F. Hill, and C. Leitch. 2003. *Entrepreneurship Education and Training*. Aldershot: Ashgate.

Hofstede, G. 1991. *Cultures and Organizations: Software of the Mind*. London: McGraw-Hill.

Hofstede, G. 2003. *Culture's Consequences: Comparing Values, Behaviors, Institutions and Organizations Across Nations*. 2nd ed. Newbury Park: Sage Publications.

Hofstede, G., N. Noorderhaven, A. R. Thurik, L. M. Uhlaner, A. R. M. Wennekers, and R. E. Wildeman. 2004. "Culture's Role in Entrepreneurship: Self-Employment Out of Dissatisfaction." In *Innovation, Entrepreneurship and Culture*, edited by T. E. Brown, and J. M. Ulijn, 162–203. Cheltenham: Edward Elgar.

Inglehart, R. 1997. *Modernization and Postmodernization*. Princeton: Princeton University Press.

Krueger, N. F. 2000. "The Cognitive Infrastructure of Opportunity Emergence." *Entrepreneurship Theory and Practice* 24 (3): 5–23.

Krueger, N. F. 2003. "The Cognitive Psychology of Entrepreneurship." In *Handbook of Entrepreneurship Research: An Interdisciplinary Survey and Introduction*, edited by Z. J. Acs, and D. B. Audretsch, 105–140. London: Kluwer.

Krueger, N. F., and A. L. Carsrud. 1993. "Entrepreneurial Intentions: Applying the Theory of Planned Behavior." *Entrepreneurship and Regional Development* 5 (4): 315–330.

Levie, J. 2007. "Immigration, In-Migration, Ethnicity and Entrepreneurship in the United Kingdom." *Small Business Economics* 28 (2–3): 143–169.

Liñán, F., J. Fernández, and I. Romero. 2013. "Necessity and Opportunity Entrepreneurship: The Mediating Effect of Culture." *Revista de Economía Mundial* 33: 21–47.

Liñán, F., G. Nabi, and N. Krueger. 2013. "British and Spanish Entrepreneurial Intentions: A Comparative Study." *Revista de Economía Mundial* 33: 73–103.

Liñán, F., D. Urbano, and M. Guerrero. 2011. "Regional Variations in Entrepreneurial Cognitions: Start-Up Intentions of University Students in Spain." *Entrepreneurship and Regional Development* 23 (3–4): 187–215.

McGrath, R. G., I. C. MacMillan, E. A. Yang, and W. Tsai. 1992. "Does Culture Endure, or Is It Malleable: Issues for Entrepreneurial Economic-Development." *Journal of Business Venturing* 7 (6): 441–458.

Moriano, J. A., I. Jaén, and F. Liñán. 2013. "Individualism in the Formation of Entrepreneurial Intention: The Interplay of Personal and Cultural Values." Paper presented at the 2nd GIKA Conference, Valencia, July, 9–11.

Mueller, S. L., and A. S. Thomas. 2001. "Culture and Entrepreneurial Potential: A Nine Country Study of Locus of Control and Innovativeness." *Journal of Business Venturing* 16 (1): 51–75.

Nabi, G., and F. Liñán. 2011. "Graduate Entrepreneurship in the Developing World: Intentions, Education and Development." *Education + Training* 53 (5): 325–334.

Pinillos, M. J., and L. Reyes. 2011. "Relationship Between Individualist–Collectivist Culture and Entrepreneurial Activity: Evidence from Global Entrepreneurship Monitor Data." *Small Business Economics* 37: 23–37.

Schwartz, S. H. 2004. "Mapping and Interpreting Cultural Differences around the World." In *Comparing Cultures, Dimensions of Culture in a Comparative Perspective*, edited by H. Vinken, J. Soeters, and P. Ester, 43–73. Leiden, The Netherlands: Brill.

Vinogradov, E., and L. Kolvereid. 2007. "Cultural Background, Human Capital and Self-Employment Rates Among Immigrants in Norway." *Entrepreneurship and Regional Development* 19 (4): 359–376.

Is there an entrepreneurial culture? A review of empirical research

James C. Hayton and Gabriella Cacciotti

Warwick Business School, University of Warwick, Coventry, UK

The literature on the association between cultural values and entrepreneurial beliefs, motives and behaviours has grown significantly over the last decade. Through its influence on beliefs, motives and behaviours, culture can magnify or mitigate the impact of institutional and economic conditions upon entrepreneurial activity. Understanding the impact of national culture, alone and in interaction with other contextual factors, is important for refining our knowledge of how entrepreneurs think and act. We present a review of the literature with the goal of distilling the major findings, points of consensus and points of disagreement, as well as identify major gaps. Research has advanced significantly with respect to examining complex interactions among cultural, economic and institutional factors. As a result, a more complex and nuanced view of culture's consequences is slowly emerging. However, work that connects culture to individual motives, beliefs and values has not built significantly upon earlier work on entrepreneurial cognition. Evidence for the mediating processes linking culture and behaviour remains sparse and inconsistent, often dogged by methodological challenges. Our review suggests that we can be less confident, rather than more, in the existence of a single entrepreneurial culture. We conclude with suggestions for future research.

1. Introduction

One of the oldest research questions in the field of entrepreneurship is how and to what extent does national culture influence entrepreneurial action, the rate of new firm formation and ultimately economic development (e.g. McClelland 1961; Weber 1930; Schumpeter 1934)? It has long been established that the level of entrepreneurial activity varies across countries and regions and this variation has been associated with both economic and social benefits (e.g. Audretsch and Thurik 2001; Birley 1987; van Praag and Versloot 2007; van Stel 2005; Wennekers, Uhlaner, and Thurik 2002). As with many topics in an applied field, scholars from diverse disciplinary backgrounds have addressed this question (Hayton, George, and Zahra 2002). However, often such disciplinary diversity can lead to challenges with respect to the incremental development of a knowledge base as scholars emphasize different theoretical lenses, languages, research questions and methods. In particular, the recent expansion in published empirical research on this topic raises the question of whether the convergence observed by Hayton, George, and Zahra (2002) towards a single view of entrepreneurial culture continues to be tenable. In contrast, does recent research create a more nuanced, but less consistent story about what aspects of culture support entrepreneurial decision and action? Understanding the real impact of culture, and the ways in which culture may moderate, or be mitigated by contextual factors such as institutions and economic development, has great significance for theorizing about, and empirically studying entrepreneurial behaviour around the world. It is also of importance for policy-makers concerned with promoting entrepreneurial activity. It is from this perspective that it is of value to review, organize and evaluate what we now know.

Hofstede (2001, 9) described culture as a 'collective programming of the mind that distinguishes the members of one group or category of people from another.' We therefore define culture as the values, beliefs and expected behaviours that are sufficiently common across people within (or from) a given geographic region as to be considered as shared (e.g. Herbig 1994; Hofstede 1980). To the extent that cultural values lead to an acceptance of uncertainty and risk taking, they are expected to be supportive of the creativity and innovation underlying entrepreneurial action. Entrepreneurial actions are facilitated both by formal institutions (e.g. property rights, enforceable contracts) and by socially shared beliefs and values that reward or inhibit the necessary behaviours (e.g. innovation, creativity, risk taking; Hayton, George, and Zahra 2002; Herbig and Miller 1992; Herbig 1994; Hofstede 1980). It is because of this subtle but widespread influence of culture that it is necessary to seek a deeper understanding of the phenomenon. For the purposes of this review, we assume a broad definition of entrepreneurship that includes growth oriented new-venture creation, but also extends to small and micro-enterprises that do not typically lead to employment growth beyond self-employment (Bhide 2000).

We take as a starting point the review by Hayton, George, and Zahra (2002), which offered a review of behavioural research into 'culture's consequences' for entrepreneurship, to borrow from Hofstede's famous title (Hofstede 1980). We focus on empirical research in order to get an accurate gauge on what we now know, and particularly what we have learned over the past decade of research. To identify articles for inclusion, we searched the ABI-Inform and Business Source Premier databases for references to national culture and entrepreneurship. These databases include extensive collections of journals that most frequently publish entrepreneurship and cross-cultural behavioural research (e.g. *Journal of Business Venturing, Entrepreneurship Theory and Practice, Entrepreneurship and Regional Development, Journal of International Business Studies, Academy of Management Journal* and *Strategic Entrepreneurship Journal*). We also examined the reference lists of all studies found through our search to identify articles not discovered through a search of the databases. We have only included single or multi-country studies that address the significance of culture, however defined or operationalized, for entrepreneurship. In all, seven studies have been excluded on the grounds that they do not measure national culture, but only infer it from country (Uhlaner and Thurik 2007; Freytag and Thurik 2007; Beugelsdijk 2007; Beugelsdijk and Noorderhaven 2004; Swierczek and Quang 2004; Stewart et al. 2003; De Pillis and Reardon 2007). In addition to the 21 empirical studies already identified in Hayton, George, and Zahra (2002), we found an additional 21 empirical studies published from 2001 to 2012.

Our review of the recent research on culture and entrepreneurship revealed research streams previously identified by Hayton, George, and Zahra (2002).[1] Rather than proposing a new analytical framework, we preferred to examine the research questions, methods and results of the studies in those research streams for two reasons: this organization of the research is still appropriate; and it allows us to directly evaluate the extent to which knowledge has been updated over the past decade, and areas where research is still needed. The first research stream addresses the impact of national culture on rates of innovation and entrepreneurship at the national or regional level. The second stream focuses on the relationship between culture and the beliefs, motives, values and cognitions of entrepreneurs across regional and national boundaries. This second stream is itself divided into two parts. The first presents evidence for differences across regions or countries in terms of the individual beliefs, motives and values associated with entrepreneurial behaviour. The second focuses on the existence of an entrepreneurial mindset, and reflects a test of the 'deviance' hypothesis – i.e. that by necessity, entrepreneurs somehow deviate from cultural norms. At the end of our review of each of these streams of research, we offer a summary that provides a critical evaluation of the state of the art with respect to culture's consequences. In the last sections of the paper, we revise the model of national culture and entrepreneurship suggested by Hayton, George, and Zahra (2002), and conclude by offering suggestions for future research.

2. National culture and entrepreneurship at the national or regional level

A growing number of studies have addressed the relationship between national or regional culture and aggregate levels of entrepreneurship (Davidsson 1995; Davidsson and Wiklund 1997; Rinne, Steel, and Fairweather 2012; Shane 1992, 1993; Stephan and Uhlaner 2010; Sun 2009; Williams and McGuire 2010). These studies are summarized in Table 1.

2.1. *Culture and national rates of innovation*

We can subdivide studies at the national level based upon the operationalization of the dependent variable. Several studies have examined the relationship between culture and aggregate rates of innovation (Shane 1992, 1993; Sun 2009; Rinne, Steel, and Fairweather 2012; Williams and McGuire 2010). Shane's (1992, 1993) studies provided preliminary evidence that Hofstede's cultural dimensions of individualism, power distance and uncertainty avoidance were significantly associated with national rates of innovation, after controlling for national wealth. However, Shane (1993) reported that the association between individualism, power distance and innovation rates was not stable over time. Sun (2009) and Rinne, Steel, and Fairweather (2012) offer mixed support for Shane's (1992, 1993) by using different sources for innovation rates (Porter and Stern 2001; INSEAD 2009). While both studies also suggest an association between individualism, power distance and innovation capability, they only examine a single time period, and do not control for other potential confounding factors such as GDP or stage of economic development.

In contrast with previous studies, Williams and McGuire reframed Hofstede's culture variables and created an aggregate measure of culture to examine its relationship with innovation at national level. They propose that 'culture is a multidimensional phenomenon whose constituent parts interact to create the whole' (2010, 393) and the diverse aspects of culture should be taken together in order to measure the effect of culture at national level of analysis. Therefore, in this study culture is treated as a single latent variable reflecting three dimensions: power proximity, uncertainty acceptance and individualism. They found that when national culture was operationalized in this way, these combined dimensions were positively associated with economic creativity, and indirectly with innovation.

2.2. *Culture and new firm formation*

Following the early empirical research by Davidsson (1995) and Davidsson and Wiklund (1997), three studies have explored the relationship between national culture and entrepreneurial activity in the last decade (Stephan and Uhlaner 2010; Wennekers et al.

Table 1. Studies of national culture and entrepreneurship at the country level.

Authors	Research question	Major variables (independent/dependent)	Sample/data source(s)	Major findings
Shane (1992)	What is the association between national culture and national rates of innovation?	Individualism, power distance (Hofstede 1980)/national rates of innovation	33 countries/cultural values based on Hofstede's (1980) result and compared with per capita rates of innovation in 1967, 1971, 1976 and 1980.	National rates of innovation are positively correlated with individualism and power distance.
Shane (1993)	What effect does national culture have on national rates of innovation?	Individualism, power distance, uncertainty avoidance, and masculinity (Hofstede 1980)/national rates of innovation	33 countries/cultural values based upon Hofstede's (1980) results and compared with per capita rates of innovation in 1975 and 1980.	National rates of innovation are positively correlated with individualism and negatively correlated with uncertainty avoidance and power distance.
Davidsson (1995)	What is the interaction among structural characteristics, culture, beliefs and concerning entrepreneurship, and entrepreneurial intentions?	· An entrepreneurial values index that includes dimensions such as achievement motivation, locus of control, need for autonomy, and change orientation. · Entrepreneurial belief: societal contribution, financial payoff, perceived risk, social status. · Values: change orientation, need for achievement, need for autonomy, Jante-mentality competitiveness. · Beliefs: social contribution, financial payoff, perceived risk, social status workload, know-how, cultural values measured by survey/rates of new-firm formation	2200 individuals; 6 regions in Sweden/survey	Scores on the entrepreneurial values index are correlated with regional rates of new-firm formation.
Davidsson and Wiklund (1997)	Controlling for economic/structural factors is culture associated with differences in rates of new-firm formation?		1313 individuals; 6 regions in Sweden/survey	Cultural values and beliefs have a small but statistically significant association with regional rates of new firm formation.

(Continued)

Table 1 – *continued*

Authors	Research question	Major variables (independent/dependent)	Sample/data source(s)	Major findings
Wennekers et al. (2007)	Does the cultural attitudes towards uncertainty influence the rate of business ownership?	Uncertainty influence/rates of business ownership	21 OECD countries/survey	There is a direct and positive relationship between uncertainty avoidance and business ownership.
Sun (2009)	What is the influence of national cultures on innovation capability?	Individualism, power distance, uncertainty avoidance and masculinity/innovation capability	2 previous studies: Hofstede (1991, 2001) and Porter and Stern (2001)	Individualism, power distance and uncertainty avoidance are correlated with national innovation capability.
Williams and McGuire (2010)	How does culture affect national prosperity?	Aggregation of power proximity, uncertainty acceptance and individualism/national prosperity	63 countries/cultural values based on Hofstede's (1980, 2001) results	Culture affects national prosperity by influencing economic creativity, which leads to innovation implementation. The latter influences directly national prosperity.
Stephan and Uhlaner (2010)	Do cultural descriptive norms explain cross-national differences in entrepreneurship rate and in antecedent supply-side and demand-side variables?	SSC and PBC/entrepreneurship rates	40 countries/GLOBE project data	The social capital is the aspect of culture that drives both the overall level and the quality of national entrepreneurship.
Rinne, Steel, and Fairweather (2012)	What is the association between Hofstede's measures of cultural values and innovation?	Hofstede's cultural values/global innovation index (GII)	66 countries/cultural values based on Hofstede, Hofstede, and Minkov (2010) result and compared with rates of innovation from INSEAD, 2009	There is a strong negative relationship between power distance and GII innovation scores as well as a strong positive relationship between individualism and GII innovation scores.
Pinillos and Reyes (2011)	What is the relationship between culture and entrepreneurial activity?	Individualism–collectivism/entrepreneurial activity	52 countries /secondary (GEM)	For lower levels of development there is a negative association between individualism and entrepreneurship, and when development is high, this relationship becomes positive.

2007; Pinillos and Reyes 2011). In these studies, entrepreneurial activity was operationalized as new firm formation or firm ownership rates.

Wennekers et al. (2007) examined the relationship between uncertainty avoidance and variation in business ownership rates across countries. Using data from a sample of 21 countries in 1976, 1990 and 2004, Wennekers et al.'s (2007) results showed that, contrary to prior evidence, high uncertainty avoidance could actually push individuals towards self-employment. Their hypotheses rest on the proposition that in uncertainty avoiding countries, entrepreneurship is the route through which innovators may pursue their objectives, while in less restrictive environments, entrepreneurial individuals may be able to pursue their goals within the context of employment. However, they found that this relationship was not stable over time. In addition, the authors report a negative moderating influence of uncertainty avoidance on the relationship between GDP per capita and business ownership: the effect of GDP on entrepreneurship rates is observed to be smaller in low-uncertainty avoidance countries than in high-uncertainty avoidance countries. This study provides evidence that the role of uncertainty avoidance is complex and may not be reducible to a simple, linear association.

Pinillos and Reyes (2011) also questioned the assumption of a simple linear association between culture and entrepreneurial activity. They observed that despite arguments that individualism is positively associated with entrepreneurship, there are many countries characterized by collectivist orientation which also exhibit high levels of entrepreneurial activity. Using data from the global entrepreneurship monitor project, these authors showed that for lower levels of development, there was a negative association between individualism and entrepreneurship, and when development was high, this relationship became positive.

A study by Stephan and Uhlaner (2010) also contradicts the established view on individualistic cultures being supportive of entrepreneurship. They used descriptive norms rather than cultural values to predict variations in cross-national entrepreneurship. According to the values approach, culture is measured as the aggregation of individual scores of values and preferences. In contrast, descriptive norms are measured by asking respondents to describe characteristic behaviours displayed by most people within their culture. Only if there is adequate evidence for agreement, are they then aggregated to a higher level of regional or national cultural values. Thus a values-based approach reflects a more direct measure, but depends upon the representativeness of the sample. The descriptive norms approach is an indirect measure, but depends upon the knowledge that respondents possess of the typical behaviours. Based on data from the GLOBE project, Stephan and Uhlaner (2010) identified two higher order factors: performance-based culture (PBC) and socially supportive culture (SSC). The first factor, PBC, is described by Stephan and Uhlaner (2010, 1351) as 'a culture that rewards individual accomplishments as opposed to collective membership, family relationships or position, and in which systematic, future-oriented planning is viewed as a key way to achieve high performance.' The most representative societies were those belonging to the Anglo, Germanic Europe and Nordic Europe country cluster. Latin American, Latin and Eastern Europe cluster showed the lowest score on PBC, while Confucian and Southern Asian countries were in the middle. The second factor, SSC, reflects high human orientation and low assertiveness. Southern and Confucian Asian countries as well as Anglo and Nordic European societies scored very high on SSC. Germanic, Eastern and Latin European societies showed low scores, whereas Latin American countries were in the middle. The authors go on to argue that SSC reflects 'a descriptive norm based on repeated experiences of supportiveness and helpfulness' (2010, 1351). Notwithstanding this conceptual and methodological contribution, the results of the study are somewhat disappointing. In direct contrast to Williams and McGuire (2010), Stephan and Uhlaner do not find any significant relationship between PBC and entrepreneurship, although SSC is related to several different measures of entrepreneurial activity. However, their hypothesized mediation relationships are not supported, thus failing to provide evidence for how or why SSC influences entrepreneurship.

Perhaps the most interesting aspect of this study is that in contrast to the broad assumption that performance-oriented cultures are most supportive of entrepreneurship (e. g. Williams and McGuire 2010), this research suggests an important role for cooperative and supportive cultures. It is plausible that higher social capital enhances weak ties among individuals of a population, increasing the number of opportunities discovered (Granovetter 1973), or that it reduces transaction costs.

2.3. *Summary*

Since Hayton, George, and Zahra's (2002) review, there have been six new published articles that explore the significance of culture for aggregate measures of entrepreneurship and innovation. The recent empirical studies provide further evidence for the association of cultural values with a diverse range of indicators of entrepreneurial activity.

Unfortunately, much of the evidence does not yet point to consensus on effects. On the topic of innovation, there have been several studies suggesting that individualism, uncertainty acceptance and power proximity are all associated with this outcome (Shane 1992, 1993; Sun 2009; Williams and McGuire 2010; Rinne, Steel, and Fairweather 2012). However, there is evidence for temporal instability (e.g. Shane 1993; Wennekers et al. 2007), which suggests caution. McGrath et al. (1992) find that individualism, uncertainty avoidance and materialist values are relatively enduring cultural values and only attitudes towards power distance appear to change significantly over time. If observed, instability cannot be attributed to changes in values, then it must be caused by the influence of unmeasured variables. Possibilities include shifts in global markets leading to growing pressures for innovation causing increases in investments by governments and businesses. Similarly, the increasingly global nature of the innovation process and the effects of knowledge spillovers from multinational enterprises may also be diminishing culture's influence on variations in innovation rates. This is the observation of Wennekers et al. (2007) who suggest that changes in the global competitive environment may account for the observed instability in culture's influence. Given the dynamism of the extra-national environment and its influence on both demand and supply factors influencing entrepreneurship, future research investigating culture's role needs to address this possibility for changes in relationships – both magnitude and direction – over time.

There has not been much consensus in research examining entrepreneurship rates, startup rates and firm formations (e.g. Davidsson 1995; Davidsson and Wiklind 1997; Stephan and Uhlaner 2010). However, contemporary research is beginning to reveal the interactions between culture and economic development in ways that allow for dynamism in the influence of culture, without suggesting instability in cultural values themselves. Pinillos and Reyes (2011) show that the association between individualism and entrepreneurial activity varies with the stage of economic development. Stephan and Uhlaner's (2010) work appears to directly contradict established views on which cultural dimensions are most supportive by revealing the significance of SSC, while finding the more masculine, performance oriented, individualist cultural characteristics to be non-significant. The significance of Stephan and Uhlaner's SSC dimension does make sense of why we can observe high rates of entrepreneurship in collectivist countries, satisfying one of the main criticisms of Pinillos and Reyes (2011) and a concern that was raised two decades ago by McGrath, MacMillan, and Scheinberg (1992) of whether the U.S. centric definition of an entrepreneurship supportive culture was universally appropriate. It appears that a model of entrepreneurial culture involving high individualism, uncertainty tolerance and low power distance is appropriate only under higher levels of economic development. There is now some support for Hayton, George, and Zahra's (2002) proposition that culture moderates the influence of economic variables (Wennekers et al. 2007).

One common methodological approach that has been challenged is the tendency to treat the dimensions of culture as discrete factors. Some scholars have recently provided evidence that these factors may either be combined into a global measure (e.g. Williams and McGuire 2010) or that they can be reduced to a smaller number of superordinate dimensions (e.g. Stephan and Uhlaner 2010). The advantage of such an approach is that it simplifies subsequent empirical analysis and facilitates clustering of similar countries according to a small number of dimensions (e.g. Stephan and Uhlaner 2010). The risk is that such clustering loses theoretical meaning and empirical information. For example, Williams and McGuire find that power proximity, uncertainty acceptance and individualism reflect a single underlying latent construct. By operationalizing culture in this way, they allow the components to be substitutable, but do not allow for possible interactions among them. Notably, the global culture factor identified by Williams and McGuire (2010) includes three components that are consistent with Stephan and Uhlaner's (2010) PBC dimension, and yet their results were not consistent. These conflicting results suggest caution with respect to the practice of reducing cultural dimensions to a single score or index.

The research question, samples, data sources, major findings and dimensions of culture measured in this group of studies are summarized in Table 1. Hayton, George, and Zahra (2002) criticized the literature for its reliance on small samples. Rinne, Steel, and Fairweather (2012) and Williams and McGuire (2010) are examples of studies with larger samples, which have contributed somewhat to ameliorating this concern. Ultimately, a limiting factor in studies at the national level is the number of countries for which data exist. One way to overcome such a challenge is by studying culture at the regional level (e.g. Davidsson 1995).

The second limitation that Hayton, George, and Zahra (2002) had identified within this literature was the lack of integration of institutional and cultural factors in single studies. Only Wennekers et al. (2007) attempt an integration of culture with institutional factors. Their theoretical approach is to examine how both cultural and institutional forces moderate the expected payoff from entrepreneurial action. It would be valuable to be able to extend such an analysis beyond uncertainty avoidance to other cultural values.

A fundamental assumption that is implicit in much of the research reviewed so far is that culture influences the motives, values and beliefs of individuals within a population so as to create a larger supply of potential entrepreneurs (Davidsson and Wiklund 1997). This question is examined directly in the second stream of research.

3. National culture and the individual characteristics of entrepreneurs

A growing number of studies have empirically examined the relationship between national culture and the entrepreneurial characteristics, or traits, of individuals. We divide these studies into two groups according to the focus. Some studies address the question of whether entrepreneurs differ in terms of their motives, beliefs or values across countries and why that is the case. These are summarized in Table 2. A second group of studies asks the question of whether a universal entrepreneurial 'mindset' exists that is more powerful

Table 2. Studies of national culture and characteristics of entrepreneurs.

Authors	Research question	Major variables (independent/ dependent)	Sample/data source(s)	Major findings
Scheinberg and MacMillan (1988)	Are the motives of entrepreneurs to start a business similar or different across cultures?	National culture/motives of entrepreneurs to start a business	1402 entrepreneurs; 11 countries/ survey	Indicators of motives represent six dimensions: need for approval, perceived instrumentality of wealth, communitarianism, need for personal development, need for independence and need for escape. The importance of these motives varies systematically across cultures.
Shane, Kolvereid, and Westhead (1991)	Are there significant differences across culture and/or gender in reasons given for business start up?	Cultural values/reasons given for business start up	597 entrepreneurs: 3 countries/ cultural values based upon Hofstede's (1980)	Reasons for starting a business reflect four underlying dimensions: recognition of achievement, independence from others, learning and development, and roles. The emphasis on each of these reasons varies systematically across countries.
Mueller and Thomas (2000)	Do entrepreneurial traits vary systematically across cultures?	Individualism, uncertainty avoidance/entrepreneurial traits	1790 students; 9 countries/survey	Cultures high in individualism are correlated with an internal locus of control. Cultures high in individualism and low in uncertainty avoidance rate highest on a measure of entrepreneurial orientation (innovativeness plus internal locus of control).
Thomas and Mueller (2000)	How prevalent are four key entrepreneurial traits (innovativeness, locus of control, risk taking, energy) across culture?	Power distance, uncertainty avoidance, individualism, masculinity/entrepreneurial traits (innovativeness, locus of control, risk taking, energy)	1790 students; 9 countries/survey	Entrepreneurial traits (internal locus of control, risk taking, high-energy levels) decrease as cultural distance from the USA increases.

Mitchell et al. (2000)	Does the presence of cognitive scripts associated with venture creation decisions vary significantly across cultures?	Individualism power distance, cognitive scripts/venture creation decisions	54; 27 from Hamamatsu, 25 from Kyoto, and 2 from Hamamatsu/ Survey	Individualism and power distance are associated with entrepreneurial cognitive scripts and the venture creation decisions.
Autio et al. (2001)	Does the Ajzen's model predict entrepreneurial intent across countries?	Perceived behavioural control, subjective norm, attitude towards the behaviour, cultural values/ entrepreneurial intent	3445 students in Finland, Sweden and the USA/survey	The international comparisons indicate a good robustness of the Ajzen's model and perceived behavioural control emerges as the most important determinant of entrepreneurial intent.
Stewart et al. (2003)	Does the relationship between entrepreneurial disposition and goal orientations differ between the USA and Russian entrepreneurs?	Individualism/collectivism, power distance, uncertainty avoidance and masculinity/ entrepreneurial motive disposition (need for achievement, risk taking, and innovativeness)	518 individuals; 427 in the USA and 91 in Russia/survey (cultural values based on Hofstede's indices)	Only achievement motivation is an important cultural variant in entrepreneurship. The significant higher levels of achievement motivation in both (macro and micro entrepreneurs) types of U.S entrepreneurs relative to their Russian counterparts is indicative of the individualistic, masculine nature of Hofstede's (1980) description of U.S culture.
Kristiansen and Indarti (2004)	What is the impact of different economic and cultural contexts on entrepreneurial intentions?	Need for achievement, locus of control and self-efficacy, cultural values/entrepreneurial intention	251 students; 121 from Norway and 130 from Indonesia/survey	The degree of entrepreneurial intention among Indonesian students is significantly higher than among Norwegian students.
Urban (2006)	Do different cultural values influence proclivity towards entrepreneurship across ethnic groups?	Individualism/collectivism, power distance, uncertainty avoidance, masculinity and long-term orientation/proclivity towards entrepreneurship	150 MBA students/survey (cultural values assessed through the value survey module 94)	Cultural values do not have a strong and clear relationship with entrepreneurial intentions.

(Continued)

Table 2 – *continued*

Authors	Research question	Major variables (independent/dependent)	Sample/data source(s)	Major findings
Lee-Ross and Mitchell (2007)	What is the relationship culture and entrepreneurial characteristics in the Torres Straits?	Individualism, power distance, uncertainty avoidance and masculinity/perceptual entrepreneurial traits	61 Torres Strait entrepreneurs/semi-structured interviews	Torres Strait entrepreneurs show sizable perceptual trait differences compared with Western theory.
Garcia-Cabrera and Garcia-Soto (2008)	Are the cultural values associated in the literature with venture creation generalizable to different cultural contexts? Are there intra-cultural differences in a country generating differences in the entrepreneurial behaviour of its population?	Individualism and masculinity/locus of control	448 individuals in Cape Verde/survey (cultural values measured using the instrument developed by Hofstede in 1982 VSM82)	Individualistic cultural orientation has a positive and direct effect on the locus of control which, in turn, influences entrepreneurial behaviour through educational level.
Pruett et al. (2009)	Do cultural, social and psychological factor predict entrepreneurial intentions?	Individualism/collectivism, power distance, uncertainty avoidance and masculinity/entrepreneurial intention	1058 students from the USA, China and Spain/survey (cultural values based on Hofstede's indices)	Country, personal entrepreneurial exposure and social barriers explain only a small part of a student's entrepreneurial intention.
Linan and Chen (2009)	Does culture influence the applicability of the entrepreneurial intention model (Ajzen model TPB) to different countries (Spain and Taiwan)?	Personal attitude, subjective norm and perceived behavioural control, individualism/collectivism, power distance, uncertainty avoidance and masculinity/entrepreneurial intention	519; 387 from Spain and 132 from Taiwan/survey (cultural values based on Hofstede's indices)	The three motivational antecedents (personal attitude, subjective norm, and perceived behavioural control) explained the formation of entrepreneurial intention in both countries, with cultural values determining the strength of the relationships. Subjective norm exerts a stronger effect on personal attitude and perceived behavioural control in the less individualistic country.

Author	Research question	Constructs/variables	Sample/method	Findings
Aoyama (2009)	What role does the regional culture play in shaping entrepreneurship?	Regional legacy/incentives, motivations and perceptions for contemporary entrepreneurship	54; 27 from Hamamatsu, 25 from Kyoto, and 2 from Hamamatsu/Kyoto/Survey	The regional legacy shapes incentives, motivations and perceptions for contemporary entrepreneurship.
Nguyen et al. (2009)	How do culture and institutions influence different aspects of entrepreneurship?	Individualism, power distance, uncertainty avoidance and Confucian cultural values, institutional aspects/entrepreneurial intention, desire, and confidence	398 undergraduate business students; 121 from the USA; 154 from Vietnam; 123 from Taiwan/survey (cultural values based on Hofstede's indices)	Neither the cultural values nor institutional development could fully explain the cross-national differences in entrepreneurship.
Engle et al. (2010)	Can the Ajzen model be used to predict entrepreneurial intent across countries with different cultures?	Attitude towards behaviour, social norms and perceived control, cultural cluster (language, geography, religion, history)/entrepreneurial intent	1748 students from 12 countries representative of 10 regional cultural clusters from House et al.'s study (2004)/survey	The three model elements (attitude towards behaviour, social norms and perceived control) that predict entrepreneurial intent differ greatly between countries. Only two countries (Finland and Russia) have all three model antecedents on intention as statistically significant predictors.
Goktan and Gunay (2011)	What is the relationship between culture and entrepreneurial cognition?	Hofstede's cultural values/likelihood of venture creation, aspiration of the entrepreneur for the new venture and opportunity evaluation	113 students from the USA and 119 from Turkey/survey	Culture and entrepreneurial cognition are significantly interrelated.
Moriano et al. (2012)	What is the role of culture in the formation of entrepreneurial intention?	Cultural values, entrepreneurial attitudes, self efficacy, subjective norms/entrepreneurial intention	1074 students in six different countries (Germany, India, Iran, Poland, Spain and the Netherlands)/survey (cultural values based on Hofstede's indices)	Results support culture universal effects of attitudes and perceived self-efficacy on entrepreneurial career intentions, but cultural variation in the effects of subjective norms.

than national culture in influencing entrepreneurship. We first examine the studies focusing on cross-cultural differences in motives, beliefs and values.

3.1. *Cultural variations in the beliefs, motives or values of entrepreneurs*

3.1.1. *Values and motives*

Earlier studies examining the association between national culture and entrepreneurial motives and values showed strong evidence that self-reported reasons for starting a business vary systematically with variations in culture along dimensions of individualism, power distance and masculinity (Scheinberg and MacMillan 1998; Shane, Kolvereid, and Westhead 1991). A recent study by Pruett et al. (2009), examining differences in motives and barriers regarding start-ups in the USA, China and Spain, parallels these findings. Chinese respondents emphasized money as the primary motive to start a business, compared with Spanish and U.S. individuals. This is explained through differences in the power distance dimension of culture, in which China scores relatively highly. Such variation in cultural tolerance of status inequality might explain Chinese entrepreneurs' greater espoused desire for money (and, therefore, greater social status) as a motive for business formation.

In a study involving interviews with 54 entrepreneurs (founders and cofounders) in Japan, Aoyama (2009) presents qualitative evidence that the mind-set, in terms of incentives, motivations, perceptions and codes of conduct among Japan's information technology entrepreneurs, is shaped by regional culture and context. While an impressive array of interview data is reported, the analysis lacks the precision of a quantitative analysis for presenting more than impressionistic evidence or testing specific hypotheses. It does, however, present further evidence that culture operates at the regional as well as national level, even within a national culture that is reputed to be strong, homogeneous and internally consistent as that of Japan.

Stewart et al. (2003) present an interesting comparison of the motive dispositions (need for achievement, risk taking and innovativeness), measured using the Jackson Personality Research Form, of growth and non-growth-oriented entrepreneurs in the USA and Russia. While the U.S. growth-oriented entrepreneurs are consistently higher than all others on the three motive disposition measures, the Russian entrepreneurs only differ significantly from U.S. entrepreneurs on need for achievement. Achievement motivation theory suggests that this is a learned disposition (McClelland et al. 1953), and therefore would be subject to influence from cultural norms and values. As with McClelland's (1961) study, the work of Stewart et al. (2003) supports this interpretation. The significantly higher levels of achievement motivation in both types of U.S. entrepreneurs relative to their Russian counterparts are suggestive of the influence of the individualistic, masculine nature of U.S. culture in contrast to the more feminine and collectivistic culture that characterizes Russia (Hofstede 1980). However, the observation that Russian entrepreneurs have lower levels of achievement motivation somewhat undermines arguments for the universal importance of this motive.

3.1.2. *Entrepreneurial traits*

Thomas and Mueller (2000) examined whether traits associated with entrepreneurship – innovativeness, locus of control, risk-taking propensity and energy – differ systematically with cultural distance from the USA. In a second study, Mueller and Thomas (2000) offer evidence that internal locus of control is dominant in individualistic cultures and that innovativeness and internal locus of control are prevalent in cultures high in individualism and low in uncertainty avoidance. At the time, these findings led to the conclusion that cultures high in individualism and uncertainty avoidance are supportive of entrepreneurship. A limitation is that the subjects were students, and neither study linked these traits to entrepreneurial outcomes. Furthermore, recent evidence of high rates of entrepreneurship in traditionally collectivist and uncertainty avoiding cultures (e.g. Pinillos and Reyes 2011) suggests that we should be cautious in drawing strong conclusions.

In their study in Cape Verde, Garcia-Cabrera and Garcia-Soto (2008) propose that individualism is linked to locus of control, which in turn only influences entrepreneurial behaviour indirectly through education level. While conceptually plausible, the authors do not present a strong test of this double mediation effect (e.g. Baron and Kenny 1986). Therefore, further evidence is needed that such a causal chain can explain the impact of culture. In contrast, Kristiansen and Indarti (2004) did not find strong differences in locus of control among Indonesian and Norwegian students. Rather, they showed that, in these countries that differ in cultural characteristics such as individualism/collectivism, differences in entrepreneurial intentions are explained by differences in need for achievement and self-efficacy. This study also leads to the conclusion that in order to trace links between culture and entrepreneurial traits, it is necessary to consider multiple dimensions of culture and multiple theoretically relevant traits.

Lee-Ross and Mitchell (2007) replicated the association between entrepreneurial traits and Hofstede's dimensions of culture in the Torres Strait Islands. In their qualitative study, 61 Torres Strait entrepreneurs perceived sizable trait differences compared to models derived from Western studies. This finding highlights an important issue. Much research has focused on high-GDP countries in which opportunity-based entrepreneurial behaviour is more prevalent than necessity-based entrepreneurship. This suggests that the form of entrepreneurial behaviour may represent an important boundary condition on theoretical frameworks linking culture to entrepreneurship.

3.1.3. *Entrepreneurial intentions*

Some recent studies have investigated the effects of cultural values on entrepreneurial intentions (Linan and Chen 2009; Engle et al. 2010; Urban 2006; Autio et al. 2001; Moriano et al. 2012). These studies used the theory of planned behaviour (TPB; Ajzen 1991) to analyse entrepreneurial intentions in specific countries (Autio et al. 2001; Urban 2006) or to compare Azjen's model across countries with different cultures (Linan and Chen 2009; Moriano et al. 2012; Engle et al. 2010). Urban (2006) measured the relationship between specific configurations of Hofstede's (1990) cultural dimensions and entrepreneurial intentions in South Africa, which is characterized as a highly diverse, multi-cultural society. This is a setting in which it is possible to test the effects of diverse cultural norms in a single country. Entrepreneurial intentions were hypothesized to be positively influenced by moderate individualism/collectivism, low uncertainty avoidance, high masculinity, low power distance and high long-term orientation. Unfortunately, the results suggest that, at least within this single country context, differences in cultural values do not have a strong and clear relationship with entrepreneurial intentions. Urban (2006) interpreted such finding with the inability of culture – as it has been measured in the study – to predict differences in entrepreneurship. However, cross-national differences in entrepreneurship might be best explained by a broader set of institutions in addition to culture (Busenitz, Gomez, and Spencer 2000). In that case, diversity in cultural norms without institutional diversity may not be sufficiently powerful to influence behaviour.

Comparative studies suggest that the three motivational antecedents (personal attitude, subjective norm and perceived behavioural control) explain the formation of entrepreneurial intention in different countries, with cultural values determining the strength of the relationships (Linan and Chen 2009; Moriano et al. 2012; Engle et al. 2010). In a twist on the standard TPB framework, Linan and Chen found that subjective norms have only an indirect effect, influencing intention through personal attitude and perceived behavioural control. Linan and Chen suggest that culture and social differences may influence perceptions of the three motivational antecedents. The way we see the world may be culturally influenced, while the internal cognitive mechanisms through which we elaborate our views are universal.

Moriano et al. (2012) found that subjective norms are the least important predictors of students' entrepreneurial intentions across cultures and the only predictors whose influence varies across cultures. However, contrary to their expectations, the influence of subjective norms did not vary along the countries' collectivism/individualism. Like Urban (2006), Moriano and colleagues attribute these findings to the operational definition of culture through country data collection (House et al. 2004), and advocate the use of direct measures of culture (e.g. Stephan and Uhlaner 2010).

Nguyen et al. (2009) examined variations in entrepreneurial potential in three countries: Vietnam, Taiwan and the USA. They defined entrepreneurial potential as the desire to create new ventures, the intention to create new ventures and the confidence in creating new ventures. The construct therefore represents an elaboration of the TPB framework. Their results suggest that the interaction between culture and institutional factors explains cross-national differences in entrepreneurship. However, contrary to their hypotheses, Vietnam scored higher on intention to create new ventures than both the USA and Taiwan. Vietnam also scored higher than Taiwan on the confidence in creating new ventures. Nguyen and colleagues argued that these findings could be explained by considering both institutional and cultural factors. In Vietnam, renovation policies brought institutional development that encouraged new venture creation. Moreover, these policies increased the levels of uncertainty, which were perceived as opportunities by Confucian entrepreneurs.

3.1.4. *Cognitions*

Empirical research linking national culture to the cognitive processes of entrepreneurs is limited and offers mixed results (Goktan and Gunay 2011; Mitchell et al. 2000). One of the earlier contributions by Mitchell et al. (2000) examined whether entrepreneurial cognitive scripts vary across cultures. They report that cognitive scripts that vary across cultures according to individualism and power distance are associated with the venture creation. However, they found that the direction of association was not consistent across specific scripts. A script describing knowledge of appropriable ideas was negatively associated with individualism and positively associated with power distance. In contrast, a script describing access to resources was positively associated with individualism and negatively associated with power distance. Thus, while entrepreneurial cognitive scripts were associated with cultural variation, this research does not support the notion that one culture is superior to another.

Notwithstanding their empirical contributions on the interrelation between culture and entrepreneurial cognition, neither of these two studies (Goktan and Gunay 2011; Mitchell et al. 2000) disentangles the effect of culture and nation on entrepreneurial cognition. Such limitation is addressed by Tan (2002), who compared the influence of cultural and national context on the perceptions and orientations of mainland Chinese, Chinese American and

Caucasian American entrepreneurs. He found that, while mainland Chinese entrepreneurs differed significantly in perceptions and orientations from both Chinese American and Caucasian Americans, the latter two groups did not differ significantly. This led Tan to suggest that differences normally attributed to culture might actually stem from differences in the national environment.

3.2. *Entrepreneurial mindset across cultures*

A question that has received limited empirical evaluation is whether there is an entrepreneurial culture that distinguishes entrepreneurs from non-entrepreneurs (Baum et al. 1993; McGrath, MacMillan, Yang and Tsai 1992; McGrath and MacMillan 1992; Tan 2002; Mitchell et al. 2002). These studies are summarized in Table 3.

Baum et al. (1993) compared entrepreneurs and managers in the USA and Israel in terms of motivation. They found that, across both countries, both the need for autonomy and, surprisingly, need for affiliation are higher in entrepreneurs than in non-entrepreneurs, although the latter was only marginally significant. Thus, the findings for an entrepreneurial 'type' across cultures were only weakly supported in this study.

While it makes a very interesting contribution in terms of the universality of motives, a limitation of Baum et al.'s study is that the authors do not make a strong connection between dimensions of national culture and the entrepreneurial traits. In contrast, McGrath, MacMillan, Yang and Tsai (1992) examine whether entrepreneurs and non-entrepreneurs differ in terms of Hosftede's dimensions of culture. McGrath, MacMillan, Yang and Tsai (1992) compared entrepreneurs with non-entrepreneurs in 13 countries. They found that entrepreneurs were comparatively higher in power distance, individualism and masculinity and lower in uncertainty avoidance than non-entrepreneurs, suggesting the possibility of an 'entrepreneurial culture'. In a related study, McGrath and MacMillan (1992) report that entrepreneurs were more likely to believe in taking the initiative and control of their destiny, were willing to take charge and direct others and were positively oriented towards adaptation and change. Mitchell et al. (2002) surveyed 990 individuals in 11 countries to explore differences in cognitions between entrepreneurs and non-business people, the universality of entrepreneurs' ways of thinking and influence of national culture on these cognitions. Their analysis shows that entrepreneurs and business non-entrepreneurs differ on arrangements, willingness and ability cognitions across countries. This was in addition to country-based differences in cognitive scripts among entrepreneurs.

This collection of studies suggests there may be a common entrepreneurial 'culture' or 'type' that transcends national culture. However, national culture may moderate the strength of traits, beliefs and perceptions related to entrepreneurship. This is consistent with the work of Tan (2002), which has shown how culture can be displaced in favour of entrepreneurial beliefs in some contexts, but not others.

3.3. *Summary*

In contrast to research seeking cultural explanations for different entrepreneurial outcomes, this literature compares whether entrepreneurs are different, from non-entrepreneurs and from other entrepreneurs, across countries. The literature on entrepreneurial motives and traits across cultures has revealed one fact quite consistently: self-reported motives vary consistently across countries (e.g. Pruett et al. 2009; Scheinberg and MacMillan 1988; Shane, Kolvereid, and Westhead 1991; Stewart et al. 2003) and

Table 3. Studies of national culture and characteristics of entrepreneurs and non-entrepreneurs.

Authors	Research question	Major variables (independent/dependent)	Sample/data source(s)	Major findings
McGrath and MacMillan (1992)	Across cultures, do entrepreneurs share the common perceptions about non-entrepreneurs?	National culture/shared perception among entrepreneurs about non-entrepreneurs	770 entrepreneurs: 14 countries/survey	Across diverse cultures there is a common set of perceptions held by entrepreneurs about non-entrepreneurs.
McGrath, MacMillan, Yang and Tsai (1992)	Is there a set of values that are held by entrepreneurs vs. non-entrepreneurs across cultures?	Entrepreneur, non-entrepreneur/power distance, individualism, uncertainty, avoidance, masculinity-femininity	1217 entrepreneurs, 1206 non-entrepreneurs: 9 countries/survey	Across cultures, entrepreneurs score high in power distance, individualism, and masculinity and low in uncertainty avoidance.
Baum et al. (1993)	Does national culture moderate the association between individual needs and chosen work role (entrepreneur vs. manager)?	Individual needs, national culture/chosen work role (entrepreneur vs. manager)	370 Israeli and U.S. entrepreneurs and managers/survey	Israeli entrepreneurs report higher need for achievement and affiliation and lower need for dominance than do Israeli managers. U.S. entrepreneurs do not differ significantly from U.S. managers.
Tan (2002)	Do the cultural and national effect differ in their influence on entrepreneurs' perception of the environment and their strategic orientation?	Hofstede's cultural values/entrepreneurs' perception of the environment and their strategic orientation	53 Mainland Chinese entrepreneurs; 62 Chinese American entrepreneurs; 85 Caucasian American entrepreneurs/survey	National differences have a more significant impact than cultural differences on entrepreneurial beliefs.
Mitchell et al. (2002)	Are entrepreneurial cognitions universal? (To what extent do entrepreneurial cognitions differ by national culture?)	National culture/entrepreneurial cognitions	990 respondents; 11 countries (418 entrepreneur and 572 non-entrepreneurs)/survey	There are country-based differences for 8 of the 10 proposed cognition constructs. Individuals who possess 'professional entrepreneurial cognition' have cognitions that are distinct from non-entrepreneurs. Moreover, the pattern of country representation within an empirically developed set of entrepreneurial archetypes differs among countries.

regions within countries (e.g. Aoyama 2009). A criticism raised previously by Hayton, George, and Zahra (2002, 47) was that if culture is assumed to be 'an aggregation of individual values and beliefs, it is not surprising that measures of cultural values are correlated with measures of individual values ...' The same argument applies to traits. The result is a tautology: when differences in the national level are derived from the aggregation of individual differences, it is hardly surprising that conceptually related individual differences are predicted based on nationality.

Work on entrepreneurial intentions only partially overcomes this problem. The TPB represents a dominant approach to theorizing about entrepreneurial motivation. In principle, we would expect that the components of the TPB to be subject to influence by both cultural and institutional factors. That is, beliefs concerning the social desirability and personal desirability of entrepreneurship are plausibly influenced by the cultural environment. Both culture and institutions would also be expected to influence entrepreneurial self-efficacy, or at least moderate the influence of such perceived behavioural control upon intentions. Despite this conceptual plausibility, due to methodological shortcomings, the studies in this area have yet to fulfil the promise of explaining the process through which culture influences intentions to behave entrepreneurially (e.g. Engle et al. 2010; Urban 2006).

Research on variations in cognitions across cultures holds promise similar to that of the intentions view. That is, by examining how culture as an exogenous factor influences perceptions and cognitions, it is possible to develop plausible, testable and non-tautological models of culture's influence. This may be direct or indirect. Interestingly, very limited research has been conducted on the influence of culture on cognition. That which has been conducted suggests systematic differences, although so far no coherent framework has been worked out and successfully tested.

The question of mindset appears to have largely fallen out of fashion, with the most recent study by Tan (2002) representing the only new contribution since Hayton, George, and Zahra's (2002) review. The evidence suggests that entrepreneurs as a group do share a number of common traits. McGrath, MacMillan, Yang and Tsai (1992) find higher individualism, masculinity and less uncertainty avoidance. This suggests that entrepreneurs' individual values, therefore, differ from the dominant culture in the way suggested by Baum et al. (1993). Furthermore, there may be some commonality in traits such as achievement, control, flexibility and tolerance of risk (Baum et al. 1993; McGrath, MacMillan, Yang and Tsai 1992). Little is known, however, about the process of this interaction between individual differences and national norms, or the cognitive processes through which these elements interact, or indeed the outcomes of these cognitive processes. For example, if being an entrepreneur involves extreme deviation from national cultural norms, what is the impact of such deviation for individuals, or the achievement of entrepreneurial objectives? A further question that arises is whether the 'entrepreneurial mindset' is converging globally, or whether there may be different forms of this mindset according to temporal (Shane 1993; Wennekers et al. 2007), economic (Pinillos and Reyes 2011; Wennekers et al. 2007) and geographic contexts (e.g. Stephan and Uhlaner 2010). Rather than abandoning this question, work is needed to integrate these moderators and also to consider the processes through which individual differences and collective values interact.

4. Revisiting the model of national culture and entrepreneurship

Hayton, George, and Zahra (2002) proposed a framework linking culture with entrepreneurship. In that model, cultural values, needs and motives, cognitions, beliefs and behaviours were each treated as correlated, but independent, factors that moderate the influence of institutional and economic context variables on entrepreneurial outcomes. To some extent, recent evidence provides support for the moderating role of culture on this relationship (e.g. Wennekers et al. 2007; Pinillos and Reyes 2011). We therefore do not want to dismiss this model as incorrect. However, it is designed to serve a specific purpose: to more completely account for contextual factors in understanding rates of entrepreneurship. A weakness of that model is that it does not account for the internal psychological, and particularly cognitive processes, through which culture, institution and economy influence individual decision-making and action. The studies reviewed show that national cultural values do influence, or at least correlate with individual motives, motive dispositions, traits and cognitions that are associated with being an entrepreneur. What is now required are studies that successfully connect the causal chain from cultural values through individual motives, traits and cognitions, to behaviours and aggregate measures of behavioural outcomes. Unfortunately, the literature may be referred to conservatively as 'messy'. A clean up is in order before such connections may be made in a coherent fashion. Such a clean up would involve a systematic consideration of culture along with dimensions of institutional environments (Busenitz, Gomez, and Spencer 2000) and connections with one or more of the sets of variables identified above. Entrepreneurial cognitions may be the most precise of these variables, although behavioural intentions are an alternative, and well-established framework, to employ.

The path forward should begin without the encumbrance of the 'standard entrepreneurial model': i.e. that need for achievement, locus of control and risk taking represent the meaningful differentiators. The evidence for this perspective is at best mixed, especially when it comes to differentiating entrepreneurs from managers. The standard model also implies that there is one best way regardless of institutional and economic contexts. This view is clearly contradicted by empirical reality. It is important to understand how individual difference variables or individual cognitions are influenced by both culture and institutions and how these factors interact. Once these relationships have been framed and tested, a fully mediated model becomes a realistic possibility. A starting point for such an integration may be the framework suggested by Busenitz and Lau (1996). Their framework, reproduced in Figure 1, places cognitions at the centre of a process, mediating between the combined main effects of culture, individual differences and contextual factors. To our knowledge, this conceptual framework has yet to be subjected to empirical examination.

An advantage of a cognitive approach is that it holds the possibility for integration of stable individual differences as antecedents to cognitive processing along with cultural and situational factors. However, Busenitz and Lau (1996) do not develop the connections between specific cultural and institutional dimensions and cognitive structure or process variables. This is where the proverbial rubber meets the road in seeking an explanation for culture's consequences.

5. Conclusion

This review has revealed a number of significant challenges. First, evidence has begun to accumulate that individualism and low uncertainty avoidance are not always positively associated with entrepreneurial behaviour. It is essential to look beyond and consider the types of entrepreneurship and the economic context for action. There remains a dearth of studies that examine the interactions among culture and institutions. Yet these and other variables, such as rates of inward investment, national innovation or entrepreneurship

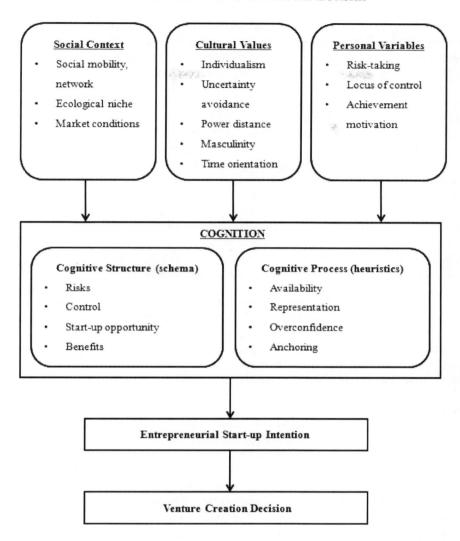

Figure 1. A cross-cultural cognitive model of venture creation (Busenitz and Lau 1996).

policies can be expected to interact with cultural factors. However, such associations are highly complex and potentially challenging to study using macro-level data.

We believe that the next stage in the evolution of this literature should be the development of more rigorous theoretical frameworks. First, future research needs to clarify the distinctions and connections among traits and dispositional motives, values, cognitions and cognitive processes. The conceptual framework provided in the previous section provides a logical foundation for this integration (Busenitz and Lau 1996). Such an approach holds the possibility of sidestepping problems caused by taking a more macroscopic view. That is, if the focus of research shifts towards an explanatory model of when and how specific cognitions (e.g. schema, scripts, perceptions or preferences) arise in contexts characterized by known institutional contexts and measured cultural values, then the currently observed inconsistencies across studies may be explained. It is evident that the role of individualism may be contingent on economic development; uncertainty avoidance may be expressed in different ways (sometimes approaching and sometimes avoiding entrepreneurship). Thus a focus on cognitions, and cross-cultural cognitive studies, may help overcome these observed 'inconsistencies' or rather nuances in what was once a taken-for-granted view of culture's consequences.

It is important that researchers in the future provide a more coherent framing of the distinctions among cultural values, and individually held values, individual difference variables and subjective norms. In addition to coherent framing, variables must be operationalized in a way which avoids the tautology of asking individuals questions about values that are expected to reflect cultural values for entrepreneurship, when those cultural values are hypothesized to represent aggregations of individual values. Taking a cognitive approach holds the possibility for better distinguishing between the exogenous factors (internal and external) and the processes by which these factors influence behaviour. Whether it is by examining knowledge structures (Mitchell et al. 2000), expectancies or other cognitive elements, this distinction needs to be maintained.

Second, future research needs to address the reasons for some inconsistences in findings. While the intuition that culture matters is still a powerful one, the evidence of predictable associations between culture and entrepreneurial outcomes at regional and national levels is remarkably mixed, perhaps more so now than 10 years earlier. This might be due to the use of different samples, different measures of entrepreneurship and/or the way national culture is operationalized. Future studies need to take account of at least two generic forms of entrepreneurship: necessity and opportunity. These reflect differences in context as well as differences in motive. It has become apparent that old distinctions thought to predict national rates of entrepreneurial activity do not hold up when that activity is broadly conceived. One way to address this would be to use type of activity as a boundary condition. An alternative is to include stage of economic development as a moderator and attempt to incorporate both types of entrepreneurship in a single framework. The latter approach would rest on an assumption that the same intermediate variables are relevant to both outcomes. Such an assumption might be most tenable with cognitive variables. Lastly, we suggest that researchers speculate on the use of different measures of national culture (e.g. cultural values vs. cultural norms). If the problem is in the way culture is operationalized, perhaps the use of cultural norms rather than cultural values will help solve inconsistencies in findings.

We have come a long way in understanding culture's consequences for entrepreneurship. However, as with any complex phenomenon, the closer we look, the more complexity we see. Unravelling this complexity is essential, not least because cultural contexts may moderate the impact of policies intended to influence entrepreneurial behaviours.

Note

1. We do not include in our review research on the relationship between culture and corporate entrepreneurship. This is due to space constraints, given the expansion of research in independent entrepreneurship, and also the relative stagnation in the literature on corporate entrepreneurship with respect to the issue of culture.

References

Ajzen, Icek. 1991. "The Theory of Planned Behavior." *Organizational Behavior and Human Decision Processes* 50: 179–211.

Aoyama, Yuko. 2009. "Entrepreneurship and Regional Culture: The Case of Hamamatsu and Kyoto, Japan." *Regional Studies* 43 (3): 495–512.

Audretsch, D. B., and A. R. Thurik. 2001. "What is New About the New Economy: Sources of Growth in the Managed and Entrepreneurial Economies." *Industrial and Corporate Change* 19: 795–821.

Autio, Erkko, R. H. Keeley, M. Klofsten, G. G. C. Parker, and Michael Hay. 2001. "Entrepreneurial Intent Among Students in Scandinavia and in the USA." *Enterprise and Innovation Management Studies* 2 (2): 145–160.

Baron, R. M., and D. A. Kenny. 1986. "The Moderator–Mediator Variable Distinction in Social Psychological Research: Conceptual, Strategic, and Statistical Considerations." *Journal of Personality and Social Psychology* 51: 1173–1182.

Baum, J. R., J. D. Olian, Miriam Erez, E. R. Schnell, K. G. Smith, H. P. Sims, J. S. Scully, and K. A. Smith. 1993. "Nationality and Work Role Interactions: A Cultural Contrast of Israeli and U.S. Entrepreneurs' Versus Managers' Needs." *Journal of Business Venturing* 8: 449–512.

Beugelsdijk, Sjoerd. 2007. "Entrepreneurial Culture, Regional Innovativeness and Economic Growth." *Journal of Evolutionary Economics* 17: 187–210.

Beugelsdijk, Sjoerd, and Niels Noorderhaven. 2004. "Entrepreneurial Attitude and Economic Growth: A Cross-Section of 54 Regions." *Annals of Regional Science* 38: 199–218.

Bhide, Amar. 2000. *The Origin and Evolution of New Business.* New York: Oxford University Press.

Birley, Sue. 1987. "New Ventures and Employment Growth." *Journal of Business Venturing* 2: 155–165.

Busenitz, L. W., Carolina Gomez, and J. W. Spencer. 2000. "Country Institutional Profiles: Unlocking Entrepreneurial Phenomena." *Academy of Management Journal* 43: 994–1003.

Busenitz, L. W., and C. M. Lau. 1996. "A Cross-Cultural Cognitive Model of New Venture Creation." *Entrepreneurship Theory and Practice* 20: 25–39.

Davidsson, Per. 1995. "Culture, Structure and Regional Levels of Entrepreneurship." *Entrepreneurship and Regional Development* 7: 41–62.

Davidsson, Per, and Johan Wiklund. 1997. "Values, Beliefs and Regional Variations in New Firm Formation Rates." *Journal of Economic Psychology* 18: 179–199.

De Pillis, E., and K. K. Reardon. 2007. "The Influence of Personality Traits and Persuasive Messages on Entrepreneurial Intention: A Cross-Cultural Comparison." *Career Development International* 12 (4): 382–396.

Engle, R. L., Nikolav Dimitriadi, J. V. Gavidia, Christopher Schlaegel, Servane Delanoe, Irene Alvarado, Xiaohong He, Samuel Buame, and Birgitta Wolff. 2010. "Entrepreneurial Intent: A Twelve-Country Evaluation of Ajzen's Model of Planned Behavior." *International Journal of Entrepreneurial Behavior & Research* 16 (1): 35–37.

Freytag, Andreas, and Roy Thurik. 2007. "Entrepreneurship and Its Determinants in a Cross-Country Setting." *Journal of Evolutionary Economics* 17: 117–131.

Garcia-Cabrera, A. M., and M. G. Garcia-Soto. 2008. "Cultural Differences and Entrepreneurial Behavior: An Intra-Country Cross-Cultural Analysis in Cape Verde." *Entrepreneurship & Regional Development: An International Journal* 20 (5): 451–483.

Goktan, A. B., and Gonca Gunay. 2011. "Is Entrepreneurial Cognition Culturally Bound? A Comparative Study Conducted in Turkey and United States." *Journal of Small Business and Entrepreneurship* 24 (4): 445–470.

Granovetter, M. S. 1973. "The Strength of Weak Ties." *American Journal of Sociology* 78 (6): 1360–1380.

Hayton, J. C., Gerard George, and S. AZahra. 2002. "National Culture and Entrepreneurship: A Review of Behavioral Research." *Entrepreneurship: Theory & Practice* 26 (4): 33–52.

Herbig, Paul. 1994. *The Innovation Matrix: Culture and Structure Prerequisites to Innovation.* Westport, CT: Quorum.

Herbig, P. A., and J. C. Miller. 1992. "Culture and Technology: Does the Traffic Move in Both Directions?" *Journal of Global Marketing* 6: 75–104.

Hofstede, Geert. 1980. *Culture's Consequences: International Differences in Work Related Values.* Beverly Hills, CA: Sage.

Hofstede, Geert. 1990. *Cultures and Organizations: Software of the Mind.* New York: McGraw Hill.

Hofstede, Geert. 1991. *Cultures and Organizations: Software of the Mind.* New York: McGraw Hill.

Hofstede, Geert. 2001. *Culture's Consequences: Comparing Values, Behaviors, Institutions, and Organizations Across Nations.* Thousand Oaks, CA: Sage.

Hofstede, Geert, G. J. Hofstede, and Michael Minkov. 2010. *Cultures and Organizations: Software of the Mind.* 3rd ed. New York, NY: McGraw Hill.

House, R. J., P. W. Hanges, Mansour Javadan, P. W. Dorfman, and Vipin Gupta. 2004. *Culture, Leadership and Organization: The GLOBE Study of 62 Societies.* Thousand Oaks, CA: Sage.

INSEAD. 2009. "Global Innovation Index-2009." http://www.elab.insead.edu

Kristiansen, Stein, and Nurul Indarti. 2004. "Entrepreneurial Intention Among Indonesian and Norwegian Students." *Journal of Enterprising Culture* 12 (1): 55–78.

Lee-Ross, Darren, and Benjamin Mitchell. 2007. "Doing Business in the Torres Straits: A Study of the Relationship Between Culture and the Nature of Indigenous Entrepreneurship." *Journal of Developmental Entrepreneurship* 12 (2): 199–216.

Linan, Francisco, and Yi-Wen Chen. 2009. "Development and Cross-Cultural Application of Specific Instrument to Measure Entrepreneurial Intentions." *Entrepreneurship: Theory and Practice* 33 (3): 593–617.

McClelland, D. C. 1961. *The Achieving Society.* Princeton, NJ: Van Nostrand.

McClelland, D. C., J. W. Atkinson, R. A. Clark, and E. L. Lowell. 1953. *The Achievement Motive.* New York: Appleton-Century-Crofts.

McGrath, R. G., and I. C. MacMillan. 1992. "More like Each Other than Anyone Else? A Cross-Cultural Study of Entrepreneurial Perceptions." *Journal of Business Venturing* 7: 419–429.

McGrath, R. G., I. C. MacMillan, and S. Scheinberg. 1992. "Elitists, Risk-Takers, and Rugged Individualists? An Exploratory Analysis of Cultural Differences Between Entrepreneurs and Non-Entrepreneurs." *Journal of Business Venturing* 7: 115–135.

McGrath, R. G., I. C. MacMillan, E. A. Yang, and William Tsai. 1992. "Does Culture Endure, or is It Malleable? Issues for Entrepreneurial Economic Development." *Journal of Business Venturing* 7: 441–458.

Mitchell, R. K., J. B. Smith, E. A. Morse, K. W. Seawright, A. M. Peredo, and Brian McKenzie. 2002. "Are Entrepreneurial Cognitions Universal? Assessing Entrepreneurial Cognitions Across Cultures." *Entrepreneurship: Theory and Practice* 26 (4): 9–32.

Mitchell, R. K., Brock Smith, K. W. Seawright, and E. A. Morse. 2000. "Cross-Cultural Cognitions and the Venture Creation Decision." *Academy of Management Journal* 43: 974–993.

Moriano, J. A., Mirjan Gorgievski, Mariola Laguna, Ute Stephan, and Kiumars Zarafshani. 2012. "A Cross Cultural Approach to Understanding Entrepreneurial Intention." *Journal of Career Development* 39 (2): 162–185.

Mueller, S. L., and A. S. Thomas. 2000. "Culture and Entrepreneurial Potential: A Nine Country Study of Locus of Control and Innovativeness." *Journal of Business Venturing* 16: 51–75.

Nguyen, T. V., S. E. Bryant, Jerman Rose, Chiung-Hui Tseng, and Supara Kapasuwan. 2009. "Cultural Values, Market, Institutions, and Entrepreneurship Potential: A Comparative Study of the Unites States, Taiwan, and Vietnam." *Journal of Developmental Entrepreneurship* 14 (1): 21–37.

Pinillos, M. J., and Luisa Reyes. 2011. "Relationship Between Individualist–Collectivist Culture and Entrepreneurial Activity: Evidence from Global Entrepreneurship Monitor Data." *Small Business Economics* 37: 23–37.

Porter, M. E., and Scott Stern. 2001. "Innovation: Location Matters." *MIT Sloan Management Review*.

Pruett, Mark, Rachel Shinnar, Bryan Toney, Francisco Llopis, and Jerry Fox. 2009. "Explaining Entrepreneurial Intentions of University Students: A Cross-Cultural Study." *International Journal of Entrepreneurial Behaviour & Research* 15 (6): 571–594.

Rinne, Tiffany, G. D. Steel, and John Fairweather. 2012. "Hofstede and Shane Revisited: The Role of Power Distance and Individualism in National-Level Innovation Success." *Cross-Cultural Research* 46 (2): 91–108.

Scheinberg, Sari, and I. C. MacMillan. 1988. "An 11 Country Study of Motivations to Start a Business." In *Frontiers of Entrepreneurship Research*, edited by Kirchoff Bruce, W. A. Long, W. E. McMullan, K. H. Vesper, and W. E. Wetzel. Wellesley, MA: Babson College.

Shane, Scott. 1992. "Why do Some Societies Invent more than Others?" *Journal of Business Venturing* 7: 29–46.

Shane, Scott. 1993. "Cultural Influences on National Rates of Innovation." *Journal of Business Venturing* 8: 59–73.

Shane, Scott, Lars Kolvereid, and Paul Westhead. 1991. "An Exploratory Examination of the Reasons Leading to New Firm Formation Across Country and Gender." *Journal of Business Venturing* 6: 431–446.

Stephan, Ute, and L. M. Uhlaner. 2010. "Performance-Based vs. Socially Supportive Culture: A Cross-National Study of Descriptive Norms and Entrepreneurship." *Journal of International Business Studies* 41: 1347–1364.

Stewart, W. H., Jr, J. C. Carland, J. W. Carland, W. E. Watson, and Sweo Robert. 2003. "Entrepreneurial Dispositions and Goal Orientation: A Comparative Exploration of United States and Russian Entrepreneurs." *Journal of Small Business Management* 41 (1): 27–46.

Sun, Hongyi. 2009. "A Meta-Analysis on the Influence of National Culture on Innovation Capability." *International Journal of Entrepreneurship and Innovation Management* 10 (3/4): 353–360.

Swierczek, F. W., and Troung Quang. 2004. "Entrepreneurial Cultures in Asia: Business Policy or Cultural Imperative." *Journal of Enterprising Culture* 12 (2): 127–145.

Tan, Justin. 2002. "Culture, Nation, and Entrepreneurial Strategic Orientations: Implications for an Emerging Economy." *Entrepreneurship: Theory and Practice* 26 (4): 95–111.

Thomas, A. S., and S. L. Mueller. 2000. "A Case for Comparative Entrepreneurship: Assessing the Relevance of Culture." *Journal of International Business Studies* 31: 287–301.

Uhlaner, L. M., and A. R. Thurik. 2007. "Post-Materialism Influencing Total Entrepreneurial Activity Across Nations." *Journal of Evolutionary Economics* 17: 161–185.

Urban, Boris. 2006. "Entrepreneurship in the Rainbow Nation: Effect of Cultural Values and ESE on Intentions." *Journal of Developmental Entrepreneurship* 11 (3): 171–186.

van Praag, M., and P. H. Versloot. 2007. "What is the Value of Entrepreneurship? A Review of Recent Research." *Small Business Economics* 29 (4): 351–382.

van Stel, A. J. 2005. "COMPENDIA: Harmonizing Business Ownership Data Across Countries and Over Time." *International Entrepreneurship and Management Journal* 1 (1): 105–123.

Weber, Max. 1930. *The Protestant Ethic and the Spirit of Capitalism*. New York: Scribners.

Wennekers, Sander, Roy Thurik, Andr van Stel, and Niels Noorderhaven. 2007. "Uncertainty Avoidance and the Rate of Business Ownership Across 21 OECD Countries, 1976–2004." *Journal of Evolutionary Economics* 17: 133–160.

Wennekers, Sander, L. M. Uhlaner, and Roy Thurik. 2002. "Entrepreneurship and Its Conditions: A Macro Perspective." *International Journal of Entrepreneurship Education* 1: 25–64.

Williams, L. K., and S. J. McGuire. 2010. "Economic Creativity and Innovation Implementation: The Entrepreneurial Drivers of Growth? Evidence from 63 Countries." *Small Business Economics* 34: 391–412.

National culture and cultural orientations of owners affecting the innovation–growth relationship in five countries

Andreas Rauch[a], Michael Frese[b], Zhong-Ming Wang[c], Jens Unger[d], Maria Lozada[d], Vita Kupcha[d] and Tanja Spirina[d]

[a]Innovation Incubator, Leuphana University Lüneburg, Lüneburg, Germany; [b]Department of Management & Organization, National University of Singapore Business School, Singapore; [c]School of Management, Zhejiang University, Hangzhou, China; [d]Department of Work and Organizational Psychology, University of Gießen, Gießen, Germany

This study tests the cross-cultural validity of the relationship between innovation and growth in a sample of 857 business owners from five different countries: China, Germany, the Netherlands, Peru and Russia. We found that innovation is effective in each country, suggesting universal relationships. In addition, cultural variables moderated the innovation–growth relationship. Finally, our cross-level operator analysis revealed that both cultural orientations of owners and national culture explain variance in innovation–growth relationships. Thus, we found interactions across difference levels of culture, which have theoretical and practical implications for cross-cultural entrepreneurship research.

1. Introduction

The relationship between innovation and growth has been studied extensively in entrepreneurship research. Although there is evidence that innovation is positively related to growth (Rosenbusch, Brinckmann, and Bausch 2011), the strength of this relationship is affected by moderators including firm-level factors (Coad and Rao 2008; Rosenbusch, Brinckmann, and Bausch 2011), industry-level factors (Freel and Robson 2004; Stam and Wennberg 2009), external linkages (Mansury and Love 2008) and environmental conditions (Jansen, van Den Bosch, and Volberda 2006).

Culture has been suggested to affect the relationship between innovation and growth (Rosenbusch, Brinckmann, and Bausch 2011). However, the details as well as the generalizability of the innovation–growth relationship across cultures are unknown. Moreover, practitioners would be interested to know whether innovation affects growth in certain contexts or not. Therefore, the aim of this study is threefold. First, we investigate the innovation–growth relationship of businesses in different countries. Specifically, we examine whether the innovation–growth relationship is universally valid in different national contexts or whether it is culturally specific. Theoretically, economics has often assumed universally valid relationships between innovation and growth. However, some scholars argued that innovation needs to be aligned to the cultural, economic and institutional context in order to produce positive outcomes (Busenitz, Gomez, and Spencer

2000). This paper combines both arguments by hypothesizing universal relationships to growth as well as specific moderators of culture and cultural orientation of owners on the innovation–growth relationship.

Second, we conceptualize culture as a moderator affecting the innovation–growth relationship. Most cross-cultural entrepreneurship research has studied direct relationships between culture and entrepreneurial activities while conceptualizing culture as an independent variable (Hayton, George, and Zahra 2002; Kreiser et al. 2010; Pinillos and Reyes 2011; Shane, Venkataraman, and MacMillan 1995; Wennekers et al. 2007). Our approach conceptualizes culture as a moderator variable. This is in line with newer cross-cultural approaches (Erez 2010; Shane, Venkataraman, and MacMillan 1995; Tung, Walls, and Frese 2007). This approach assumes that it is possible to develop innovation in any culture, but that the hurdles to be addressed are dependent on the culture. To our knowledge, this moderator hypothesis has not been addressed in the previous research.

Third, we argue that innovation implementation is a firm-level activity, which should be affected by individual-level and country-level culture. Thus, our study adds to the literature about cultural differences in entrepreneurship by looking at the cultural orientations of entrepreneurs (König et al. 2007). Thereby, we examine whether individual orientations replicate national cultural effects. Addressing cross-country differences in innovativeness solely at the country level assumes that national culture directly affects the behaviour of business firms; this assumption may sometimes be true but not always (Erez 2010). Moreover, the additional layer of analysis allows understanding the processes by which national culture can have an influence on the innovation–growth relationship. Studies measuring culture at one single level of analysis necessarily assume similar relationships between constructs at different levels of analysis (Chen, Bliese, and Mathieu 2005; Erez 2010; Erez and Gati 2004). This assumption is oversimplified because individual-level cultural orientations may not always have the same effects as the national culture.

We compare business owners in five divergent contexts: China, Germany, the Netherlands, Peru and Russia. These countries vary considerably on a number of dimensions such as geography, socio-economic system and development, traditions, cultural practices and values. Finding the same relationships between innovation and growth in such divergent countries would indicate the existence of cultural universals (Norenzayan and Heine 2005). Finding differences between these countries would indicate that entrepreneurship theory needs to consider 'cultural specifics' by studying contingency theory.

2. Theory development

Figure 1 displays the conceptual model of our study. We first explain the role of innovations and of national culture and cultural orientations of owners.

2.1. *The role of innovation on growth*

Innovation includes the successful introduction of new products/services, new production methods, new markets, new supply methods and the new organization of industries (e.g. Schumpeter 1935). Innovation is a core characteristic of entrepreneurship (Drucker 1993; Schumpeter 1935). Innovations are important because they help to maintain a flexible and durable organization. In addition, innovations stimulate learning processes that increase competitive advantages (Zahra and George 2002). Moreover, product innovations help to maintain the market share, and process innovations help to produce below current price

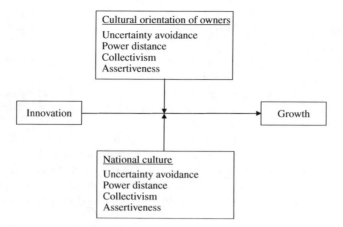

Figure 1. The conceptual model of the study.

levels (Heunks 1998). Innovations thus help firms to achieve a competitive advantage; therefore, they should be related to growth (Brouwer and Kleinknecht 1996; Heunks 1998; Stam and Wennberg 2009). However, the positive effect of innovation on growth is not uncontested (Christensen and Raynor 2003). For example, some studies reported no effect (Cooke, Clifton, and Oleaga 2005; Freel 2000) or even a negative effect (Freel and Robson 2004). Rosenbusch, Brinckmann, and Bausch (2011) performed a meta-analysis of 42 studies and reported a positive relationship between innovation and success across studies ($r = 0.133$). Therefore, our first hypothesis is a replication hypothesis:

Hypothesis 1:   There is a positive relationship between innovation and growth.

2.2. *The role of national culture and cultural orientations of owners*

The meta-analysis by Rosenbusch, Brinckmann, and Bausch (2011) indicated that the innovation–performance relationship is moderated by third variables (compare also Coad and Rao 2008; Freel and Robson 2004; Mansury and Love 2008; Stam and Wennberg 2009). Particularly, these results indicated that collectivism is one such moderator variable. Our study builds on this meta-analysis by examining additional dimensions of culture and by looking at both national and individual cultural dimensions.

Culture represents patterns of characteristic behaviours displayed by most people within a culture as observed by members of that culture (Fischer et al. 2009). Our study addresses four dimensions of culture at both the national level and the level of business owners that are important for innovation: uncertainty avoidance, collectivism, power distance and assertiveness. Uncertainty avoidance, collectivism and power distance have been related to entrepreneurship, innovation and growth in previous studies (Hayton, George, and Zahra 2002; Mueller and Thomas 2000; Shane and Kolvereid 1995). Uncertainty avoidance describes the extent to which members of a group feel threatened by uncertain and unknown situations (Hofstede 1991). Power distance reflects the extent to which people accept that power should be stratified and concentrated at higher levels of organizations or governments (Hofstede 1991; House et al. 2007). Collectivism reflects the degree to which people express pride in and loyalty to their in-groups such as a family or an organization. Assertiveness refers to the degree to which individuals are assertive, confrontational and aggressive in social relationships (House et al. 2007). We used assertiveness as an additional dimension of culture from the GLOBE study because it is related to Hofstede's masculinity index without tapping the gender role aspect of masculinity (Dickson, Den Hartog, and Mitchelson 2003). Moreover, assertiveness emphasizes initiative, competition and rewarding performance. Therefore, assertiveness may be important in the context of our study because it is closely related to the competitiveness associated with entrepreneurship (Lumpkin and Dess 1996).

Culture is a multilevel construct (Erez and Gati 2004). For example, an entrepreneur belonging to a national culture is nested in an entrepreneurial subculture and, moreover, establishes an own organizational culture in his venture (Tung, Walls, and Frese 2007). Thus, there are differences of national culture on the whole and of the cultural orientations of entrepreneurs (McGrath, MacMillan, and Scheinberg 1992). Our study predicts innovation–growth relationships and, thus, focuses on the firm level of analysis. Consequently, looking at the national culture alone is not sufficient for analysing the impact of culture on innovation. An important additional level of culture is the level of the cultural orientation of business owners, because this level is directly related to the practices that the owner implements in his business (König et al. 2007). Owners and managers of businesses have a strong influence on the specific practices in their enterprises (Frese 2000). Cultural practices reveal how owners go about managing their business (Schein 1992). Therefore, cultural orientations of business owners provide a starting point for the development of an organizational culture (Schein 1992). We assume that owners support a culture they consider to be related to growth (Schein 1992).

Studying culture at two levels of analysis requires identifying the nature of relationships between the different levels of culture. Most approaches assume that different levels of culture affect the relationship between innovation and performance in the same way. For example, studies exploring the effect of one level of culture (e.g. the country level) on innovation–performance relationships assume that culture affects, in a linear way, the behaviours and consequences at the firm level (e.g. Rosenbusch, Brinckmann, and Bausch 2011). This is a plausible assumption because most models of culture assume that a misalignment between different levels of culture creates a tension that reduces performance (Erez and Eagly 1993). However, there are exceptions to this rule – the different levels of culture do not necessarily correspond with each other (Morris, Davis, and Allen 1994). For example, a clash between individual and national levels of uncertainty avoidance may drive people into entrepreneurship (Noorderhaven et al. 2004). Similarly, an owner from a national culture low in uncertainty avoidance may try to reduce uncertainty in his firm, aiming to stimulate a safe environment for innovation. Thus, we propose that the innovation–growth relationship depends on whether the analysis is performed at the national level or at the level of the business owner. We now develop hypotheses on how the different levels of culture affect the proposed relationships.

2.3. *The effect of culture on the relationship between innovation and growth*

2.3.1. *Uncertainty avoidance*

Entrepreneurs face high uncertainty (Kirzner 1997; Knight 1921), and this needs to be addressed in order to recognize and exploit opportunities successfully (McMullen and Shepherd 2006).

We argue that uncertainty avoidance may be functional at the level of business owners to increase the relationship between innovation and growth. Innovation increases uncertainty because innovations increase firm risks (Sorescu and Spanjol 2008), involve huge resource commitments (Li and Atuahene-Gima 2001) and implicate investments into an unknown future. Such uncertainty harms entrepreneurial behaviour (McMullen and Shepherd 2006; Shane and Venkataraman 2000) and produces hesitancy, indecisiveness and procrastination (Casson 1982). Therefore, owners high in uncertainty avoidance attempt to reduce the uncertainty associated with innovation in the business, for example, by creating a safe environment for experimentation, by establishing plans and milestones for goal achievements and by launching routines for innovation implementation. Moreover, the emphasis on planning associated with high uncertainty avoidance helps to implement innovations faster while reducing the likelihood of expensive mistakes (Nakata and Sivakumar 1996). Thus, high uncertainty avoidance orientation helps to establish a protected firm environment that minimizes the uncertainty associated with innovation (Morris, Avila, and Allen 1993) and, therefore, leads to growth.

At the country level, uncertainty avoidance may inhibit innovation implementation, thereby reducing the relationship between innovation and growth. By definition, uncertainty avoidance creates resistance towards risk, innovation and change (Hofstede 1991; Shane 1993), suggesting that high uncertainty avoidant countries have little support for entrepreneurship and innovation (Hayton, George, and Zahra 2002). For example, in countries high in uncertainty avoidance, innovation acceptance is lower because customers prefer established products and services, and investors invest in ventures that reduce risk. Therefore, high uncertainty avoidance reduces the chance to grow from innovation.

Hypothesis 2a: The relationship between innovation and growth is stronger if the cultural orientation of owners is high in uncertainty avoidance when compared to owners with cultural orientations of low uncertainty avoidance.

Hypothesis 2b: The relationship between innovation and growth is stronger in countries with low levels of uncertainty avoidance than in countries with high levels of uncertainty avoidance.

2.3.2. *Power distance*

Power distance is related to resistance to change, because members of a culture high in power distance are dependent on their supervisor and are not used to taking personal initiative and adapting to changes (Hofstede 1991). Moreover, power distance is associated with maintaining the *status quo* and established barriers to novelty and change (Geletkanycz 1997). As a consequence, power distance has been argued to be negatively related to entrepreneurship activity (Hayton, George, and Zahra 2002). Empirically, the relationship between power distance and innovation is inconsistent. While Shane (1992) and Dwyer, Mesak, and Hsu (2005) reported positive relationships between power distance and innovation, Shane (1993) reported negative relationships. This suggests that moderators may be operative here.

We argue that high power distance may be functional to innovation implementation at the level of the cultural orientation of the owner. High power distance can produce a higher adherence to strategies already established in a firm and enables entrepreneurs to envision and implement novel ideas and strategies. The centralized authority associated with high power distance helps to institutionalize innovation implementation and to overcome the resistance associated with innovation (Geletkanycz 1997; Nakata and Sivakumar 1996). Moreover, innovation implementation requires control to ensure that the complex efforts associated with innovation result in the implementation of new products and services

(Nakata and Sivakumar 1996). Finally, research has shown that powerful authorities motivate employees to act innovatively (Elenkov and Manev 2005; Vaccaro et al. 2012) and help to monitor the realization and commercialization of innovations (Burgers, van Den Bosch, and Volberda 2008). Thus, owners high in power distance foster successful innovation implementation and, thereby, facilitate business growth.

At the country level, it may be difficult to implement innovation successfully in countries high in power distance because power distance refers to maintaining the *status quo* and resistance to change (Hofstede 1991). Therefore, customers might not be willing to accept innovations. Moreover, the bureaucratic structures of countries high in power distance aim to maintain the distribution of power and, thereby, build barriers for the initiatives of innovative entrepreneurs. Thus, there is little incentive for innovation in high power distance countries. As a consequence, it is difficult to implement innovation and change, which, in turn, reduces the innovation–growth relationship.

Hypothesis 3a: The relationship between innovation and growth is stronger if the cultural orientation of owners is high in power distance when compared to owners with cultural orientations of low power distance.

Hypothesis 3b: The relationship between innovation and growth is stronger in countries with low levels of power distance than in countries with high levels of power distance.

2.3.3. *Collectivism*

Individualism has been related to innovation and entrepreneurship because entrepreneurship is an activity of enterprising individuals who are individually rewarded (Hayton, George, and Zahra 2002). Moreover, innovation involves personal risk to overcome resistance to innovations (Shane 1993). A number of studies have investigated the relationship between individualism and innovation (Morris, Avila, and Allen 1993; Shane, Venkataraman, and MacMillan 1995; Taras, Kirkman, and Steel 2010).

With regard to innovation–growth relationships, collectivism seems to be important at the firm level (Triandis 1984). Successful innovation implementation is an effort of multiple persons (Klein and Sorra 1996); therefore, innovation implementation may well benefit from a collectivistic culture (Nakata and Sivakumar 1996). The effectiveness of innovation should increase when employees and management jointly pursue agreed upon goals and share the risk of failure. Moreover, high collectivism fosters collaboration and teamwork needed to address the challenges, resistance and efforts required for successful innovation implementation (Lechler 2001). Therefore, collectivistic orientations of owners affect the effectiveness of innovation.

With regard to the effect of country-level collectivism on the innovation–growth relationship, one has to consider the cohesive nature of collectivistic societies. Collective cultures provide more opportunities for communicating the new product innovations to employees, investors and customers (Dwyer, Mesak, and Hsu 2005). Thus, collectivism and cohesive networks support the commercialization of products because they support the interaction with customers, suppliers and other stakeholders (Rowley, Behrens, and Krackhardt 2000; Van de Ven 1986). This makes it more likely that the market accepts the innovations introduced by entrepreneurs. The general tendency for cooperation reduces the transaction costs in collective societies (Fukuyama 2001), and macro-level social capital (such as civic associations) should provide the resources to implement innovations successfully (Stephan and Uhlander 2010). As a consequence, there is a positive relationship between innovation and growth in countries high in collectivism (Rosenbusch, Brinckmann, and Bausch 2011). Thus:

Hypothesis 4a: The relationship between innovation and growth is stronger if the cultural orientation of owners is high in collectivism when compared to owners with cultural orientations of low collectivism.

Hypothesis 4b: The relationship between innovation and growth is stronger in countries with high levels of collectivism than in countries with low levels of collectivism.

2.3.4. *Assertiveness*

To our knowledge, assertiveness has not been related to entrepreneurial behaviour in previous studies. Assertiveness stresses a preference for competition, an emphasis on results over relationship and having a 'can-do' attitude (House et al. 2007). The strong emphasis of competitiveness and aggressiveness suggests a high responsiveness to the environment and to competitive threats (Lumpkin and Dess 2001). At the level of the business owner, assertiveness helps to implement innovation, because assertiveness helps to shape the environment to one's advantage in order to achieve results, and it emphasizes initiatives to establish a competitive market position. Moreover, assertiveness is related to the emergence of leadership (Stogdill 1948) and, specifically, it is associated with an emphasis on employees' initiative and support (Brodbeck et al. 2000). Such a leadership style should help successful innovation implementation.

However, at the national level, we assume that assertiveness reduces the relationship between innovation and growth. In high assertive countries, firms either defend their market position or aggressively enter the markets of their competitors, for example, by cutting prices (Venkatraman 1989). In this way, firms reduce opportunities and, moreover, innovations cannot be exploited to their full potential, which, in turn, reduces the innovation–growth relationship.

Hypothesis 5a: The relationship between innovation and growth is stronger if the cultural orientation of owners is high in assertiveness when compared to owners with cultural orientations of low assertiveness.

Hypothesis 5b: The relationship between innovation and growth is stronger in countries with low levels of assertiveness than in countries with high levels of assertiveness.

3. Methods

3.1. *Sample*

3.1.1. *The selection of countries*

The study compares five samples of business owners/managers from China, Germany, the Netherlands, Peru and Russia. We selected these countries based on two criteria (Franke and Richey 2010). First, it was our aim to include diverse cultures. Only high diversity of cultures allows testing the case for universality (Norenzayan and Heine 2005). Moreover, we chose the samples from high- and low-income countries (Heinrich, Heine, and Norenzayan 2010). We used these selection criteria because we assume that innovation has a different meaning in countries with a weak or a strong economy. For example, the innovativeness of firms increases with increasing levels of economic development

(Kelley, Singer, and Herrington 2011). Moreover, a high prevalence of opportunity-driven entrepreneurship should support innovation and growth.

We selected Peru for its high entrepreneurship rates (Kelley, Singer, and Herrington 2011). Peru is classified as an upper-middle-income country (World Bank 2012), ranking high in the Human Development Index (Human Development Statistical Annex 2011). China is located in a different continent, and it is an upper-middle-income country as well (World Bank 2012), ranking slightly lower in the Human Development Index than Peru. However, both countries differ considerably. For example, there is twice the necessity entrepreneurship in China than in Peru (Kelley, Singer, and Herrington 2011). China is a country high in uncertainty avoidance. We also selected the high-income countries, Germany and the Netherlands, both ranking high in the Human Development Index and low on entrepreneurship. Although both countries are located in Europe, they differ considerably in terms of their cultural values; Germany is higher in uncertainty avoidance and power distance than the Netherlands. Finally, we selected Russia because this country shares some economic similarities to China and Peru but, at the same time, it has considerably lower prevalence rates of entrepreneurship.

3.1.2. *The selection of participants*

To make the samples comparable, the participants were selected using three criteria: first, participants had to be owners and managers of their business (Stewart and Roth 2001). Second, they had at least one employee, because there is a qualitative difference between owners who work alone and owners who have employees (Frese 2000). Third, we selected industries that exist in all five countries: car and machinery components manufacturing, software development, hotel and catering and building and construction. This guaranteed a minimum amount of comparability across the five countries.

The national teams translated the English version of the instruments into the language of their home country. Since the Netherlands, Peru and Russia joined the investigation subsequently to Germany and China, the data were collected in the period between 2005 and 2008. All data were collected prior to the collapse of the Lehman Brothers in 2008. Therefore, we assume that the global economic conditions have not changed dramatically during the study period.

All investigators were trained to ensure that procedures, interviews and coding guidelines were the same across countries. Randomization within industries was done by using registration lists of the local Chambers of Commerce, Yellow Pages and some snowball sampling.

In China, 289 business owners from the area of Hangzhou in the Zheijang Province participated in our survey; the response rate was 62%. The German sample was drawn in the Rhine-Main area and consists of 302 owners; the response rate was 43%. The sample from the Netherlands consists of 87 business owners; the response rate was 13%. In Peru, 220 owners from the Arequipa region were contacted of which 112 participated, resulting in a response rate of 49%. In Russia, 67 owners from the area of Moscow participated in the survey; the response rate was 35%. The differences in these response rates are comparable with those reported in other cross-national surveys (Harzing 2000). Most participants did not only own and manage their business, but had also founded them (82% in China, 67% in Germany, 61% in the Netherlands, 78% in Peru and 86% in Russia). The owners' firms were small to medium sized, although the Chinese firms were bigger than the firms included in the other samples (the average number of full-time employees was 140 in China, 10 in Germany, 18 in the Netherlands, 8 in Peru and 14 in Russia).

3.2. *Measures*

In order to reduce common method variance, we used multiple sources of information: a standardized interview, a questionnaire and secondary data.

3.2.1. *Innovation*

We measured innovation outcomes because input innovations are biased towards bigger companies and, moreover, produce lower correlations with performance than outcome innovations (Rosenbusch, Brinckmann, and Bausch 2011). Innovation was ascertained in the interview. The interviewer explained the concept of innovation and then asked the participant about the introduction of new products, services, marketing strategies and processes innovations in a similar manner as the instrument used by Heunks (1998). Subsequently, the interviewee was asked to describe each innovation in detail. The answers were transcribed, and two coders independently coded the degree of innovation on a five-point scale with a '1' for being not at all innovative, a '2' for not innovative (rather copied than new), a '3' for neither/nor, a '4' for innovative (among the first movers) and a '5' for very innovative (first mover). The interrater reliabilities were 0.73 in China, 0.86 in Germany, 0.85 in the Netherlands, 0.63 in Peru and 0.96 in Russia.

3.2.2. *Culture*

Culture has been assessed by both values and practices (Stephan and Uhlander 2010). In this study, we used practices (House et al. 2007) because they describe typical behaviours within a society. Since entrepreneurship is a set of behaviours initiated by entrepreneurs (Gartner 1988), cultural practices should affect innovation and success of entrepreneurs. We measured the same dimensions of culture for assessing the national culture and the cultural orientation of owners: uncertainty avoidance, power distance, collectivism and assertiveness.

The scores of the *national culture* were taken from the GLOBE study (House et al. 2007), because GLOBE provides more recent data on culture and, moreover, it avoids many problems associated with Hofstede's (1991) survey (Ailon 2008). The GLOBE data were aggregated at the country level. We measured *Cultural orientations of owners* in a questionnaire that is based on the GLOBE framework (König et al. 2007). The questionnaire consists of scenarios related to the practices owners apply in their businesses. Each scenario provides two behavioural options that represent high and low values of a cultural dimension. For example, a scenario for power distance states 'imagine that one of your employees challenges an established rule in your business'. The behavioural options for this item are 'you ask your employee to make suggestions on how to change the rule' and 'you tell your employee to accept the rule'. Cronbach's alphas were 0.77 for uncertainty avoidance, 0.81 for power distance, 0.66 for collectivism and 0.87 for assertiveness. The reliability of collectivism is low. Although scenarios show lower internal consistencies than Likert items (Chan and Schmitt 1997), they tend to have high retest reliabilities (König et al. 2007).

3.2.3. *Growth*

Growth was measured in the interview by asking about the number of employees over the last three years. Growth in employment has been frequently used in entrepreneurship research and is positively correlated to other indicators of growth such as sales growth (Combs, Crook, and Shook 2005; Delmar 1997). Growth was calculated using the Birch (1987) index. This measure combines absolute and relative changes in the number of employees within the last three years. Thereby, this measure reduces a bias towards any particular firm size. We explored the validity of our dependent variables for the German sample by comparing them with the Hoppenstedt data that were available for 15 firms in our sample. Hoppenstedt publishes financial information of enterprises in Germany (http://www.hoppenstedt.de). The agreement in the number of employees was $r = 0.95$ in the three years evaluated. Moreover, growth correlated with the Hoppenstedt data on the number of employees ($r = 0.57$) and sales levels ($r = 0.41$).

We controlled for company age. Moreover, our design included enterprises from four different industries and, therefore, we controlled for the type of industry. An additional difference in the characteristics of firms in different countries might be firm size. In order to test whether our results are biased by firm size, we conducted robustness tests controlling for sales levels and found similar results.

3.3. *Analysis*

Since our design included two levels of culture, our analysis needed to account for cross-level effects. While there are a number of different techniques available to account for cross-level effects, the number of lower level and upper level entities required to estimate cross-level interactions is not really known (Mathieu and Chen 2011). Clearly, our design involving five upper level units restricts our analysis. Therefore, we used two different analytical techniques to test our hypotheses. First, we used the cross-level operator (CLOP) analysis (James and Williams 2000). CLOP can be used to test the interaction effects of higher level variables and lower level variables on lower level outcomes (Klein and Kozlowski 2000). The method is conceptually related to hierarchical linear modelling (HLM) and provides similar parameter estimates (Klein and Kozlowski 2000). CLOP can be used when the number of higher level observations does not allow the use of HLM (Blau 1995; Fischer et al. 2007). Accordingly, we used a hierarchical regression analysis including control variables in the first step. In the second step, firm-level variables (innovation and cultural orientations of owners), and in the third step, the firm-level interactions between innovation and cultural orientations of owners were included in the equation. In the fourth step, we included country-level culture in the equation. Finally, we tested the cross-level interactions by entering the interaction term between innovation and national culture in the fifth step of the equation (Bedeian, Kemery, and Mossholder 1989). We mean centred independent variables to create the interaction terms.

We complemented the CLOP analysis by additional robustness tests, adapting techniques used in the literature about the person-culture fit that dummy codes higher level variables (Friedman et al. 2010; Parkes, Bochner, and Schneider 2001; Ramesh and Gelfand 2010). We first entered control variables in the regression analysis. Moreover, we dummy coded the countries on the respective cultural practice, using the mean values of the cultural practices. In the second step, firm-level variables (innovation and cultural orientations of owners), and in the third step, the firm-level interactions between innovation and the cultural orientation of owners were included in the equation. Finally, the interaction between the national culture (dummy coded) and innovation was included in the fourth step of the regression analysis.

4. Results

Table 1 displays the mean values of study variables for all five countries, and Table 2 presents the intercorrelations. In general, the correlations were in the expected direction.

Table 1. Descriptive statistics of study variables: means (standard deviations).

	China	Germany	Netherlands	Peru	Russia
Uncertainty avoidance, culture[a]	4.94	5.22	4.70	3.55	2.88
Uncertainty avoidance, orientation	4.23 (0.90)	4.37 (0.67)	4.41 (0.91)	2.72 (0.77)	2.83 (0.96)
Power distance, culture[a]	5.04	5.25	4.11	5.25	5.52
Power distance, orientation	4.64 (0.90)	4.26 (0.83)	4.16 (0.92)	3.05 (1.05)	3.22 (0.99)
Collectivism, culture[a]	5.80	4.02	3.70	5.55	5.63
Collectivism, orientation	4.74 (0.94)	4.45 (0.94)	4.84 (0.89)	2.34 (0.94)	3.27 (1.18)
Assertiveness, culture[a]	3.76	4.55	4.32	4.07	3.68
Assertiveness, orientation	5.08 (0.83)	5.25 (0.60)	5.37 (0.58)	1.78 (0.81)	2.16 (0.99)
Innovation	2.30 (0.74)	1.50 (0.55)	1.40 (0.51)	1.99 (0.99)	2.81 (0.75)
Growth	48.31 (100.39)	0.51 (3.41)	2.83 (5.11)	1.28 (6.36)	3.07 (6.56)

[a] Value scores from the GLOBE study (House et al. 2007) (standard deviations not reported).

Moreover, the intercorrelations of cultural orientations were high. We addressed this multicollinearity by running separate regressions for each cultural dimension in the multivariate analyses.

We tested Hypothesis 1 by performing a regression analysis testing whether innovation predicts growth when controlling for country dummies (Table 3). As our results indicated, innovation was related to growth ($\beta = 0.10$, $p < 0.05$), and the explained variance was 1%. Thus, Hypothesis 1 was supported.

Hypothesis 2a predicted that the innovation–growth relationship is stronger if cultural orientations of owners are high in uncertainty avoidance when compared with that in low uncertainty avoidance. Step 3 in Table 4 displays our test of Hypothesis 2a. The interaction terms increased explained variance significantly ($\Delta R^2 = 0.02$, $p < 0.01$). Moreover, the interaction effect between innovation and uncertainty avoidance was positive and significant ($\beta = 0.14$, $p < 0.01$). We plotted the interaction and found that the innovation–growth relationship was higher for owners high in uncertainty avoidance

Table 2. Intercorrelations of study variables across all five countries.

	1	2	3	4	5	6	7	8	9	10	11
1. Growth											
2. Innovation[a]	0.34**										
3. Uncertainty avoidance	0.04	−0.12**									
4. Power distance	0.17**	0.01	0.49**								
5. Collectivism	0.16**	−0.01	0.45**	0.45**							
6. Assertiveness	0.10*	−0.16**	0.60**	0.52**	0.67**						
7. Manufacturing	0.15**	0.11**	−0.02	0.09*	−0.02	−0.07					
8. Software development	−0.01	0.12**	−0.02	0	0	−0.04	−0.31**				
9. Construction	−0.07	−0.15**	0.05	−0.08*	−0.03	0	−0.34**	−0.35**			
10. Hotel/catering	−0.06	−0.04	−0.07	−0.02	0	0.05	−0.29**	−0.30**	−0.33**		
11. Firm age	−0.03	−0.19**	−0.02	0	−0.01	0.03	0.01	−0.11**	0.07*	0.01	

Note: *$p < 0.05$; **$p < 0.01$.
[a]Spearman's coefficient.

Table 3. Regression analysis: the effect of innovation on performance in cross-country analysis.

	Growth	Growth
Car/machinery manufacturing	0.05	0.06
Software development	0.01	0.01
Building/construction	−0.02	−0.01
Hotel	−0.05	−0.02
Age of enterprise	0.02	0.02
Germany[a]	−0.37**	−0.34**
Peru[a]	−0.28**	−0.27**
Netherlands[a]	−0.23**	−0.18**
Russia[a]	−0.23**	−0.25**
Innovation		0.10*
R^2	0.14	0.15
ΔR^2	0.14	0.01
F for ΔR^2	12.51**	5.32*
df1, df2	9,670	1,669

Note: *$p < 0.05$; **$p < 0.01$.
[a] Dummy codings. The comparison dummy is China. Growth was higher in China leading to negative effects for the other countries.

(Figure 2). Our robustness test replicated this result. Therefore, Hypothesis 2a was supported. Hypothesis 2b predicted that country-level uncertainty avoidance negatively moderates the relationship between innovation and growth. Step 5 of the regressions displayed in Table 4 tested Hypothesis 2b. As expected, the interaction between innovation and uncertainty avoidance explained growth ($\beta = 0.14$, $p < 0.01$) and increased explained variance by 1%. However, the interaction was in the wrong direction (Figure 3). The innovation–growth relationship was higher in countries high in uncertainty avoidance than in countries low in uncertainty avoidance. This result was replicated in our robustness test. Thus, Hypothesis 2b was not supported.

Hypothesis 3a assumed that the cultural orientation of owners in power distance positively moderates the innovation–growth relationship. The third column in Table 5

Table 4. CLOP analysis: uncertainty avoidance and innovation predicting growth.

	1	2	3	4	5
Car/machinery manufacturing	0.22*	0.16	0.13	0.13	0.14
Software development	0.04	0	0	−0.03	−0.02
Hotel/catering	0.03	0.03	0	−0.02	−0.01
Building/construction	0.05	0.05	0.04	0.02	0.03
Age of enterprise	−0.02	−0.02	−0.01	−0.02	−0.02
Innovation		0.19**	0.23**	0.26**	0.29**
Uncertainty avoidance, orientation		0.06	0.03	−0.09	−0.08
Innovation × uncertainty avoidance, orientation			0.14**	0.12**	0.04
Uncertainty avoidance, culture				0.21**	0.19**
Innovation × uncertainty avoidance, culture					0.14*
R^2	0.03	0.07	0.08	0.11	0.12
ΔR^2	0.03	0.04	0.02	0.03	0.01
F for ΔR^2	3.55**	9.88**	9.50**	16.07**	5.66*
df1, df2	5,534	2,532	1,531	1,530	1,529

Note: Displayed coefficients are standardized betas. *$p < 0.05$; **$p < 0.01$.

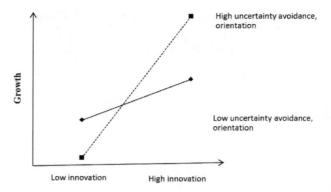

Figure 2. Uncertainty avoidance (orientation) moderating the relationship between innovation and growth.

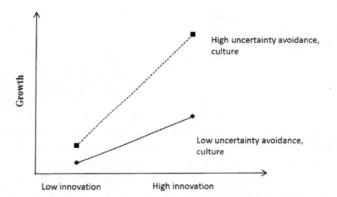

Figure 3. Uncertainty avoidance (culture) moderating the relationship between innovation and growth.

Table 5. CLOP analysis: power distance and innovation predicting growth.

	1	2	3	4	5
Car/machinery manufacturing	0.23*	0.13	0.12	0.21	0.21
Software development	0.05	−0.02	−0.01	0.06	0.06
Hotel/catering	0.02	−0.01	−0.01	0.07	0.07
Building/construction	0.05	0.02	0.03	0.12	0.12
Age of enterprise	−0.02	−0.02	−0.01	−0.01	−0.01
Innovation		0.21**	0.22**	0.24**	0.25**
Power distance, orientation		0.16**	0.13**	0.12**	0.10*
Innovation × power distance, orientation			0.17**	0.16**	0.14**
Power distance culture				−0.08	−0.12*
Innovation × power distance, culture					−0.09
R^2	0.04	0.10	0.12	0.13	0.13
ΔR^2	0.04	0.06	0.03	0.01	0.01
F for ΔR^2	3.97**	18.00**	16.23**	2.80	3.69
df1, df2	5,537	2,535	1,534	1,533	1,532

Note: Displayed coefficients are standardized betas. *$p < 0.05$; **$p < 0.01$.

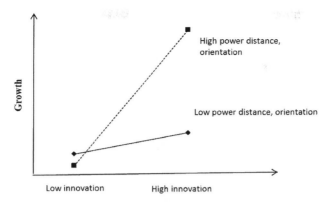

Figure 4. Power distance (orientation) moderating the relationship between innovation and growth.

displays the analysis applied for testing Hypothesis 3a. When we entered the interaction term between innovation and owner's power distance orientation into the regression equation, the interaction was positive and significant ($\beta = 0.17$, $p < 0.01$), and explained variance was 3%. Figure 4 shows that innovation had stronger effects on growth when owners were high in power distance than owners with low power distance. The result was replicated when controlling for the dummy variable power distance culture. Thus, Hypothesis 3a was supported. According to Hypothesis 3b, the innovation–growth relationship is higher in countries with low levels of power distance than in countries with high power distance. As Table 5 displays, the interaction between innovation and power distance culture was not significant ($\beta = -0.09$, ns). However, the robustness test indicated that the interaction between culture and innovation was significant and that the relationship between innovation and growth was higher in countries low in power distance than in countries high in power distance. Since the CLOP analysis and the robustness test did not reveal consistent results, we conclude that Hypothesis 3b was not supported.

Hypothesis 4a assumed that owner's collectivism moderates positively the innovation–growth relationship. When we entered the owner's collectivistic orientation in the regression as displayed in Table 6, the interaction was significant ($\beta = 0.14$,

Table 6. CLOP analysis: collectivism and innovation predicting growth.

	1	2	3	4	5
Car/machinery manufacturing	0.23*	0.20	0.15	0.04	0.03
Software development	0.05	0.03	0	−0.06	−0.05
Hotel/catering	0.03	0.04	0.02	−0.06	−0.07
Building/construction	0.05	0.08	0.05	−0.02	−0.02
Age of enterprise	−0.02	−0.02	0	0.02	0.02
Innovation		0.21**	0.24**	0.15**	0.11*
Collectivism, orientation		0.17**	0.16**	0.21**	0.19**
Innovation × collectivism, orientation			0.13**	0.10*	0.14**
Collectivism, culture				0.20**	0.23**
Innovation × collectivism, culture					0.14**
R^2	0.04	0.10	0.12	0.14	0.16
ΔR^2	0.04	0.07	0.02	0.03	0.02
F for ΔR^2	3.97**	19.61**	9.38**	15.48**	10.28**
df1, df2	5,537	2,535	1,534	1,533	1,532

Note: Displayed coefficients are standardized betas. *$p < 0.05$; **$p < 0.01$.

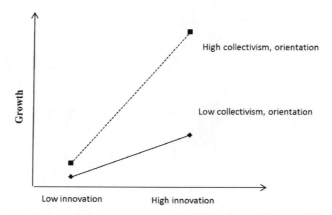

Figure 5. Collectivism (orientation) moderating the relationship between innovation and growth.

$p < 0.01$), increasing explained variance by 2%. Figure 5 shows that innovation was more strongly related to growth if the collectivistic orientation of owners was high as opposed to low collectivism. This result was replicated in our robustness test. Thus, Hypothesis 4a was supported. In addition, Table 6 shows support for our hypothesis that the innovation–growth relationship is stronger in collectivistic countries than in individualistic countries (Hypothesis 4b). We found that the interaction between innovation and collectivism culture was significant ($\beta = 0.14$, $p < 0.01$). Moreover, Figure 6 depicts the finding that innovation was positively correlated with growth in countries high in collectivism, whereas in countries low in collectivism, innovation was related to decreased growth. This result was replicated in our robustness test. Thus, our results supported Hypothesis 4b.

Hypothesis 5a proposed that assertiveness of owners positively moderates the innovation–growth relationship. The third column in Table 7 displays the test of Hypothesis 5a. The inclusion of the interaction term increased explained variance significantly ($\Delta R^2 = 0.02$, $p < 0.01$), and the interaction term was significant ($\beta = 0.15$, $p < 0.01$). Moreover, the moderation effect was in the expected direction: The relationship between innovation and growth was stronger when owners had a high assertiveness orientation (Figure 7). Thus, Hypothesis 5a was supported. Hypothesis 5b assumed that country-level

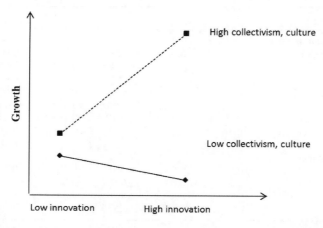

Figure 6. Collectivism (culture) moderating the relationship between innovation and growth.

Table 7. CLOP analysis: assertiveness and innovation predicting growth.

	1	2	3	4	5
Car/machinery manufacturing	0.23*	0.20	0.16	0.12	0.10
Software development	0.05	0.03	0.01	0.02	0.02
Hotel/catering	0.03	0.03	0.03	0.02	0
Building/construction	0.05	0.07	0.06	0.06	0.05
Age of enterprise	−0.02	−0.02	−0.01	0.02	0.02
Innovation		0.23**	0.28**	0.19**	0.17**
Assertiveness, orientation		0.16**	0.13**	0.18**	0.17**
Innovation × assertiveness, orientation			0.15**	0.12**	0.14**
Assertiveness, culture				−0.20**	−0.20**
Innovation × assertiveness, culture					−0.10*
R^2	0.04	0.10	0.12	0.14	0.15
ΔR^2	0.04	0.06	0.02	0.03	0.01
F for ΔR^2	3.93**	18.32**	12.22**	16.19**	4.93*
df1, df2	5,541	2,539	1,538	1,537	1,536

Note: Displayed coefficients are standardized betas. $*p < 0.05$; $**p < 0.01$.

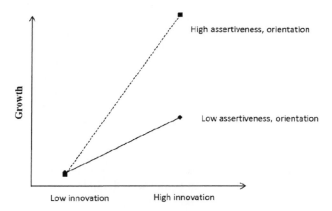

Figure 7. Assertiveness (orientation) moderating the relationship between innovation and growth.

assertiveness negatively moderated the relationship between innovation and growth. The last column in Table 7 indicates that the interaction term was significant ($\beta = -0.10$, $p < 0.05$) and increased explained variance by 1%. In addition, high assertiveness was associated with a low relationship between innovation and growth (Figure 8). This result was replicated in the robustness test. Thus, Hypothesis 5b was supported.

5. Discussion

This study investigated the innovation–growth relationship in different cultural contexts. The results indicated that innovation predicts growth fairly well in cross-country analyses when we hold the effect of the country constant. Thus, we established evidence for the universal validity of innovation–growth relationships. Second, cultural variables moderated the relationships between innovation and growth (Rosenbusch, Brinckmann, and Bausch 2011). Third, both national culture and cultural orientations of owners explained variation in innovation–growth relationships. Sometimes, the two levels of culture affected this relationship in the same way. In other instances, country-level culture

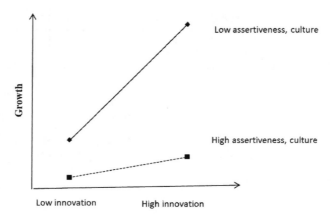

Figure 8. Assertiveness (culture) moderating the relationship between innovation and growth.

and owner-level culture differentially influenced this relationship and, therefore, both levels need to be assessed when studying growth across countries.

Our study contributes to the literature in three ways. First, our results suggest that innovation is correlated with growth in different contexts. Thus, to some extent this relationship is universally valid. At the same time, the strength of this relationship varies considerably across different contexts. This result explains some of the conflicting findings reported in the innovation–growth literature. For example, studies conducted in countries low in collectivism and high in assertiveness such as the USA (Edelman, Brush, and Manolova 2005; McGee, Dowling, and Megginson 1995) and the UK (Cooke, Clifton, and Oleaga 2005; Freel 2000) reported small and insignificant relationships between innovation and growth. In collectivistic countries, there is a stronger relationship between innovation and performance (Rosenbusch, Brinckmann, and Bausch 2011). Thus, our results contribute to the literature by explaining why the innovation–growth relationship is sometimes strong and sometimes weak.

Second, most previous research conceptualized culture as an independent variable that affects entrepreneurship behaviour (Freytag and Thurik 2007; Hayton, George, and Zahra 2002; Stephan and Uhlander 2010). Although this research provided valuable insights, it is more useful to test whether innovation is functional in certain cultural contexts. Thereby, one addresses both the boundaries and the predictive validity of entrepreneurship theories. Such an approach would probably result in a reassessment of cross-cultural theorizing in entrepreneurship research. For example, Hayton, George, and Zahra (2002, 34) noted that 'entrepreneurship is facilitated by cultures that are high in individualism, low in power distance, and low in uncertainty avoidance'. However, we found that high collectivism and high power distance can very well be functional for effective innovation implementation. Only recently, the entrepreneurship literature has begun to conceptualize culture as a moderator variable (Tung, Walls, and Frese 2007; van der Vegt, van de Vliert, and Huang 2005; Zhao, Li, and Rauch 2012). Our results contribute to this line of research.

Third, our study investigated both owner's cultural orientations and national culture. Most previous studies ascertained culture only at one single level of analysis (exceptions are Autio, Pathak, and Wennberg 2013; Bosma and Schutjens 2011; Stuetzer et al. 2013). This is problematic, because such studies suffer from ecological fallacy, specifically of generalizing from relationships at the country level to relationships at the individual level

(Brett et al. 1997). Moreover, such studies assume a homological model of cross-cultural differences. However, our results indicate that such designs are oversimplified, because the effect of culture on innovation–growth relationships is sometimes different at different levels of analysis. Thus, a theoretical contribution of our study emphasizes the necessity to conceptualize different levels of culture, which allows researchers to achieve more consistent results in cross-cultural entrepreneurship research.

We did not expect a positive moderator effect of country-level uncertainty avoidance. Possibly, only very few entrepreneurs choose innovative strategies in countries high in uncertainty avoidance. As a consequence, innovations might be more easily exploited to their full potential. In addition, the GLOBE index of uncertainty avoidance addresses the extent to which societies try to increase the predictability of future events (Stephan and Uhlander 2010). Predictability is, to a certain extent, required for successful innovation implementation and, therefore, may affect the innovation–growth relationship positively.

5.1. *Limitations*

Our results need to be interpreted in light of some limitations. First, our country-level analysis is based on a small sample size. Owner's cultural orientation and innovation are nested in countries and, therefore, performing an analysis that does not separate the different levels of analysis in an equation is problematic (compare, e.g. Mitchell et al. 2000; Steensma et al. 2000). Although the number of studies included in our analysis does not allow running an HLM, we addressed the problem by performing a CLOP analysis and additional robustness tests.

The culture-specific effects require additional investigation, because the countries included in our study differ not only in culture but in other ways as well. For example, the economic (Audretsch, Grilo, and Thurik 2011; Bosma and Harding 2006; Carree et al. 2002) or institutional environment (Acs and Karlsson 2002; Lee, Peng, and Barney 2007) may impact reported relationships and there might be temporal effects as well (Freel and Robson 2004). We cannot rule out such influences. Therefore, future research should examine and compare alternative explanations. Our study addressed the effect of culture on performance relationships; testing relationships across countries is less vulnerable to biases than testing mean differences.

Although we analysed two levels of cultures, participants were embedded in two additional levels of culture, i.e. the industry level and the regional level. We selected four specific industries and, consequently, it is unclear whether the same relationships hold in other industries. For example, different industries may develop different subcultures that might affect innovation–growth relationships. Similarly, our findings might be confounded by regional culture. There are some objections whether national culture is meaningful in large countries such as China or Russia, where regional culture might have important implications for firms. In addition, because we could not study a random sample of businesses in each country, we studied entrepreneurs from a particular region within the countries, which might not be representative for the entire country. Nevertheless, every cross-cultural national study including Hofstede (1991) and GLOBE (House et al. 2007) has regional biases; however, the questions often refer to the cultural national level and, therefore, there are fewer problems when interpreting the results (cf. also Schloesser et al. (2013) for an example that regional and sample differences do not play an important role when the answer format is correct). Moreover, we could not identify measures of culture at the regional level (Davidsson and Wiklund 1997; Stuetzer et al. 2013) and, therefore, relied on country-level indicators of culture. Finally, because the national value results were taken from GLOBE, they were from a different sample and more likely from a different region. Hence, any correlation that appears as a result of different regions would then lead to lower relationships. Thus, our results reveal conservative effects. Future research should examine the cultural consequences of additional levels of culture.

Fourth, we used the dependent variable employment growth. Although conceptually different, employment growth is correlated with other growth indicators such as sales growth (Delmar 1997; Weinzimmer, Nystrom, and Freeman 1998). However, the relationship between growth and profitability is only moderate (Combs, Crook, and Shook 2005) and sometimes even absent (Markman and Gartner 2002). In addition, employment growth is a relatively specific performance criterion. It is more likely to identify culture-specific effects at a specific level of abstractness (Norenzayan and Heine 2005). Future research should test whether culture has the same role in predicting other performance criteria.

Fifth, similar to other studies, we cannot rule out reversed causality. For example, growing firms might have more resources required for innovations, an effect that might be more prevalent in certain cultural contexts. However, there is evidence that scarce resources do not constrain the relationship between innovation and performance (Mansury and Love 2008). Moreover, the innovation–performance relationship is higher for new firms than for established firms (Rosenbusch, Brinckmann, and Bausch 2011). These results indicate that resources accumulated via prior growth might not increase innovations.

A strength of our study is the use of different sources of information, of data sources from different countries and the inclusion of interaction terms; these strategies reduce common method variance (Chang, Van Witteloostuijn, and Eden 2010).

5.2. Practical implications

Practically, entrepreneurs should enforce cultural orientations emphasizing uncertainty avoidance, power distance, collectivism and assertiveness. This may be difficult to accomplish in countries that are high in individualism and low in uncertainty avoidance. However, in order to facilitate successful innovation implementation, entrepreneurs should create a safe environment for innovation, emphasizing firms' collective outcomes, predictability, competition and accomplishment. Moreover, practitioners and businesses counsellors suggesting innovation need to consider that the effect of innovation depends on the cultural context that may either help or hinder successful innovation implementation. There are policy implications as well. First, some cultures have comparatively low levels of innovation (Hayton, George, and Zahra 2002; Shane 1993; Shane and Kolvereid 1995). However, firms that do innovate in such cultures are generating growth. Thus, it is advisable to support innovative firms even in cultures with low innovation rates. In addition, it may be ill-advised to support innovation implementation in cultures that reduce the relationship between innovation and growth such as individualistic cultures. In such cultures, non-innovative strategies may very well be successful.

Funding

This study was supported by a grant of the German Research Foundation (Deutsche Forschungsgemeinschaft) [grant number FR 638/23-1]. The authors gratefully acknowledge this.

References

Acs, Z., and C. Karlsson. 2002. "Introduction to Institutions, Entrepreneurship and Firm Growth: From Sweden to the OECD." *Small Business Economics* 19 (3): 183–187.

Ailon, G. 2008. "Mirror, Mirror on the Wall: Culture's Consequences in a Value Test of Its Own Design." *Academy of Management Review* 33 (4): 885–904.

Audretsch, D. B., I. Grilo, and A. R. Thurik. 2011. "Globalizazion, Entrepreneurship, and the Region." In *Hanbook of Research on Entrepreneurship and Regional Development*, edited by M. Fritsch, 11–32. Northhampton, MA: Edward Elgar.

Autio, E., S. Pathak, and K. Wennberg. 2013. "Consequences of Cultural Practices for Entrepreneurial Behaviors." *Journal of International Business Studies* 44 (2): 334–362.

Bedeian, A. G., E. R. Kemery, and K. W. Mossholder. 1989. "Testing for Cross-Level Interactions: An Empirical Demonstration." *Behavioral Science* 34 (1): 70–78.

Birch, D. L. 1987. *Job Creation in America*. New York: Free Press.

Blau, G. 1995. "Influence of Group Lateness on Individual Lateness: A Cross-Level Examination." *Academy of Management Journal* 38 (5): 1483–1496.

Bosma, N., and R. Harding. 2006. *Global Entrepreneurship Monitor 2006 Global Summary Results*. Babson College and London Business School.

Bosma, N., and V. Schutjens. 2011. "Understanding Regional Variation in Entrepreneurial Activity and Entrepreneurial Attitude in Europe." *The Annals of Regional Science* 47 (3): 711–742.

Brett, J. M., C. H. Trinsley, M. Janssens, Z. I. Berness, and A. L. Lytle. 1997. "New Approaches to the Study of Culture in Industrial/Organizational Psychology." In *New Perspectives in International Industrial/Organizatioal Psychology*, edited by P. C. Earley, and M. Erez. San Francisco, CA: New Lexington Press.

Brodbeck, F. C., M. Frese, S. Akerblom, G. Audia, G. Bakacsi, H. Bendova, D. Bodega, et al. 2000. "Cultural Variation of Leadership Prototypes Across 22 European Countries." *Journal of Occupational and Organizational Psychology* 73 (1): 1–29.

Brouwer, E., and A. Kleinknecht. 1996. "Small Business Presence and Sales of Innovative Products: A Micro-Econometric Analysis." *Small Business Economics* 8 (3): 189–201.

Burgers, J. H., F. A. J. van Den Bosch, and H. W. Volberda. 2008. "Why New Business Development Projects Fail: Coping with the Differences of Technological Versus Market Knowledge." *Managing Through Projects in Knowledge-Based Environments* 41 (1): 55–73.

Busenitz, L. W., G. Gomez, and J. W. Spencer. 2000. "Country Institutional Profiles: Unlocking Entrepreneurial Phenomena." *Academy of Management Journal* 43 (5): 994–1003.

Carree, M., A. van Stel, R. Thurik, and S. Wennekers. 2002. "Economic Development and Business Ownership: An Analysis Using Data of 23 OECD Countries in the Period 1976–1996." *Small Business Economics* 19 (3): 271–290.

Casson, M. 1982. *The Entrepreneur: An Economic Theory*. Totowa, NJ: Barnes and Noble Books.

Chan, D., and N. Schmitt. 1997. "Video-Based Versus Paper-and-Pencil Method of Assessment in Situational Judgment Tests: Subgroup Differences in Test Performance and Face Validity Perceptions." *Journal of Applied Psychology* 82 (1): 143–159.

Chang, S.-J., A. Van Witteloostuijn, and L. Eden. 2010. "From the Editors: Common Method Variance in International Business Research." *Journal of Interantional Business Studies* 41 (2): 178–184.

Chen, G., P. D. Bliese, and J. E. Mathieu. 2005. "Conceptual Framework and Statistical Procedures for Delineating and Testing Multi-Level Theories." *Organizational Research Methods* 8 (4): 375–409.

Christensen, C. M., and M. E. Raynor. 2003. *The Innovator's Solution: Creating and Sustaining Successful Growth*. Boston, MA: Harvard Business School Press.

Coad, A., and R. Rao. 2008. "Innovation and Firm Growth in High-Tech Sectors: A Quantile Regression Approach." *Research Policy* 37 (4): 633–648.

Combs, J. G., T. R. Crook, and C. L. Shook. 2005. "The Dimensionality of Organizational Performance and Its Implications for Strategic Management Research." In *Research

Methodology in Strategic Management, edited by D. J. Ketchen and D. D. Bergh, 259–286. San Diego, CA: Elsevir.

Cooke, P., N. Clifton, and M. Oleaga. 2005. "Social Capital, Firm Embeddedness and Regional Development." *Regional Studies* 39 (8): 1065–1077.

Davidsson, P., and J. Wiklund. 1997. "Values, Beliefs and Regional Variations in New Firm Formation Rates." *Journal of Economic Psychology* 18 (2–3): 179–199.

Delmar, F. 1997. "Measuring Growth: Methodological Considerations and Empirical Results." In *Entrepreneurship and SME Research: On Its Way to the New Millenium*, edited by R. Donkels, and A. Miettinen, 190–216. Aldershot, UK: Ashgate.

Dickson, M. W., D. N. Den Hartog, and J. K. Mitchelson. 2003. "Research on Leadership in a Cross-Cultural Context: Making Progress, and Raising New Questions." *Leadership Quarterly* 14 (6): 729–768.

Drucker, P. F. 1993. *Innovation and Entrepreneurship*. New York: Harper Business.

Dwyer, S., H. Mesak, and M. Hsu. 2005. "An Exploratory Examination of the Influence of National Culture on Cross-National Product." *Journal of International Marketing* 13 (2): 1–27.

Edelman, L. F., C. G. Brush, and T. Manolova. 2005. "Co-alignment in the Resource–Performance Relationship: Strategy as Mediator." *Journal of Business Venturing* 20 (3): 359–383.

Elenkov, D. S., and I. M. Manev. 2005. "Top Management Leadership and Influence on Innovation: The Role of Sociocultural Context." *Journal of Management* 31 (3): 381–402.

Erez, M. 2010. "Cross Cultural and Global Issues in Organizational Psychology." In *Handbook of Industrial and Organizationoal Psychology*, edited by S. Zadeck. Washington, DC: The American Psychological association.

Erez, M., and P. C. Eagly. 1993. *Culture, Self-Identity, and Work*. New York: Oxford University Press.

Erez, M., and A. Gati. 2004. "A Dynamic, Multi-Level Model of Culture: From the Microlevel of the Individual to the Macro Level of a Global Culture." *Applied Psychology: An International Review* 53 (4): 583–598.

Fischer, R., M. C. Ferreira, E. Assmar, P. Redford, C. Harb, S. Glazer, and B. S. Cheng. 2009. "Individualism-Collectivism as Descriptive Norms: Development of a Subjective Norm Approach to Culture Measurement." *Journal of Cross-Cultural Psychology* 40 (2): 187–213.

Fischer, R., P. B. Smith, B. Richey, M. C. Ferreira, E. M. L. Assmar, J. Maes, and S. Stumpf. 2007. "How do Organizations Allocate Rewards? The Predictive Validity of National Values, Economic and Organizational Factors Across Six Nations." *Journal of Cross-Cultural Psychology* 38 (1): 3–18.

Franke, G. R., and R. G. Richey Jr. 2010. "Improving Generalizations From Multi-Country Compartisons in International Business Research." *Journal of International Business Studies* 41 (8): 1–19.

Freel, M. S. 2000. "Do Small Innovating Firms Outperform Non-Innovators?" *Small Business Economics* 14 (3): 195–210.

Freel, M. S., and P. J. A. Robson. 2004. "Small Firm Innovation, Growth and Performance: Evidence From Scotland and Northern England." *International Small Business Journal* 22 (6): 561–575.

Frese, M. 2000. *Success and Failure of Microbusiness Owners in Africa: A New Psychological Approach*. Westport, CT: Greenwood.

Freytag, A., and R. Thurik. 2007. "Entrepreneurship and Its Determinants in a Cross-Country Setting." *Journal of Evolutionary Economics* 17 (2): 117–131.

Friedman, M., W. S. Rholes, J. Simpson, M. Bond, R. Diaz-Loving, and C. Chan. 2010. "Attachment Avoidance and the Cultural Fit Hypothesis: A Cross-Cultural Investigation." *Personal Relationships* 17 (1): 107–126.

Fukuyama, F. 2001. "Social Capital, Civil Society and Development." *Third World Quarterly* 22 (1): 7–20.

Gartner, W. B. 1988. "'Who is an Entrepreneur?' is the Wrong Question." *Entrepreneurship Theory and Practice* 12 (2): 47–68.

Geletkanycz, M. A. 1997. "The Salience of 'Culture's Consequences': The Effects of Cultural Values on Top Executive Commitment to the Status Quo." *Strategic Management Journal* 18 (8): 615–634.

Harzing, A.-W. 2000. "Cross-National Industrial Mail Surveys: Why Do Response Rates Differ between Countries?" *Industrial Marketing Management* 29 (3): 243–254.

Hayton, J. C., G. George, and S. A. Zahra. 2002. "National Culture and Entrepreneurship: A Review of Behavioral Research." *Entrepreneurship Theory and Practice* 24 (4): 33–52.

Heinrich, J., S. J. Heine, and A. Norenzayan. 2010. "The Weirdest People in the World?" *Behavioral and Brain Science* 33 (2/3): 61–135.

Heunks, F. J. 1998. "Innovation, Creativity, and Success." *Small Business Economics* 10 (3): 263–272.

Hofstede, G. 1991. *Cultures and Organizations*. London: McGraw-Hill.

House, R. J., P. J. Hanges, M. Javidan, P. W. Dorfman, and V. Gupta. 2007. *Culture, Leadership, and Organizations: The Globe Study of 62 Societies*. Thousand Oaks: Sage.

Human Development Statistical Annex. 2011. *Human Development Report*. http://hdr.undp.org/en/reports/global/hdr2011/download/

James, L., and L. Williams. 2000. "The Cross-Level Operator in Regression, ANCOVA, and Contextual Analysis." In *Multi-Level Theory, Research, and Methods in Organizations*, edited by K. Klein, and S. Kozlowski, 382–424. San Francisco, CA: Jossey-Bass.

Jansen, J. J. P., F. A. J. van Den Bosch, and H. W. Volberda. 2006. "Exploratory Innovation, Exploitative Innovation, and Performance: Effects of Organizational Antecedents and Environmental Moderators." *Management Science* 52 (11): 1661–1674.

Kelley, D. J., S. Singer, and N. Herrington. 2011. *The Global Entrepreneurship Monitor: 2011 Global Report*. Global Entrepreneurship Research Association.

Kirzner, I. M. 1997. "Entrepreneurial Discovery and the Competitive Market Process: An Austrian Approach." *Journal of Economic Literature* 35 (1): 60–85.

Klein, K. J., and S. Kozlowski. 2000. *Multi-Level Theory, Research, and Methods in Organizations*. San Francisco, CA: Jossey-Bass.

Klein, K. J., and J. S. Sorra. 1996. "The Challenge of Innovation Implementation." *Academy of Management Review* 21 (4): 1055–1080.

Knight, F. H. 1921. *Risk, Uncertainty, and Profit*. New York: Kelly and Millman.

König, C., H. Steinmetz, M. Frese, A. Rauch, and Z-M. Wang. 2007. "Scenario-Based Scales Measuring Cultural Orientations of Business Owners." *Journal of Evolutionary Economics* 17 (2): 221–229.

Kreiser, P. M., L. D. Marino, P. Dickson, and K. M. Weaver. 2010. "Cultural Infuences in Entrepreneurial Orientation: The Impact of National Culture on Risk-Taking and Proactiveness in SME's." *Entrepreneurship Theory and Practice* 34 (5): 959–983.

Lechler, T. 2001. "Social Interaction: A Determinant of Entrepreneurial Team Venture Success." *Small Business Economics* 16 (4): 263–278.

Lee, S.-H., M. W. Peng, and J. B. Barney. 2007. "Bankruptcy Law and Entrepreneurship Development: A Real Options Perspective." *Academy of Management Review* 32 (1): 257–272.

Li, H., and K. Atuahene-Gima. 2001. "Product Innovation Strategy and the Performance of New Technology Ventures in China." *Academy of Management Journal* 44 (6): 1123–1134.

Lumpkin, G. T., and G. G. Dess. 1996. "Clarifying the Entrepreneurial Orientation Construct and Linking it to Performance." *Academy of Management Review* 21 (1): 135–172.

Lumpkin, G. T., and G. G. Dess. 2001. "Linking Two Dimensions of Entrepreneurial Orientation to Firm Performance: The Moderating Role of Environment and Industry Life Cycle." *Journal of Business Venturing* 16 (5): 429–451.

Mansury, M. A., and J. H. Love. 2008. "Innovation, Productivity and Growth in US Business Services: A Firm-Level Analysis." *Technovation* 28 (1-2): 52–62.

Markman, G. D., and W. B. Gartner. 2002. "Is Extraordinary Growth Profitable? A Study of Inc. 500 High-Growth Companies." *Entrepreneurship Theory and Practice* 27 (1): 65–75.

Mathieu, J. E., and G. Chen. 2011. "The Etiology of the Multilevel Paradigm in Management Research." *Journal of Management* 37 (2): 610–641.

McGee, J. E., M. J. Dowling, and W. L. Megginson. 1995. "Cooperative Strategy and New Venture Performance: The Role of Business Strategy and Management Experience." *Strategic Management Journal* 16 (7): 565–580.

McGrath, R. G., I. C. MacMillan, and S. Scheinberg. 1992. "Elitists, Risk-Takers, and Rugged Individualists? An Exploratory Analysis of Cultural Differences Between Entrepreneurs and Non-Entrepreneurs." *Journal of Business Venturing* 7 (2): 115–135.

McMullen, J. S., and D. A. Shepherd. 2006. "Entrepreneurial Action and the Role of Uncertainty in the Theory of the Entrepreneur." *Academy of Management Review* 31 (1): 132–152.

Mitchell, R. K., B. Smith, K. W. Seawright, and E. A. Morse. 2000. "Cross-Cultural Cognitions and the Venture Creation Decision." *Academy of Management Journal* 43 (5): 974–993.

Morris, M. H., R. A. Avila, and J. Allen. 1993. "Individualism and the Modern Corporation: Implications for Innovation and Entrepreneurship." *Journal of Management* 19 (3): 595–612.

Morris, M. H., D. L. Davis, and J. W. Allen. 1994. "Fosterig Corporate Entrepreenurship: Cross-Cultural Comparisons of the Importance of Individualism Versus Collectivism." *Journal of International Business Studies* 25 (1): 65–89.

Mueller, S. L., and A. S. Thomas. 2000. "Culture and Entrepreneurial Potential: A Nine Country Study of Locus of Control and Innovativeness." *Journal of Business Venturing* 16 (1): 51–75.

Nakata, C., and K. Sivakumar. 1996. "National Culture and New Product Development: An Integrative View." *Journal of Marketing* 60 (1): 61–72.

Noorderhaven, N. G., R. Thurik, S. Wennekers, and A. van Stel. 2004. "The Role of Dissatisfaction and Per Capita Income in Explaining Self-Employment Across 15 European Countries." *Entrepreneurship Theory and Practice* 28 (5): 447–466.

Norenzayan, A., and S. Heine. 2005. "Psychological Universals: What are They and How can We Know?" *Psychological Bulletin* 131 (5): 763–784.

Parkes, L. P., S. Bochner, and S. K. Schneider. 2001. "Person–Organisation Fit Across Cultures: An Empirical Investigation of Individualism and Collectivism." *Journal of Applied Psychology* 50 (1): 81–108.

Pinillos, M.-J., and L. Reyes. 2011. "Relationship Between Individualist-Collectivist Culture and Entrepreneurial Activity: Evidence From Global Entrepreneurship Monitor Data." *Small Business Economics* 37 (1): 23–37.

Ramesh, A., and M. J. Gelfand. 2010. "Will they Stay or Will they Go? The Role of Job Embeddedness in Predicting Turnover in Individualistic and Collectivistic Cultures." *Journal of Applied Psychology* 95 (5): 807–823.

Rosenbusch, N., J. Brinckmann, and A. Bausch. 2011. "Is Innovation Always Beneficial? A Meta-Analysis of the Relationship Between Innovation and Performance in SMEs." *Journal of Business Venturing* 26 (4): 441–457.

Rowley, T., D. Behrens, and D. Krackhardt. 2000. "Redundant Governance Structures: An Analysis of Structural and Relational Embeddedness in the Steel and Semiconductor Industries." *Strategic Management Journal* 21 (3): 369–386.

Schein, E. H. 1992. *Organizational Culture and Leadership*. San Fancisco, CA: Jossey-Bass.

Schloesser, O., M. Frese, A.M. Heintze, A.M. Al-Najjar, T. Arciszewski, E.G. Besevegis, G.D. Bishop, et al. (2013) "Humane Orientation as a New Cultural Dimension of the GLOBE Project: A Validation Study of the GLOBE Scale and Out-Group Humane Orientation in 25 Countries." *Journal of Cross-Cultural Psychology* 44 (4): 535–551.

Schumpeter, J. 1935. *Theorie der wirtschaftlichen Entwicklung* [Theory of economic growth]. München: Von Duncker und Humbolt.

Shane, S. 1992. "Why Do Some Societies Invent More than Others?" *Journal of Business Venturing* 7 (1): 29–46.

Shane, S. 1993. "Cultural Infuences on National Rates of Innovation." *Journal of Business Venturing* 8 (1): 59–73.

Shane, S., and L. Kolvereid. 1995. "National Environment, Strategy, and New Venture Performance." *Journal of Small Business Management* 33 (2): 37–50.

Shane, S., and S. Venkataraman. 2000. "The Promise of Entrepreneurship as a Field of Research." *Academy of Management Review* 25 (1): 217–226.

Shane, S., S. Venkataraman, and I. MacMillan. 1995. "Cultural Differences in Innovation Championing Strategies." *Journal of Management* 21 (5): 931–952.

Sorescu, A. B., and J. Spanjol. 2008. "Innovation's Effect on Firm Value and Risk: Insights From Consumer Packaged Goods." *Joutnal of Marketing* 72 (2): 114–132.

Stam, E., and K. Wennberg. 2009. "The Roles of R&D in New Firm Growth." *Small Business Economics* 33 (1): 77–89.

Steensma, H. K., L. Marino, K. M. Weaver, and P. H. Dickson. 2000. "The Influence of National Culture on the Formation of Technological Alliances by Entrepreneurial Firms." *Academy of Management Journal* 41 (5): 951–973.

Stephan, U., and L. M. Uhlander. 2010. "Performance-Based vs Socially Supportive Culture: A Cross-National Study of Descriptive Norms and Entrepreneurship." *Journal of Interantional Business Studies* 41 (8): 1347–1364.

Stewart, W. H., and P. L. Roth. 2001. "Risk Propensity Differences Between Entrepreneurs and Managers: A Meta-Analytic Review." *Journal of Applied Psychology* 86 (1): 145–153.

Stogdill. 1948. "Personal Factors Associated with Leadership: A Survey of the Literature." *Journal of Psychology* 25 (1): 35–71.

Stuetzer, M., M. Obschonka, U. Brixy, R. Sternberg, and U. Cantner. 2013. "Regional Characteristics, Opportunity Perception and Entrepreneurial Activities." *Small Business Economics* 1–24. doi:10.1007/s11187-013-9488-6.

Taras, V., B. L. Kirkman, and P. Steel. 2010. "Examining the Impact of Culture's Consequences: A Three-Decade, Multilevel, Meta-Analytic Review of Hofstede's Cultural Value Dimensions." *Journal of Applied Psychology* 95 (3): 405–439.

Triandis, H. C. 1984. "Toward a Psychological Theory of Economic Growth." *International Journal of Psychology* 19 (1–4): 79–95.

Tung, R. L., J. Walls, and M. Frese. 2007. "Cross-Cultural Entrepreneurship: The Case of China." In *The Psychology of Entrepreneurship*, edited by J. R. Baum, M. Frese, and R. A. Baron, 265–286. Mahwah, NJ: Erlbaum.

Vaccaro, I. G., J. J. P. Jansen, F. A. J. van Den Bosch, and H. W. Volberda. 2012. "Management Innovation and Leadership: The Moderating Role of Organizational Size." *Journal of Management Studies* 49 (1): 28–51.

Van de Ven, A. H. 1986. "Central Problems in the Management of Innovation." *Management Sciences* 32 (5): 590–607.

Van der Vegt, G. S., E. van de Vliert, and X. Huang. 2005. "Location-Level Links Between Diversity and Innovative Climate Depend on National Power Distance." *The Academy of Management Journal* 48 (6): 1171–1182.

Venkatraman, N. 1989. "Strategic Orientation of Business Enterprises: The Construct, Dimensionality, and Measurement." *Management Science* 35 (8): 942–962.

Weinzimmer, L. G., P. C. Nystrom, and S. J. Freeman. 1998. "Measuring Organizational Growth: Issues, Consequences, and Guidelines." *Journal of Management* 24 (2): 235–262.

Wennekers, S., R. Thurik, A. van Stel, and N. Noorderhaven. 2007. "Uncertainty Avoidance and the Rate of Business Ownership Across 21 OECD Countries, 1976–2004." *Journal of Evolutionary Economics* 17 (2): 133–160.

World Bank. 2012. *World Development Indicators*. http://data.worldbank.org/country

Zahra, S. A., and G. George. 2002. "Absorptive Capacity: A Review, Reconceptualization, and Extension." *Academy of Management Review* 27 (2): 185–203.

Zhao, X., H. Li, and A. Rauch. 2012. "Cross-Country Differences in Entrepreneurial Activity: The Role of Cultural Practice and National Wealth." *Frontiers of Business Research in China* 6 (4): 447–474.

How culture moulds the effects of self-efficacy and fear of failure on entrepreneurship

Karl Wennberg[a,b], Saurav Pathak[c] and Erkko Autio[d,e]

[a]Stockholm School of Economics, Stockholm, Sweden; [b]The Ratio Institute, Stockholm, Sweden; [c]School of Business and Economics, Michigan Tech University, Houghton, USA; [d]Imperial College London Business School, London, UK; [e]Aalto University School of Science, Department of Industrial Engineering and Engineering Management

We use data from the Global Entrepreneurship Monitor and the Global Leadership and Organizational Behavior Effectiveness study for 42 countries to investigate how the effects of individual's self-efficacy and of fear of failure on entrepreneurial entry are contingent on national cultural practices. Using multi-level methodology, we observe that the positive effect of self-efficacy on entry is moderated by the cultural practices of institutional collectivism and performance orientation. Conversely, the negative effect of fear of failure on entry is moderated by the cultural practices of institutional collectivism and uncertainty avoidance. We discuss the implications for theory and methodological development in culture and entrepreneurship.

1. Introduction

National culture is often seen as central to entrepreneurship (Hayton, George, and Zahra 2002). Some countries are considered models of an 'entrepreneurial society,' whereas others are perceived as 'less entrepreneurial' (Freytag and Thurik 2007). Yet, findings from studies on how national culture influences individuals' entrepreneurial behaviours remain conflicting (Bowen and De Clercq 2008; Mueller and Thomas 2000; Steensma, Marino, and Weaver 2000; Stephan and Uhlaner 2010). One reason for this confusion is that few studies apply multi-level methods to test the relationship between national culture – a collective-level construct – and entrepreneurial behaviours – an individual-level construct. This paper provides a multi-level examination of the relationships between national culture and individual's entrepreneurial entry.

Cultural norms and practices are known to shape individuals' entrepreneurial behaviours, such as international orientation, start-up attempts and innovative activities (Shane 1993; Bowen and De Clercq 2008). While economics, sociology and management theories alike point to the importance of culture on the allocation of entrepreneurial efforts (Hayton, George, and Zahra 2002; Thornton 1999; Welter 2011), empirical studies on culture often disagree. For example, De Clercq, Danis, and Dakhli (2010) report a positive relationship between in-group collectivism and national rates of entrepreneurship – in contrast with much established beliefs. Wennekers, Thurik, and Stel (2007) report a positive association between the cultural disposition of uncertainty avoidance and entrepreneurial behaviours, again in contrast with the general current in research. In part, this confusion may be due to the inconsistent treatment of levels of analysis and inappropriate application of observed least squares regressions in clustered data (Davidsson and Wiklund 2001; Peterson, Arregle, and Xavier 2012). Many macro-level studies have correlated country-level measures of culture with national rates of entrepreneurship, ignoring the fact that entrepreneurship is fundamentally an individual-level endeavour (Bowen and De Clercq 2008; Stephan and Uhlaner 2010). Micro-level research in entrepreneurship, on the other hand, has often tended to use individual-level operationalizations of cultural dispositions, ignoring the fact that as an encapsulation of a shared belief system, culture is fundamentally a collective construct (Hofstede 1991). Few studies use multi-level techniques in their analyses, increasing the risk of generating 'false positives' (Hofmann, Griffi, and Gavin 2000).

Our overarching theoretical proposition is that the individual-level perceptions and motivations spurring the decision to enter entrepreneurship are contingent upon *informal* institutions, such as culture and behavioural norms. This proposition addresses an important gap since most empirical research have focused on *formal* rather than *informal institutions,* and few studies have attended to such contingencies that cross levels of analysis.

We address these gaps using cross-national data from the Global Entrepreneurship Monitor (GEM) and the Global Leadership and Organizational Behavior Effectiveness (GLOBE) study for 42 countries to test multi-level models investigating the effect of cultural traits on individuals' entrepreneurial behaviour. Cross-level moderation models reveal that several of the individual-level effects posited in entrepreneurship research are contingent upon cultural traits that operate at higher levels of analysis, testifying of the under-explored influences of national cultural context on individual's entrepreneurship. We found that the positive effect of self-efficacy on entrepreneurial entry is more pronounced in cultural landscapes that favour institutional collectivism and has higher performance orientation. Intriguingly, we also found that the negative effects of individuals' fear of failure on entry are somewhat smaller in settings with high levels of institutional collectivism. This may help explain the conflicting results in prior studies of the collectivism-entrepreneurship link (De Clercq, Danis, and Dakhli 2010; Uhlaner and Thurik 2007), highlighting the importance of research to theorize about different types of collectivism (Gelfand et al. 2004) as well as to explore what consequences collectivism brings for entrepreneurial processes, such as opportunity identification, motivation building and resource mobilization (Thessen 1997).

Empirically, our findings contribute by revealing a strong general pattern that individuals exhibiting similar perceptions may behave differently depending on their cultural context. Theoretically, this contributes by questioning prevailing individual-centric approaches to entrepreneurship, in which individuals are considered sole authors of their perceptions, dreams and actions (Davidsson 1995; Fayolle, Basso, and Bouchard 2010). We also outline contributions to methodology in entrepreneurship research and discuss insights for public policy.

2. Theory and hypotheses development

We see entrepreneurship as opportunity-seeking behaviour that operates at multiple levels of analysis (Davidsson and Wiklund 2001). This behaviour takes place within a social and cultural context that the entrepreneurs cannot escape (Jack and Anderson 2002). By investing their own and others' resources to pursue the opportunity, entrepreneurs engage in risky actions that may lead to negative consequences (Cassar 2007). When implementing novel approaches to pursuing business opportunities, entrepreneurial entry also represents a variance-inducing act by introducing novelty into the social context, exposing entrepreneurs to the judgment of others (Eckhardt and Ciuchta 2008). Intention-based theories of entrepreneurial entry suggest that individuals consider not only their own ability to succeed and the possibility of failure, but also how this action is consistent with prevailing cultural norms and practices (Krueger and Carsrud 1993). Consequently, we draw upon intention-based theories of entrepreneurial behaviours and cultural theory to develop a multi-level model of entrepreneurial entry. *Cultural practices* refers to the actual manifestation of a culture in individuals' daily lives (House et al. 2004) and is useful for theorizing about the culture–entrepreneurship link since distinctively from more abstract 'values', 'practices' are more proximate concepts dealing with the decisions important in entrepreneurship (Javidan et al. 2006). At the individual level, we expect individual self-efficacy and fear of failure to influence entry. We also expect individuals' societal context as experienced through cultural practices to moderate how these two factors affect the likelihood of entry. Our model is illustrated in Figure 1.

2.1. *Intentions, self-efficacy and entrepreneurial behaviours*

A common view is that the best predictors of individual's behaviour are the intentions towards that behaviour (Ajzen 1991). Consequently, intention-based models are commonly applied to theorize entrepreneurial entry as an intentionally planned behaviour (Krueger, Reilly, and Carsrud 2000). In this line of theory, individual's entrepreneurial intention derives from perceptions of desirability and feasibility. Feasibility requires potential firm founders to perceive entrepreneurship as a 'credible' career choice. Desirability depends on the individual values derived from his/her social and cultural environment (Shapero and Sokol 1982). In our development of this model, we view feasibility as linked to Bandura's (1977) concept of self-efficacy. Self-efficacy constitutes an individual's cognitive estimate of his or her capabilities to mobilize the motivation,

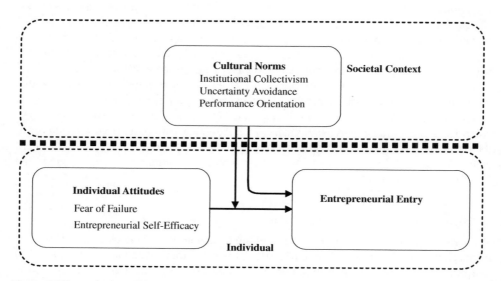

Figure 1. Theoretical model.

cognitive resources and the will of action needed to exercise control over events in one's life. Entrepreneurial self-efficacy refers to the strength of an individual's belief that he or she will or will not be capable of successfully performing the roles and tasks of an entrepreneur (Chen, Greene, and Crick 1998). Consequently, individuals view entrepreneurship as an attractive career option when they believe they have the requisite skills and abilities to act in a way that is needed to produce desired outcomes (Zhao, Seibert, and Hills 2005). As such, we expect the following:

Hypothesis 1:   An individual's *perception of entrepreneurial self-efficacy* will be positively related to his or her entrepreneurial entry.

2.2. *Fear of failure and entrepreneurial behaviours*

While the theory of self-efficacy posits that the perceived feasibility of engaging in entrepreneurship drives individuals' behaviours, there may also be negative forces that inhibit entrepreneurial intentions that lead to eventual entry. Since entrepreneurship is intimately related to uncertainty and risk taking, individual's fear of failure is a potent factor inhibiting entrepreneurial entry (Caliendo, Fossen, and Kritikos 2009). In the psychological research tradition, individual's fear of failure is thought of as a self-evaluative framework that influences how he or she defines, orients to and experiences failure in achievement situations (Heckhausen 1991), especially those related to risk-taking behaviour (Caraway et al. 2003). Fear of failure has been found to have a central influence on individuals' achievement motivation and their occupational aspirations (Burnstein 1963), including decisions to exploit a business opportunity or not (Welpe et al. 2012), and also affect regional rates of entrepreneurship (Vaillant and Lafuente 2007). We therefore expect the following:

Hypothesis 2:   An individual's *fear of failure* will be negatively related to his or her entrepreneurial entry.

2.3. *Societal institutional collectivism and entrepreneurial behaviours*

Individualism/collectivism is one of the most widely studied cultural dimensions (Smith and Bond 1993). Hofstede (1980) defined individualism as societies in which the ties between individuals are loose, and individuals' personal needs take precedence over those of the group. Conversely, in collectivist societies, individuals are more often integrated into cohesive in-groups, which protect them in exchange for group loyalty. Important for our theory is that the individualism/collectivism dimension may play out at different levels of analysis and may be reflected in both cultural values and cultural practices (Thessen 1997; Konig et al. 2007). Gelfand et al. (2004) distinguished between societal institutions (how societal institutions and practices favour group loyalty at the expense of the individual in return for the loyalty of the collective towards the individual) and in-group collectivism (the degree to which individuals identify with and emphasize the importance of social groups, such as the family). Since our interest is on the country level, we focus on institutional collectivism as a cultural practice.

A strong emphasis in the literature has been to associate entrepreneurial behaviours with individualism rather than collectivism (Shane, Kolvereid, and Westhead 1991;

Mueller and Thomas 2000; Hayton, George, and Zahra 2002), whereas some have emphasized the need for balance between the two (Thessen 1997; Pinillos and Reyes 2001). Still, empirical support for the link between individualism and entrepreneurship remains mixed (De Clercq, Danis, and Dakhli 2010; Morris, Avila, and Alien 1993; Pinillos and Reyes 2001). These conflicting findings may partly reflect inconsistent research methods as well as the oversimplified ways in which the individualism/collectivism dimension has been conceptualized and theorized. We follow Thessen (1997) by distinguishing between the *variation-generating* and *resource-mobilizing* aspects of entrepreneurship when considering the effect of individualism/collectivism on entrepreneurial activity. The variance-generating aspect refers to how entrepreneurs have to create new means-end frameworks to connect supply and demand (Shane and Venkataraman 2000), exposing themselves to how deviation from commonly accepted behaviour is tolerated. In collectivistic societies, the room for deviation is lesser since pursuing entrepreneurship may represent a potential challenge to established societal norms. The resource-mobilizing aspect of entrepreneurship refers to how entrepreneurs have to find and leverage financial, social and knowledge resources to launch a firm (Sørensen and Sorenson 2003).

Distinguishing between variance-generating and resource-mobilizing aspects helps theorize how collectivism shapes entrepreneurial entry. In societies with high-institutional collectivism, group loyalty will be favoured at the expense of individual income maximization. In return, there is a sense of collective loyalty towards the individual (House et al. 2004). Institutional collectivism may thus inhibit the effects of an individual's self-efficacy for entrepreneurial entry. In institutionally individualistic countries, tolerance for individual exuberance is higher since there are fewer institutionalized norms and social systems diminishing variance in social and economic behaviour (House et al. 2004). Also, resource-mobilizing processes may be more cumbersome in institutionally individualistic societies, in which 'every man is for himself' (Thessen 1997). Hence, the importance of individual-centric motivation marshalling resources to engage in entrepreneurship will be more important in institutionally individualistic societies because there are fewer institutionalized norms and social systems for decreasing inequality. These aspects lead us to posit that the effect of self-efficacy will exhibit a *stronger* effect on entrepreneurial entry in institutionally individualistic societies, as opposed to institutionally collectivist societies:

Hypothesis 3a: In societies characterized by *a low* level of institutional collectivism, entrepreneurial self-efficacy will be a more potent facilitator of entrepreneurial entry.

For the effect of individuals' fear of failure for entrepreneurial entry, institutional collectivism may not exhibit the same effect as self-efficacy. Institutional collectivism is depicted in societies as structures, institutions and traditions that serve to mitigate exuberant individualism but also to provide a social fabric to support individuals deemed in need of support (Welter and Smallbone 2006). Because of such aspects, individuals are substantially less likely to choose an entrepreneurial career in societies in which institutional collectivism is high, *regardless* of their fear of failure. An entrepreneurial career choice signals that the individual prioritizes his or her own interests and ambitions relative to those of the collective (Thessen 1997). If individuals do not fear the risk of failure, the context in which such risk tolerance plays out will reinforce the effect of that priority, diminishing the positive effect of low fear of failure on entrepreneurial entry in collectivistic societies. Thus, we hypothesize that the effect of *either* high or low fear of failure should be weaker in collectivist societies:

Hypothesis 3b: In societies characterized by a *low* level of institutional collectivism, fear of failure will be a more potent inhibitor of entrepreneurial entry.

2.4. *Uncertainty avoidance and entrepreneurial behaviours*

Uncertainty avoidance refers to the extent to which individuals in a society feel threatened in ambiguous situations, the extent to which they prefer order and rule-based reduction of uncertainty, and how they tolerate uncertainty in general (Sully de Luque and Javidan 2004). Also here, the findings of empirical studies to date are conflicting (Shane 1993; Wennekers, Thurik, and Stel 2007). In Hofstede's definition, uncertainty avoidance is 'the extent to which the members of a culture feel threatened by uncertain or unknown situations' (Hofstede 1991, 113). Relevant for entrepreneurship, uncertainty avoidance affects the extent to which individuals in a given society feel threatened by ambiguity; prefer rule-based mechanisms for uncertainty reduction; and seek orderliness, consistency, structure and formalized processes in their lives (Wennekers et al. 2010). Based on these arguments, we expect that in societies with high-uncertainty avoidance, individuals exhibiting a high fear of failure will be more likely to also exhibit reservations towards entrepreneurship. Conversely, the effect of self-efficacy should be particularly strong in societies with low-uncertainty avoidance. Therefore, we hypothesize the following:

Hypothesis 4a: In societies characterized by a *low* degree of uncertainty avoidance, entrepreneurial self-efficacy will be a more potent facilitator of entrepreneurial entry.

Hypothesis 4b: In societies characterized by a *high* degree of uncertainty avoidance, fear of failure will be a more potent inhibitor of entrepreneurial entry.

2.5. *Performance orientation*

Performance orientation reflects the extent to which a community encourages and rewards innovation, high standards and performance improvement (Javidan 2004). Perhaps the best known elaboration of this construct was provided by Weber (1930), who considered this cultural trait to be a key distinguishing aspect between Catholic and Protestant religions. The Protestant work ethic emphasizes the punctilious performance of everyday work as an intrinsically valuable calling in its own right and highlights the importance of work-related accomplishment as an important goal in life. The cultural uses of this construct, to our knowledge, have been limited to Konig et al.'s (2007) creation of scenario-based measures of entrepreneurs' cultural orientations. In his review, Javidan (2004, 245) associated performance orientation with, for example, valuing training and development, emphasizing results rather than people, emphasizing competitiveness and materialism, setting demanding targets, having a 'can-do' attitude, appreciating feedback as necessary for improvement, taking initiative, providing bonuses and financial rewards, and believing that anyone can succeed if they try hard enough. These values are often associated with entrepreneurship (Davidsson 1995; Stephan and Uhlaner 2010). Individuals choosing the entrepreneurial career option set a high bar for themselves (Cassar 2007). The entrepreneurial career option also forces the individual to take initiative, and few would choose this option if they believed they could not succeed. Therefore, we hypothesize that performance orientation will positively moderate the effect of self-efficacy on entrepreneurial entry:

Hypothesis 5a: In societies characterized by a *high* degree of performance orientation, entrepreneurial self-efficacy will be a more potent facilitator of entrepreneurial entry.

Performance orientation might also come at a cost if performance can be directed at a variety of activities. While self-efficacy may influence the performance of both managers and entrepreneurs (Chen, Greene, and Crick 1998), a societal emphasis on high performance may lead individuals towards activities with the highest predicted economic outcome rather than towards activities that are more uncertain. It has been widely documented that on average, individuals with equal skills and experience have higher economic returns as paid workers than as entrepreneurs – a career from which some reap economic returns but most earn little (Hamilton 2000). Hence, in cultural settings in which professionalism, performance and perseverance are seen as virtues, potential loss from engaging in more uncertain economic activities (if they do not pay off) may lead individuals to shun away from entrepreneurship if they are fearful of failing (Vaillant and Lafuente 2007). Thus, a society's performance orientation may enhance the effect of both self-efficacy and fear of failure on entry:

Hypothesis 5b: In societies characterized by a *high* degree of performance orientation, fear of failure will be a more potent inhibitor of entrepreneurial entry.

3. Methodology

3.1. *Data*

We test our predictions using 8 years of survey data from the GEM data-set (Reynolds, Bosma, and Autio 2005). We combined this with data on national cultural attributes collected by the GLOBE study (House et al. 2004). Together, 42 countries and 324,566 (unweighted) individual-level interviews from 2001 to 2008 were available after combining both data sources. We added exogenous controls of national-level attributes – *country's population* and *gross domestic product (GDP) per capita* and two additional cultural measures – obtained from the International Monetary Fund, EuroStat and GLOBE data-sets, respectively.

3.2. *Variables*

The dependent variable in our analysis is *individual-level entrepreneurial entry*. GEM identifies three types of entrepreneurs: nascent entrepreneurs, new entrepreneurs and established entrepreneurs. Since we do not know which nascent entrepreneurs actually go ahead and launch ventures, and that established entrepreneurs may be thought of as incumbents, the most salient operationalization of entrepreneurial entry comes from identifying 'new' entrepreneurs (Delmar and Davidsson 2000). GEM defines these as 'owner-managers of new firms less than 42 months old' – consistent with other studies of entrepreneurial entrants (Cassar 2007; Folta, Delmar, and Wennberg 2010; Zahra, Ireland, and Hitt 2000). Overall, 12,788 of 324,566 (3.94%) individuals interviewed qualified as new entrepreneurs, which we coded as a dummy variable (1 = 'entry'). Table 1 indicates the number of interviews and percentage rates of entrepreneurship by country averaged over 2001–2008.

The GEM data-set has been widely used in research, affirming its suitability for the study of entrepreneurship (Freytag and Thurik 2007; Bowen and De Clercq 2008). A potential limitation of the GEM data-set for our purposes, however, is that it captures any kind of entrepreneurial activity, including self-employment.

Table 1. Sample descriptives.

Country	N	Entrepreneurial entry (%)	Institutional collectivism	Performance orientation	Uncertainty avoidance
Argentina	5391	4.75	3.66	3.63	3.63
Australia	4616	4.57	4.31	4.37	4.40
Austria	1594	4.02	4.34	4.47	5.10
Bolivia	1330	14.66	3.96	3.57	3.30
Brazil	5133	10.40	3.94	4.11	3.74
Canada	3661	3.52	4.36	4.46	4.54
China	5899	9.85	4.67	4.37	4.81
Colombia	4338	14.18	3.84	3.93	3.62
Denmark	12,165	2.48	4.93	4.40	5.32
Ecuador	800	11.75	3.82	4.06	3.63
Egypt	1286	6.69	4.36	4.15	3.97
Finland	6076	3.18	4.77	4.02	5.11
France	10,021	0.61	4.20	4.43	4.66
Germany	21,800	2.08	3.97	4.42	5.35
Greece	3819	3.59	3.41	3.34	3.52
Hong Kong	2728	2.93	4.03	4.69	4.17
Hungary	6529	2.63	3.63	3.50	3.26
India	4232	5.10	4.25	4.11	4.02
Indonesia	1458	11.18	4.27	4.14	3.92
Ireland	2959	5.44	4.57	4.30	4.25
Israel	4700	2.49	4.40	4.03	3.97
Italy	3231	1.64	3.75	3.66	3.85
Japan	5387	2.08	5.23	4.22	4.07
Malaysia	988	10.43	4.45	4.16	4.59
Mexico	5331	2.42	3.95	3.97	4.06
Netherlands	8800	2.85	4.62	4.46	4.81
New Zealand	1898	6.38	4.96	4.86	4.86
Philippines	1450	18.34	4.37	4.21	3.69
Poland	2491	1.53	4.51	3.96	3.71
Portugal	1425	4.49	4.02	3.65	3.96
Russia	3175	1.48	4.57	3.53	3.09
Singapore	6179	2.80	4.77	4.81	5.16
Slovenia	6598	2.30	4.09	3.62	3.76
South Africa	7516	2.57	4.50	4.40	4.36
South Korea	4065	8.07	5.20	4.53	3.52
Spain	64,412	3.89	3.87	4.00	3.95
Sweden	6877	1.76	5.26	3.67	5.36
Switzerland	5647	3.88	4.20	5.04	5.42
Thailand	6055	10.55	3.88	3.84	3.79
Turkey	3779	4.66	4.02	3.82	3.67
UK	56,335	3.31	4.31	4.16	4.70
USA	12,392	3.47	4.21	4.45	4.15

Notes: N is the number of observations. Percentage of entrepreneurial entry represents the percentage of respondents per country who are identified as nascent or new entrepreneurs.
Source: GEM (2001–2008).
National scores for the cultural practices – namely, institutional collectivism, uncertainty avoidance and performance orientation – were obtained from the GLOBE survey.

3.2.1. *Individual-level (Level 1) predictors*

Individual's motivations and perceptions are fundamental predictors of entrepreneurial entry (Krueger and Carsrud 1993). In this study, we considered two such factors frequently theorized as central for entrepreneurial entry – *fear of failure* and *self-efficacy* in entrepreneurial efforts – both obtained from GEM. To minimize bias caused by cultural interpretations (i.e. intention-based variables such as scales of self-efficacy may be judged differentially across cultures, Liñán and Chen 2009), only dichotomous (yes/no) scales were used. Although dichotomous scales limit variability and in turn nuance in findings, prior research suggests this is preferable to bias caused by cultural interpretations of scales (Hult et al. 2008; Runyan et al., 2012).

Fear of failure was captured using a dummy variable ($1 =$ yes if individuals were fearful of failure, $0 =$ if not) that measures an individual's lack of confidence in his or her ability to cope with endogenous or exogenous uncertainty associated with new business venture creation as well as the fear of anticipated consequences of such failure (Vaillant and Lafuente 2007).

Entrepreneurial self-efficacy indicates whether individuals think they possess the knowledge, skills and experience required to start a new business ($1 =$ yes, $0 =$ if not) (Krueger, Reilly, and Carsrud 2000).

3.2.2. *Country-level (Level 2) predictors*

We used three cultural attributes as practiced at the country level: institutional collectivism, uncertainty avoidance and performance orientation. GLOBE measures *societal institutional collectivism* as the degree to which (1) societal institutions and practices favour group loyalty even at the expense of the individual in return for the loyalty of the collective towards the individual and (2) the degree to which the common good is preferred over private good in societal decision-making. *Uncertainty avoidance* societal practice is measured as the degree to which individuals in a given society feel threatened by ambiguity and prefer rule-based mechanisms, orderliness and clearly articulated expectations even at the cost of experimentation and innovation. *Performance orientation* reflects the society's current practices regarding innovation, improvement and reward systems. In essence, performance orientation measures the extent to which a given society is perceived to encourage and reward performance improvement.

GLOBE measures of national cultural attributes are based on a survey of more than 17,000 middle managers in 951 organizations in 63 countries or cultural regions. Cultural attributes were measured with 7-point Likert-type scales, with cultural scores presented as regression-predicted scores that correct for response bias. We chose to use practice variables ('as is') since our theory development emphasized cultural influences as experienced by individuals in their cultural contexts. Appendix 1 shows the wordings of the items used to measure the individual-level as well as the country-level predictors in this study.

3.2.3. *Interaction terms*

Six interaction terms were generated to test our hypotheses. Mean standardized Z-scores of each of the three cultural predictors were multiplied with each of the two individual-level perceptual variables to yield the six interaction terms.

3.2.4. *Individual-level controls*

Entrepreneurial entry may be influenced by factors other than an individual's perceptions. We controlled for a number of demographic characteristics, obtained from the GEM data-set, that have been shown to strongly correlate with entrepreneurial entry.

3.2.4.1. Age and age squared. An individual's age is an important influence on entrepreneurial entry (Bosma et al. 2009). We controlled for individuals' age as well as the mean-centred squared term of age in order to capture curvilinear effects.

3.2.4.2. Gender. Another important influence on entrepreneurial motivation is gender, with women typically being less willing to enter than men. In our data, female is coded as 2 and male as 1.

3.2.4.3. Education and household income tier. Both education and household income have been associated with entrepreneurial entry (Vinogradov and Kolvereid 2007). In GEM, education is operationalized using five categories: 'none' (0), 'some secondary' (1), 'secondary' (2), 'post-secondary' (3) and 'graduate' educational experience (4). Household income includes three categories: 'lower middle' (1), 'middle' (2) and 'upper middle' (3) tiers.

3.2.5. *Country-level controls*

We also controlled for two additional measures of cultural orientation[3] – *in-group collectivism* and *assertiveness*. These two indicators were also obtained from the GLOBE survey. The GEM research suggests that a country's level of economic development influences the nature and distribution of entrepreneurial activity (Pinillos and Reyes 2001). We control for *GDP per capita* and *population size* (in millions) for each country from 2001 to 2008.

The three cultural predictors and control variables were z-standardized because they were collected from separate sources, so raw scores for each of them would have different interpretations. Standardizing them also yielded a reference point based upon which relative effects could be interpreted.

3.3. *Research design and analysis*

Since culture is a collective construct theorizing about societal structures (Hofstede 1991), studies using individual-level perceptions of culture may suffer from the ecological fallacy by assuming that collective-level attributes are directly reflected in individual behaviours (Peterson, Arregle, and Xavier 2012). Conversely, studies of entrepreneurship on the individual or firm levels of analyses often suffer from the individualistic fallacy of ignoring the broader context within which individuals are embedded (Stenholm, Acs, and Wuebker 2013). Multi-level designs help avoid these fallacies by allowing simultaneous consideration of country-level and individual-level factors. Our data-set constitutes a cross-sectional panel grouped by country, combining observations at the individual and country levels. Such data necessitate multi-level techniques for analysis (Hofmann, Griffi, and Gavin 2000). Our models are based on random-effect logistic regression for which an individual's probability of entrepreneurial entry is a dichotomous outcome, estimated from individual-level factors (Level 1), country-level factors (Level 2) and cross-level interactions between the two.

Our objective was to examine the (1) the individual-level effects of *entrepreneurial self-efficacy* and *fear of failure* and (2) the interaction effects by which the three cultural predictors moderate the effect of the individual factors on an individual's probability of entering entrepreneurship. We adopted a three-step testing strategy by first estimating the influence of individual-level predictors on entrepreneurial entry (Model 2 of Table 4). We then included both individual- and country-level predictors in Model 3. Finally, we looked into the influence of the cross-level moderation effects between country-level cultural measures and individual-level perceptions towards entrepreneurship (Model 4).

4. Results

Table 2 provides the descriptive statistics for all the predictors and controls used. Table 3 shows the correlation matrix for the individual-level variables and country-level controls and predictors. To check multicollinearity, in addition to standardizing the cultural variables, we computed the variance inflation factors (VIFs) of all variables (constitutive and interaction variables) in our model. We found low to moderate VIF values between 1.04 and 6.5, which indicates that the models are not tainted by multicollinearity.

Table 4 shows our multi-level model of individuals' probability of entrepreneurial entry. The model is reported with estimates for the fixed individual-level part (estimates of coefficients) and the random culture-level part (variance estimates). Columns 2 and 3 in Table 4 report the odds ratio (OR), where $OR > 1$ indicates a positive relationship and $OR < 1$ indicates a negative relationship. Columns 5–9 report the beta-coefficients of the logistic regression.

We note a variance of 15% (also called intraclass correlation [ICC]) in individual-level entrepreneurial entry across the 42 countries included in our study. This is shown in Column 1 of Table 4. This finding suggests that a significant proportion of entrepreneurial entry is explained by country-level factors – namely, culture in our study – thus warranting a multi-level analysis that accommodates contextual factors to explain entrepreneurial entry.

Columns 2 in Table 4 shows the influence of two individual-level predictors – namely, fear of failure and self-efficacy – on the probability of entry into entrepreneurship. The ORs show that individuals' fear of failure suppresses their probability of entering into entrepreneurship by 31% on average $(1 - 0.69, p < 0.000)$. Individuals with high self-efficacy are on average more than five times $(OR = 5.47, p < 0.000)$ more likely to enter

Table 2. Descriptive statistics.

Variables	N	Mean	SD	Min	Max
Individual-level variables					
Entrepreneurial entry	324,566	0.04	0.19	0	1
Age	324,566	43.09	14.92	18	64
Gender	324,566	1.51	0.50	1	2
Education level	324,566	2.25	1.08	0	4
Household income	324,566	1.88	0.79	1	3
Self-efficacy	324,566	0.47	0.50	0	1
Fear of failure	324,566	0.37	0.48	0	1
Country-level variables					
GDP per capita (USD)	43	31403.66	15270.17	515	67,779
Population in millions	43	88.73	208.87	2.00	1321.05
In-group collectivism	43	4.83	0.74	3.46	6.14
Assertiveness	43	4.25	0.29	3.41	4.71
Institutional collectivism	43	4.23	0.40	3.41	5.26
Performance orientation	43	4.15	0.32	3.34	5.04
Uncertainty avoidance	43	4.37	0.60	3.09	5.42

Table 3. Correlation matrix (based on $N = 324{,}566$).

Variables	1	2	3	4	5	6	7	8	9	10	11	12	13	14
Entrepreneurial entry	1.00													
Age	-0.06	1.00												
Gender	-0.04	0.04	1.00											
Education level	0.02	-0.12	0.00	1.00										
Household income	0.04	-0.03	-0.09	0.18	1.00									
Self-efficacy	0.15	-0.04	-0.16	0.07	0.11	1.00								
Fear of failure	-0.05	-0.04	0.05	-0.05	-0.04	-0.13	1.00							
GDP per capita (USD)	-0.07	0.17	0.03	0.21	0.00	-0.07	0.01	1.00						
Population in millions	0.05	-0.06	-0.04	-0.05	-0.01	0.02	-0.03	-0.39	1.00					
In-group collectivism	0.06	-0.15	-0.07	-0.21	0.08	0.06	0.08	-0.57	0.20	1.00				
Assertiveness	-0.05	0.03	-0.01	-0.04	0.03	0.02	0.04	0.30	-0.30	0.02	1.00			
Institutional collectivism	-0.02	0.05	0.02	0.17	-0.01	-0.09	-0.09	0.25	0.13	-0.58	-0.53	1.00		
Performance orientation	-0.01	0.04	0.01	0.04	-0.01	-0.03	-0.05	0.38	0.12	-0.43	0.11	0.48	1.00	
Uncertainty avoidance	-0.05	0.10	0.03	0.12	-0.04	-0.06	-0.06	0.52	0.03	-0.77	-0.09	0.65	0.69	1.00

Table 4. Effects on individual-level entrepreneurial entry (ORs for Models 2 and 3, beta-coefficients for Models 4–9).

		1	2	3	4	5	6	7	8	9
Individual-level (Level 1)										
Age			0.98*** (0.00)	0.98*** (0.00)	−0.02*** (0.00)	−0.02*** (0.00)	−0.02*** (0.00)	−0.02*** (0.00)	−0.02*** (0.00)	−0.02*** (0.00)
Age (squared)			0.99*** (0.00)	0.99*** (0.00)	−0.00*** (0.00)	−0.00*** (0.00)	−0.00*** (0.00)	−0.00*** (0.00)	−0.00*** (0.00)	−0.00*** (0.00)
Gender			0.84*** (0.01)	0.84*** (0.01)	−0.17*** (0.01)	−0.17*** (0.01)	−0.17*** (0.01)	−0.17*** (0.01)	−0.17*** (0.01)	−0.17*** (0.01)
Education			1.04*** (0.00)	1.04*** (0.00)	0.04*** (0.00)	0.04*** (0.00)	0.04*** (0.00)	0.04*** (0.00)	0.04*** (0.00)	0.04*** (0.00)
Household income			1.16*** (0.01)	1.16*** (0.01)	0.15*** (0.01)	0.15*** (0.01)	0.15*** (0.01)	0.15*** (0.01)	0.15*** (0.01)	0.15*** (0.01)
Self-efficacy	H1		5.47*** (0.14)	5.47*** (0.14)	1.70*** (0.14)	1.70*** (0.14)	1.70*** (0.14)	1.70*** (0.14)	1.70*** (0.14)	1.70*** (0.14)
Fear of failure	H2		0.69*** (0.01)	0.69*** (0.01)	−0.37*** (0.01)	−0.37*** (0.01)	−0.37*** (0.01)	−0.37*** (0.01)	−0.37*** (0.01)	−0.37*** (0.01)
Country-level (Level 2)										
GDP per capita (PPP), USD				0.99 (0.00)	−0.00 + (0.00)	−0.00 + (0.00)	−0.00 + (0.00)	−0.00 + (0.00)	−0.00 + (0.00)	−0.00 + (0.00)
Population (million)				1.01 (0.00)	0.00 (0.00)	0.00 (0.00)	0.00 (0.00)	0.00 (0.00)	0.00 (0.00)	0.00 (0.00)
In-group collectivism				1.13 (0.14)	0.12 (0.14)	0.12 (0.14)	0.12 (0.14)	0.12 (0.14)	0.12 (0.14)	0.12 (0.14)
Assertiveness				0.76** (0.07)	−0.27*** (0.07)	−0.27*** (0.07)	−0.27*** (0.07)	−0.27*** (0.07)	−0.27*** (0.07)	−0.27*** (0.07)
Institutional collectivism				0.88* (0.07)	−0.13* (0.07)	−0.13* (0.07)	−0.13* (0.07)	−0.13* (0.07)	−0.13* (0.07)	−0.13* (0.07)
Uncertainty avoidance				0.84 + (0.08)	−0.17 + (0.08)	−0.17 + (0.08)	−0.17 + (0.08)	−0.17 + (0.08)	−0.17 + (0.08)	−0.17 + (0.08)
Performance orientation				1.35*** (0.12)	0.30*** (0.12)	0.30*** (0.12)	0.30*** (0.12)	0.30*** (0.12)	0.30*** (0.12)	0.30*** (0.12)
Cross-level interactions										
Institutional collectivism * self-efficacy	H3a				**0.07** (0.02)**					
Institutional collectivism * fear of failure	H3b					**−0.04 + (0.02)**				
Uncertainty avoidance * self-efficacy	H4a						**0.24*** (0.03)**			
Uncertainty avoidance * fear of failure	H4b							**−0.15*** (0.02)**		
Performance orientation * self-efficacy	H5a								**0.07** (0.03)**	
Performance orientation * fear of failure	H5b									**−0.04 (0.02)**

(Continued)

Table 4 – continued

	1	2	3	4	5	6	7	8	9
Random part estimates									
Number of observations	324,566	324,566	324,566	324,566	324,566	324,566	324,566	324,566	324,566
Number of groups (countries)	42	42	42	42	42	42	42	42	42
Variance of random intercept	0.58 (0.08)	0.41 (0.07)	0.22 (0.05)	0.22 (0.05)	0.22 (0.05)	0.22 (0.05)	0.21 (0.04)	0.22 (0.04)	0.22 (0.04)
Variance of overall residual	3.27	3.26	3.33	3.33	3.33	3.25	3.23	3.23	3.33
% of variance, ICC or rho	15.04 (0.02)	11.18 (0.02)	6.18 (0.01)	6.18 (0.01)	6.18 (0.01)	6.34 (0.01)	6.11 (0.01)	6.23 (0.01)	6.18 (0.01)
Model fit statistics									
Prob > χ^2	–	***	***	***	***	***	***	***	***
Log likelihood	–51,721	–47,601	–47,587	–47,582	–47,582	–47,543	–47,565	–47,584	–47,586
AIC [a]	103,442	95,216	95,202	95,194	95,194	95,116	95,160	95,198	95,202
Likelihood ratio test of rho = 0 [b]	***	***	***	***	***	***	***	***	***
Likelihood ratio test of model fit [c]	–	–	*	*	*	*	*	*	*

Notes: Standard errors are in parentheses. Bold values indicate variables testing the hypotheses. ***$p < 0.001$, **$p < 0.01$, *$p < 0.05$, +$p < 0.10$. All tests of significances two-tailed. ORs in columns 2 and 3 above 1 represent a positive relationship, ORs below 1 represent a negative relationship; columns 4–9 report beta-coefficients needed to plot the interactions.

[a] AIC is Akaike's Information Criterion and is = (2*k – 2* (Log Likelihood)), where k denotes degrees of freedom. Gradually smaller values over models denote improved model fit.

[b] Statistically significant ($p < 0.001$). Likelihood ratio test of rho = 0 confirms that the country-level variance component is important.

[c] LR test performed against previous model suggests improvement in model fit.

into entrepreneurship than individuals with low self-efficacy. Combined, these findings support the individual-level hypotheses (Hypotheses 1 and 2) in that individuals' self-efficacy is positively associated with entrepreneurial entry, while fear of failure is negatively associated with entrepreneurial entry.

Column 3 in Table 4 shows the direct effects of cultural practices on entry. Although we did not formally hypothesize about these effects, summarizing them is in order. We found that a one-unit standard deviation change in institutional collectivism decreases the probability of entry by 12% $(1 - 0.88; p < 0.05)$. Furthermore, a one-unit standard deviation change in performance orientation increases probability of entry by 35% $(p < 0.001)$. This is different from the country-level study by Stephan and Uhlaner (2010), which motivates the need for studies to compare the differential effects of national culture on individual's action versus aggregate rates of entrepreneurship. We also find a one-unit standard deviation change in uncertainty avoidance decreases the probability of entry by 16%, although this is only marginally significant $(p < 0.10)$.

To investigate Hypotheses 3a–5b, we introduced cross-level moderation effects between national culture and self-efficacy as well as between national culture and fear of failure in Columns 4–9 of Table 4. The moderators were introduced sequentially to avoid multicollinearity. The estimates in Columns 4–9 reported as beta-coefficients of the logistic regression as opposed to the ORs reported in Columns 2 and 3 of Table 4 reveal statistical significances for five out of the six interaction terms (Hypothesis 5b not supported). Since cross-level interaction terms are estimated with individuals' entry as the outcome variable, the coefficients themselves are individual-level disaggregates and cannot be used to explain direction and effect size for the dependent variable across countries (Bliese and Britt 2001). We therefore plotted the marginal effects of the five significant interaction terms, holding all other variables constant at their means. This allows us to gauge the *economic significance* of the results instead of merely statistical significance. It also allows us to ascertain the directionality of cross-level effects, which cannot be inferred from the coefficients.

All figures show the computed interaction between 'high,' 'medium' and 'low' levels of cultural practices (at one standard deviation above the mean, at the mean and one standard deviation below the mean, respectively) and the perceptual variables for fear of failure and self-efficacy. Figure 2 plots the interaction between high, medium and low levels of institutional collectivism and entrepreneurial self-efficacy, which is observed in Table 4 as significant at $p < 0.01$. By comparing the end points of the lines (i.e. at low or high levels of self-efficacy), we see that the positive effect of an individual's self-efficacy on entrepreneurial entry is more pronounced in societies with low-institutional collectivism. The difference between high and low self-efficacy amounts to an 8% increase in the likelihood of entrepreneurial entry in countries where institutional collectivism is low but a 12% increase in countries where institutional collectivism is high. This affirms Hypothesis 3 and shows that the estimated effects are both statistically significant and meaningfully large.

Figure 3 plots the interaction between high, medium and low levels of institutional collectivism and fear of failure, which is moderately significant in Table 4 at $p < 0.06$. Comparing the end points of the lines (i.e. at low or high levels of fear of failure), we see that the negative effect of an individual's fear of failure on entrepreneurial entry is more pronounced in societies with low institutional collectivism; however, the influence is not very large in effect size. The difference between high and low fear of failure amounts to a 2% increase in the likelihood of entry in countries where institutional collectivism is low but only a 1% increase in countries with high institutional collectivism. This affirms Hypothesis 3b.

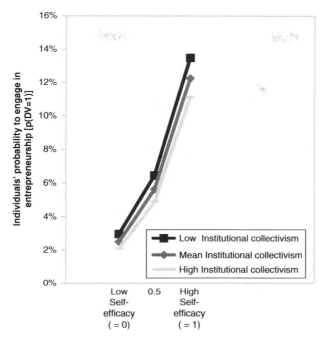

Figure 2. Interaction between country-level institutional collectivism and individual-level self-efficacy.

Figure 4 plots the interaction between high, medium and low levels of uncertainty avoidance and self-efficacy, which is observed in Table 4 as significant at $p < 0.001$. By comparing the end points of the lines, we see that the positive effect of an individual's

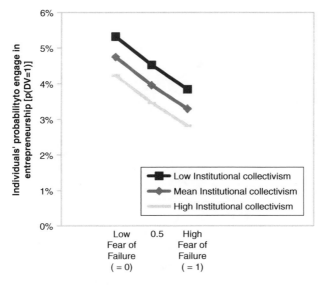

Figure 3. Interaction between country-level institutional collectivism and individual-level fear of failure.

CULTURAL VALUES AND ENTREPRENEURSHIP

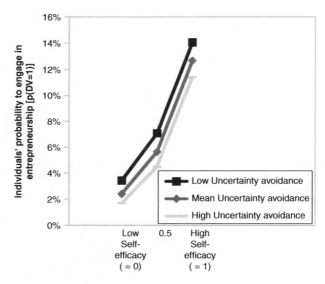

Figure 4. Interaction between country-level uncertainty avoidance and individual-level self-efficacy.

self-efficacy on entrepreneurial entry is actually marginally more pronounced in societies with *high* uncertainty avoidance. The difference between high and low self-efficacy amounts to a 11% increase in the likelihood of entrepreneurial entry in countries where uncertainty avoidance is low and a 9% increase in countries where uncertainty avoidance is high, thus rejecting Hypothesis 4a.

Figure 5 plots the interaction between uncertainty avoidance and fear of failure, observed in Table 4 as significant at $p < 0.001$. By comparing the end points of the lines,

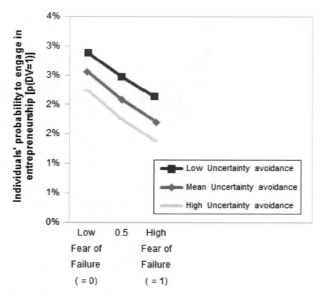

Figure 5. Interaction between country-level uncertainty avoidance and individual-level fear of failure.

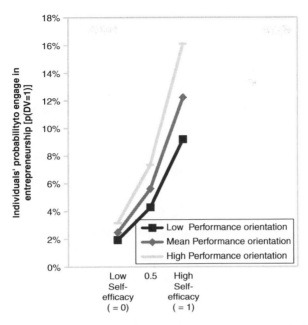

Figure 6. Interaction between country-level performance orientation and individual-level self-efficacy.

we see that the negative effect of an individual's fear of failure on entrepreneurial entry is more pronounced in societies with high uncertainty avoidance, yet while the influence is statistically significant, it is not large in effect size. The difference between high and low fear of failure amounts to a 1% decrease in the likelihood of entrepreneurial entry in countries where uncertainty avoidance is high and a 0.75% decrease in countries where uncertainty avoidance is low, weakly affirming Hypothesis 4b.

Finally, Figure 6 plots the interaction between performance orientation and self-efficacy, observed to be significant at $p < 0.05$. Comparing the end points of the lines, we see that the negative effect of an individual's fear of failure on entrepreneurial entry is more pronounced in societies with high performance orientation. The difference between high and low self-efficacy amounts to a 13% decrease in the likelihood of entrepreneurial entry in countries where performance orientation is high and a 7% decrease in countries where performance orientation is low. This affirms Hypothesis 5c in that performance orientation positively moderates how individuals' self-effiacy impacts entrepreneurial entry.

5. Discussion

This study is among the first to pinpoint some of the crucial mechanisms by which national cultural attributes and individual-level factors jointly shape entrepreneurial behaviours (Peterson, Arregle, and Xavier 2012). We observed several contingencies in how national culture moderates the effect of commonly investigated individual-level attributes through cross-level moderation effects. First and foremost, we found that the cultural traits of institutional collectivism and uncertainty avoidance in a country moderate both how individuals' fear of failure and their self-efficacy impact the likelihood of entrepreneurial entry, albeit uncertainty avoidance has a relatively much smaller influence on how individuals' fear of failure impacts their likelihood of entrepreneurial entry. We also found that the level of performance orientation slightly moderates how individuals' fear of failure impacts their likelihood of entrepreneurial entry.

These cross-level moderations show how individual's context have a direct influence on entrepreneurial entry, but also how the context moderates the effect of individual-level attributes on entrepreneurial entry. Individuals exhibiting similar perceptions may behave differently depending on the cultural context in which they are embedded. Furthermore, changes in the cultural context may induce a change in how individuals with certain attributes behave.

Our results indicate that cultural landscapes favouring institutional collectivism do not exacerbate the negative effects of individuals' fear of failure on entry. This challenges the view that always associates entrepreneurship with individualism (Mueller and Thomas 2000) and which is consistent with findings by Morris, Avila, and Alien (1993) using survey data, as well as the findings by De Clercq, Danis, and Dakhli (2010) and Pinillos and Reyes (2001) using country-level aggregates of GEM data. Pinillos and Reyes (2001) further show that the effects of individualism in a country on entrepreneurship may be dependent on the country's level of economic development. While we control for economic development, our study does not attend to country-level moderation effects since our theoretical model is concerned with country-level influences on *how individual's motivation and perceptions shape entrepreneurial behaviours*, not country-level influences on *aggregate rates of entrepreneurship*. A general theoretical explanation that may explain the unearthed relationship between institutionalized collectivism and entrepreneurship may be found in the distinction between variance-generating and resource-mobilizing aspects of entrepreneurship (Thessen 1997). Entrepreneurs need both a societal setting that allows for deviance and playfulness (Hjorth 2004) and a social fabric that facilities resource mobilization (Sørensen and Sorenson 2003).

We theorized that in cultural landscapes that favour institutional collectivism, the positive effects of an individual's self-efficacy on entry would be enhanced because the individual's belief in his or her ability to succeed would mitigate the potentially negative influence of collectivistic structures and attitudes. We found support for such an effect, which was among the strongest in our study. Our study also surprisingly showed that if a country's culture is predominantly inclined towards uncertainty avoidance, there is actually an even stronger positive association between self-efficacy and entrepreneurial entry. These two cross-level moderations highlight the fact that belief in one's ability to succeed may partly isolate individuals from the negative influences of cultural norms for entrepreneurial entry. We theorized and found weak support for a moderation effect of uncertainty avoidance on fear of failure, but societal uncertainty avoidance did not negatively moderate the effect of individual's self-efficacy, on the contrary. This is interesting because it shows that individuals with high entrepreneurial self-efficacy may help to partly insulate individuals against societal uncertainty avoidance.

Finally, we theorized on the effect of performance orientation in terms of how self-efficacy and fear of failure impact entry. We found no evidence that the effect of individual's fear of failure for entrepreneurial entry was more or less pronounced in countries with cultures that exhibit a strong performance orientation. However, we did find national performance orientation to positively moderate the effect of an individual's self-efficacy. This finding may be explained by the fact that while several cultural settings are known to put a high emphasis on results, continuous improvement and a strong work ethic (Weber 1930), many of them exhibit low rates of entrepreneurship since the economic framework is more conducive towards large firms (Henrekson and Jakobsson 2001).

Our study has several implications for entrepreneurship theory. We respond to calls for increasing the contextualization of research (Welter 2011) by studying the effect of national culture on entrepreneurship. Our multi-level perspective on culture not only allows us to *control* for contextual differences but also to *theorize* on how contextual variance affects entrepreneurship (Autio, Pathak, and Wennberg 2013; Zahra and Wright 2011). Theorizing on context is of importance in developing theory since decisions to engage in entrepreneurship involve personal tradeoffs that are influenced by contextual contingencies (Shane and Venkataraman 2000). To understand why some individuals and not others choose to pursue entrepreneurship, we need multi-level theories that consider not only individual-level characteristics but also the context within which those characteristics influence entrepreneurship (Davidsson and Wiklund 2001). This research serves as a reminder that the majority of entrepreneurship research that centres on the USA and Europe are often devoid of context, and therefore have lower generalizability in other cultural contexts (Aldrich 2009; Kim and Li 2013; Welter 2011; Zahra and Wright 2011).

We also contribute methodologically by showing the limitations of models focusing only on a single level of analysis (Davidsson and Wiklund 2001) and how these limitations can be overcome. Our paper highlights the potential danger of solely focusing on countries or regions as the unit of analysis when considering the influence of culture on entrepreneurship. Country-level studies often suffer from the individualistic fallacy of aggregating individual- or team-level entrepreneurial behaviours to that of the country level (Peterson, Arregle, and Xavier 2012). This may bias explanations at the country level, easily leading to over-socialized theory. As Hofstede notes (2001, 17), countries 'are not king size individuals. They are wholes, and their internal logic cannot be understood in the terms used for the personality dynamics of individuals. Eco-logic differs from individual psycho-logic.'

Individual-level studies using individuals' *perceptions of culture* to study their entrepreneurial behaviour may suffer from the ecological fallacy by assuming that collective attributes can be directly reflected in the behaviours and values of individuals, easily confusing individuals' perceptions and motivations with that of the national culture (Hofmann, Griffi, and Gavin 2000). Our analysis shows that while individuals' perceptions and motivations are a significant explanation of entrepreneurial behaviour, they are contingent on national cultures in intricate ways. Multi-level models allow researchers to explore more detailed analyses of the mechanisms between culture and entrepreneurship, more truthful to the levels of analysis at which those mechanisms play out (Peterson, Arregle, and Xavier 2012). The development of multi-level theories offers rich opportunities for entrepreneurship research.

Our findings also carry implications for policy practice that seeks to manipulate context in order to engender desired outcomes. In order to promote entrepreneurship, societies with high institutional collectivism should seek to promote entrepreneurial role models that emphasize entrepreneurship as an attractive norm rather than as a behaviour that conflicts with established norms. Societies with low institutional collectivism should promote an image of entrepreneurship as an act celebrating individuals rather than merely their societal contributions. Societies with low institutional collectivism could also seek to build mechanisms that mitigate the risks associated with resource investments in the pursuit of entrepreneurial growth, and similar initiatives could help mitigate the negative effect of cultural uncertainty avoidance. Finally, societies with low performance orientation might benefit from policy measures that highlight entrepreneurship as a lifestyle choice rather than merely as a way to become rich (Hjorth 2004).

Our study also comes with limitations. On the individual level, we considered two perceptions frequently associated with entrepreneurial behaviours: fear of failure and entrepreneurial self-efficacy. Obviously, entrepreneurship is influenced by other attributes such as demographics, experiences and individuals' social position, which also deserves further scrutiny. Although single-item measures were motivated due to cross-country equivalence (Hult et al. 2008; Runyan et al. 2012), further research is needed to ascertain perceptions related to entrepreneurship. Given the cross-sectional nature of the GEM data, it might also be possible that the actual act of having started a new venture enhances individuals' entrepreneurial self-efficacy and/or diminishes their fear of failure. Further research is needed to ascertain the full causal chain of these perceptions, and consider what other national cultural attributes such as assertiveness or future orientation may influence entrepreneurship. Finally, our focus on national culture – commonly seen as the most salient unit of analysis from which to derive proxies of cultural practices – could be nuanced by studying more fine-grained groupings of culture on the regional or neighbourhood level (Klyver and Foley 2012).

5.1. *Conclusion*

This study demonstrates important contingencies in how national cultural attributes affect individual-level entrepreneurial behaviours. The application of multi-level analysis techniques may unearth further important nuances in how national culture and individual attributes jointly mould individuals' entrepreneurial behaviours, and we hope future studies heed this call by challenging, developing and/or refining the theoretical models and empirical findings presented in this paper.

Acknowledgements

Financial support from the Swedish Research Council and UK Enterprise Research Centre (grant ref ES/K006614/1) are gratefully acknowledged. All errors remain ours alone.

Notes

3. GLOBE lists nine measures of cultural practices and values. We used three as predictors and two as controls because (1) 'humane orientation' and 'female egalitarianism' dropped out of equations due to multicollinearity with the seven other dimensions and (2) out of the remaining seven, two dimensions – power distance and future orientation – were never statistically significant in any model, nor in robustness checks. Hence, we dropped them from the models presented. These analyses are available upon request.

References

Ajzen I. 1991. "The Theory of Planned Behavior." *Organizational Behavior and Human Decision Processes* 50: 179–211.
Aldrich, H. E. 2009. "Lost in Space, Out of Time: How and Why We Should Study Organizations Comparatively." In *Research in the Sociology of Organizations*, edited by B. King, T. Felin, and D. Whetten. Vol. 26, 21–44. Bingley: Emerald Group.
Autio, E., S. Pathak, and K. Wennberg. 2013. "Consequences of Cultural Practices for Entrepreneurial Behaviors." *Journal of International Business Studies* 44: 334–362.
Bandura, A. 1977. *Social Learning Theory*. Englewood Cliffs, NJ: Prentice-Hall.
Bliese, P., and T. Britt. 2001. "Social Support, Group Consensus and Stressor–Strain Relationships: Social Context Matters." *Journal of Organizational Behavior* 22: 425–436.
Bosma, N., Z. Acs, E. Autio, A. Coduras, and J. Levie. 2009. *Global Entrepreneurship Monitor 2008 Executive Report: 65*. London: GERA.

Bowen, H. P., and D. De Clercq. 2008. "Institutional Context and the Allocation of Entrepreneurial Effort." *Journal of International Business Studies* 39: 1–21.

Burnstein, E. 1963. "Fear of Failure, Achievement Motivation, and Aspiring to Prestigeful Occupations." *Journal of Abnormal and Social Psychology* 67: 189–193.

Caliendo, M., F. Fossen, and A. Kritikos. 2009. "Risk Attitudes of Nascent Entrepreneurs-New Evidence from an Experimentally Validated Survey." *Small Business Economics* 32: 153–167.

Caraway, K., C. Tucker, W. Reinke, and C. Hall. 2003. "Self-Efficacy, Goal Orientation, and Fear of Failure as Predictors of School Engagement in High School Students." *Psychology in the Schools* 40: 417–427.

Cassar, G. 2007. "Money, Money, Money? A Longitudinal Investigation of Entrepreneur Career Reasons, Growth Preferences and Achieved Growth." *Entrepreneurship and Regional Development* 19: 89–107.

Chen, C., P. Greene, and A. Crick. 1998. "Does Entrepreneurial Self-Efficacy Distinguish Entrepreneurs from Managers?" *Journal of Business Venturing* 13: 295–316.

Davidsson, P. 1995. "Culture, Structure and Regional Levels of Entrepreneurship." *Entrepreneurship and Regional Development* 7 (1): 41–62.

Davidsson, P., and J. Wiklund. 2001. "Levels of Analysis in Entrepreneurship Research: Current Research Practice and Suggestions for the Future." *Entrepreneurship: Theory and Practice* 25: 81–99.

De Clercq, D., W. Danis, and M. Dakhli. 2010. "The Moderating Effect of Institutional Context on the Relationship Between Associational Activity and New Business Activity in Emerging Economies." *International Business Review* 19: 85–101.

Delmar, F., and P. Davidsson. 2000. "Where Do They Come From? Prevalence and Characteristics of Nascent Entrepreneurs." *Entrepreneurship and Regional Development* 12: 1–23.

Eckhardt, J. T., and M. P. Ciuchta. 2008. "Selected Variation: The Population-Level Implications of Multistage Selection in Entrepreneurship." *Strategic Entrepreneurship Journal* 2: 209–224.

Fayolle, A., O. Basso, and V. Bouchard. 2010. "Three Levels of Culture and Firms' Entrepreneurial Orientation: A Research Agenda." *Entrepreneurship and Regional Development* 22: 707–730.

Folta, T. B., F. Delmar, and K. Wennberg. 2010. "Hybrid Entrepreneurship." *Management Science* 56: 253–269.

Freytag, A., and R. Thurik. 2007. "Entrepreneurship and its Determinants in a Cross-Country Setting." *Journal of Evolutionary Economics* 17: 117–131.

Gelfand, M., D. Bhawuk, L. Nishii, and D. Bechtold. 2004. "Individualism and Collectivism." In *Culture, Leadership, and Organizations: The GLOBE Study of 62 Societies*, edited by R. House, P. Hanges, M. Javidan, P. Dorfman, and V. Gupta, 437–512. Thousand Oaks, CA: Sage.

Hamilton, B. H. 2000. "Does Entrepreneurship Pay? An Empirical Analysis of the Returns of Self-Employment." *Journal of Political Economy* 108: 604–631.

Hayton, J., G. George, and S. Zahra. 2002. "National Culture and Entrepreneurship: A Review of Behavioral Research." *Entrepreneurship: Theory and Practice* 26: 33.

Heckhausen, H. 1991. *Motivation and Action*. New York: Springer.

Henrekson, M., and U. Jakobsson. 2001. "Where Schumpeter Was Nearly Right – the Swedish Model and Capitalism, Socialism and Democracy." *Journal of Evolutionary Economics* 11: 331–358.

Hjorth, D. 2004. "Creating Space for Play/Invention-Concepts of Space and Organizational Entrepreneurship." *Entrepreneurship and Regional Development* 16: 413–432.

Hofmann, D., M. Griffi, and M. Gavin. 2000. "The Application of Hierarchical Linear Modeling to Organizational Research." In *Multilevel Theory, Research, and Methods in Organizations: Foundations, Extensions, and New Directions*, edited by K. J. Klein, and S. W. J. Kozlowski, 467–511. San Francisco, CA: Jossey-Bass.

Hofstede, G. 1980. *Culture's Consequences: International Differences in Work-Related Values*. Beverly Hills, CA: Sage Publishers.

Hofstede, G. 1991. *Cultures and Organizations: Software of the Mind.* Newbury: McGraw-Hill.

House, R., P. Hanges, M. Javidan, P. Dorfman, and V. Gupta. 2004. *Culture, Leadership, and Organizations: The GLOBE Study of 62 Societies.* London: Sage.

Hult, G., D. Ketchen, D. Griffith, C. Finnegan, T. Gonzalez-Padron, N. Harmancioglu, Y. Huang, M. Talay, and S. Cavusgil. 2008. "Data Equivalence in Cross-Cultural International Business Research: Assessment and Guidelines." *Journal of International Business Studies* 39: 1027–1044.

Jack, S. L., and A. R. Anderson. 2002. "The Effects of Embeddedness on the Entrepreneurial Process." *Journal of Business Venturing* 17: 467–487.

Javidan, M. 2004. "Performance Orientation." In *Culture, Leadership, and Organizations: The GLOBE Study of 62 Societies*, edited by R. House, P. Hanges, M. Javidan, P. Dorfman, and V. Gupta, 235–281. London: Sage.

Javidan, M., R. House, P. Dorfman, P. Hanges, and M. De Luque. 2006. "Conceptualizing and Measuring Cultures and their Consequences: A Comparative Review of GLOBE's and Hofstede's Approaches." *Journal of International Business Studies* 37: 897–914.

Kim, P., and M. Li. 2013. "Seeking Assurances When Taking Action: Legal Systems, Social Trust, and Starting Businesses in Emerging Economies." *Organization Studies*, forthcoming. doi:10.1177/0170840613499566.

Klyver, K., and D. Foley. 2012. "Networking and Culture in Entrepreneurship." *Entrepreneurship and Regional Development* 24: 561–588.

Konig, C., H. Steinmetz, M. Frese, A. Rauch, and Z. Wang. 2007. "Scenario-Based Scales Measuring Cultural Orientations of Business Owners." *Journal of Evolutionary Economics* 17: 211–239.

Krueger, N. F., and A. L. Carsrud. 1993. "Entrepreneurial Intentions: Applying the Theory of Planned Behavior." *Entrepreneurship and Regional Development* 5: 315–330.

Krueger, N. F., M. D. Reilly, and A. L. Carsrud. 2000. "Competing Models of Entrepreneurial Intentions." *Journal of Business Venturing* 15: 411–432.

Liñán, F., and Y. W. Chen. 2009. "Development and Cross-Cultural Application of a Specific Instrument to Measure Entrepreneurial Intentions." *Entrepreneurship Theory and Practice* 33: 593–617.

Morris, M. H., R. A. Avila, and J. Alien. 1993. "Individualism and the Modern Corporation: Implications for Innovation and Entrepreneurship." *Journal of Management* 19: 595–612.

Mueller, S. N., and A. S. Thomas. 2000. "Culture and Entrepreneurial Potential: A Nine Country Study of Locus of Control and Innovativeness." *Journal of Business Venturing* 16: 51–75.

Peterson, M. F., J.-L. Arregle, and M. Xavier. 2012. "Multilevel Models in International Business Research." *Journal of International Business Studies* 43: 451–457.

Pinillos, M. J., and L. Reyes. 2001. "Relationship Between Individualist-Collectivist Culture and Entrepreneurial Activity: Evidence from Global Entrepreneurship Monitor Data." *Small Business Economics* 37: 23–37.

Reynolds, P., N. Bosma, and E. Autio. 2005. "Global Entrepreneurship Monitor: Data Collection Design and Implementation 1998–2003." *Small Business Economics* 24: 205–231.

Runyan, R., B. Ge, B. Dong, and J. Swinney. 2012. "Entrepreneurial Orientation in Cross-Cultural Research: Assessing Measurement Invariance in the Construct." *Entrepreneurship Theory and Practice* 36: 819–836.

Shane, S. 1993. "Cultural Influences on National Rates of Innovation." *Journal of Business Venturing* 8: 59–73.

Shane, S., L. Kolvereid, and P. Westhead. 1991. "An Exploratory Examination of the Reasons Leading to New Firm Formation Across Country and Gender." *Journal of Business Venturing* 6: 431–446.

Shane, S., and S. Venkataraman. 2000. "The Promise of Entrepreneurship as a Field of Research." *Academy of Management Review* 25: 217–266.

Shapero, A., and L. Sokol. 1982. "The Social Dimensions of Entrepreneurship." In *Encylopedia of Entrepreneurship*, edited by C. A. Kent, D. L. Sexton, and K. H. Vesper, 72–90. Engelwoods Cliffs, NJ: Prentice-Hall.

Smith, P. B., and M. H. Bond. 1993. *Social Psychology Across Cultures: Analysis and Perspectives*. Hemel Hempstead: Harvester/Wheatsheaf.

Sørensen, J. B., and O. Sorenson. 2003. "From Conception to Birth: Opportunity Perception and Resource Mobilization in Entrepreneurship." *Advances in Strategic Management* 20: 89–117.

Steensma, H. K., L. Marino, and P. Weaver. 2000. "The Influence of National Culture on the Formation of Technology Alliances by Entrepreneurial Firms." *Academy of Management Journal* 43: 951–973.

Stenholm, P., Z. Acs, and R. Wuebker. 2013. "Exploring Country-Level Institutional Arrangements on the Rate and Type of Entrepreneurial Activity." *Journal of Business Venturing* 28: 176–193.

Stephan, U., and L. Uhlaner. 2010. "Performance-Based vs Socially Supportive Culture: A Cross-National Study of Descriptive Norms and Entrepreneurship." *Journal of International Business Studies* 41: 1347–1364.

Sully de Luque, M., and M. Javidan. 2004. "Uncertainty Avoidance." In *Culture, Leadership, and Organizations*, edited by R. J. House, P. J. Hanges, M. Javidan, P. W. Dorfman, and V. Gupta, 602–653. Thousand Oaks, CA: Sage.

Thessen, J. H. 1997. "Individualism, Collectivism, and Entrepreneurship: A Framework for International Comparative Research." *Journal of Business Venturing* 12: 367–384.

Thornton, P. 1999. "The Sociology of Entrepreneurship." *Annual Review of Sociology* 25: 19–46.

Uhlaner, L. M., and R. Thurik. 2007. "Postmaterialism Influencing Total Entrepreneurial Activity Across Nations." *Journal of Evolutionary Economics* 17: 161–185.

Vaillant, Y., and E. Lafuente. 2007. "Do Different Institutional Frameworks Condition the Influence of Local Fear of Failure and Entrepreneurial Examples over Entrepreneurial Activity?" *Entrepreneurship and Regional Development* 19: 313–337.

Vinogradov, E., and L. Kolvereid. 2007. "Cultural Background, Human Capital and Self Employment Rates Among Immigrants in Norway." *Entrepreneurship and Regional Development* 19: 359–376.

Weber, M. 1930. *The Protestant Ethic and the Spirit of Capitalism*. London: Allen and Undwin.

Welpe, I., M. Spörrle, D. Grichnik, T. Michl, and D. Audretsch. 2012. "Emotions and Opportunities: The Interplay of Opportunity Evaluation, Fear, Joy, and Anger as Antecedent of Entrepreneurial Exploitation." *Entrepreneurship Theory and Practice* 36: 69–96.

Welter, F. 2011. "Contextualizing Entrepreneurship – Conceptual Challenges and Ways Forward." *Entrepreneurship Theory and Practice* 35 (1): 165–184.

Welter, F., and D. Smallbone. 2006. "Exploring the Role of Trust in Entrepreneurial Activity." *Entrepreneurship Theory and Practice* 30: 465–475.

Wennekers, S., R. Thurik, A. Stel, and N. Noorderhaven. 2007. "Uncertainty Avoidance and the Rate of Business Ownership Across 21 OECD Countries, 1976–2004." *Journal of Evolutionary Economics* 17: 133–160.

Wennekers, S., R. Thurik, A. Stel, and N. Noorderhaven. 2010. "Uncertainty Avoidance and the Rate of Business Ownership Across 21 OECD Countries, 1976–2004." In *Entrepreneurship and Culture*, edited by A. Freytag, and R. Thurik, 271–299. Berlin: Springer.

Zahra, S. A., R. D. Ireland, and M. A. Hitt. 2000. "International Expansion by New Venture Firms: International Diversity, Mode of Market Entry, Technological Learning and Performance." *Academy of Management Journal* 43: 925–950.

Zahra, S. A., and M. Wright. 2011. "Entrepreneurship's Next Act." *Academy of Management Perspectives* 25: 67–83.

Zhao, H., S. E. Seibert, and G. E. Hills. 2005. "The Mediating Role of Self-Efficacy in the Development of Entrepreneurial Intentions." *Journal of Applied Psychology* 90: 1265–1272.

Appendix 1

Societal-level Institutional Collectivism: Society Practices – Sample Item (s)
In this society, leaders encourage group loyalty even if individual goals suffer: (reverse coded)

Strongly agree			Neither agree nor disagree			Strongly disagree
1	2	3	4	5	6	7

The economic system in this society is designed to maximize:

Individual interests						Collective interests
1	2	3	4	5	6	7

Uncertainty Avoidance: Society Practices (As is) – Sample Item (s)
In this society, orderliness and consistency are stressed, even at the expense of experimentation and innovation: (reverse coded)

Strongly agree			Neither agree nor disagree			Strongly disagree
1	2	3	4	5	6	7

In this society, societal requirements and instructions are spelled out in detail so citizens know what they are expected to do: (reverse coded)

Strongly agree			Neither agree nor disagree			Strongly disagree
1	2	3	4	5	6	7

Performance Orientation: Society Practices – Sample Item(s)
In this society, students are encouraged to strive for continuously improved performance: (reverse coded)

Strongly agree			Neither agree nor disagree			Strongly disagree
1	2	3	4	5	6	7

Individual-level Self-Efficacy:
You have the knowledge, skill and experience required to start a new business: YES (=1)   NO (=0)

Individual-level Fear of Failure:
Fear of failure would prevent you from starting a business: YES (=1)   NO (=0)

Survey items on the cultural practices were obtained from House et al. (2004), whereas the individual-level perception items were obtained from Reynolds et al. (2005).

The interaction between culture and sex in the formation of entrepreneurial intentions

Rotem Shneor[a], Selin Metin Camgöz[b] and Pinar Bayhan Karapinar[b]

[a]Faculty of Economics and Social Sciences, Institute of Economics, University of Agder, Norway; [b]Department of Business Administration, Hacettepe University, Ankara, Turkey

This study aims to reveal the effect of an interaction between culture and sex on the formation of entrepreneurial intentions, while building on notions of a cultural construction of gender. The study adopts the theory of planned behaviour as the setting for such exploration, as it has been proven to be robust across national contexts. The analysis is based on survey data collected from business students in Norway and Turkey. Both countries were selected as two distinct and opposite cultural constellations in accordance with the dissatisfaction approach to entrepreneurship. Turkey representing a relatively masculine, high power distance, uncertainty avoiding and collectivistic society; while Norway representing the opposite. Results show that Turkish students, regardless of sex, exhibit significantly higher levels of entrepreneurial intentions and self-efficacy. Male students, regardless of national background, exhibit higher levels of entrepreneurial intentions, self-efficacy and social norms. Finally, our study shows that the extent to which males differ from females in terms of their entrepreneurial intentions is contingent on the national cultural context from which they originate.

Introduction

Motivated by the interest to understand supportive conditions for entrepreneurial behaviour, entrepreneurship scholarship has seen an exponential growth in studies of entrepreneurial intentions and their antecedents. Entrepreneurial intentions are defined as the intent to start a business and/or to launch a new venture (Krueger 2009). Its antecedents have been robustly anchored in a number of intentionality models (Hindle, Klyver, and Jennings 2009; Iakovleva and Kolvereid 2009; Krueger and Carsrud 1993; Krueger, Reilly, and Carsrud 2000), at the core of which are elements from Shapero and Sokol's (1982) model of the entrepreneurial event (EE) and/or Ajzen's (1991) theory of planned behaviour (TPB).

Although parsimonious and robust, these models underestimate the social contextualization of the mind sets that they seek to capture (Hindle, Klyver, and Jennings 2009). Two important dimensions of social contextualization include gender roles and stereotyping, as well as national culture.

Research at the intersection of sex/gender and entrepreneurship shows that people associate masculine characteristics with entrepreneurs and that entrepreneurship is regarded as a masculine field (Ahl 2006; Gupta et al. 2009). However, when one examines the effects of sex on entrepreneurial intentions, the literature is split between those finding such effect (Kautonen, Luoto, and Tornikoski 2010; Kolvereid and Moen 1997; Kuckertz and Wagner 2010; Lee and Wong 2004; Liñán, Santos, and Fernández 2011; Yordanova 2011), implying higher levels of entrepreneurial intentions among males, and those finding no such effect (Fitzsimmons and Douglas 2011; Kolvereid 1996; Kolvereid and Isaksen 2006; Mueller 2011; Singh and DeNoble 2003; Tkachev and Kolvereid 1999). Other studies suggest indirect effect of sex via various elements of the TPB (Liñán, Urbano, and Guerrero 2011; Zhao, Hills, and Seibert 2005), or a moderator effect between entrepreneurial intentions and their antecedents (BarNir, Watson, and Hutchins 2011; Kickul et al. 2008).

Similarly, research at the intersection of national culture and entrepreneurship, mostly drawing on Hofstede's (1980, 2001) framework, is full of conflicting hypotheses and findings as well. On the one hand, there is literature suggesting that entrepreneurship is facilitated by cultures characterized by high individualism, low uncertainty avoidance, low power distance and high masculinity (Hayton, George, and Zahra 2002; Shane 1993). And, on the other, some evidence shows that the opposite – low individualism, high uncertainty avoidance, high power distance and low masculinity are more conducive to entrepreneurship (Baum et al. 1993; Hofstede et al. 2004). The former was labelled as the 'aggregate psychological traits' perspective, while the latter as the 'dissatisfaction hypothesis' (Hofstede et al. 2004). However, and more specifically, while cross-cultural studies of entrepreneurial intentions do identify significant differences between countries (i.e. Giacomin et al. 2011; Lee et al. 2006; Nguyen et al. 2009; Pruett et al. 2009), in most cases, these differences were not traced to concrete cultural explanations.

Furthermore, studies of entrepreneurial intentions that encompass both the sex/gender and cultural dimensions are rare (i.e. Mueller 2004; Shinnar, Giacomin, and Janssen 2012), and often focus on one aspect while addressing the other only marginally (i.e. Gupta et al. 2009; Mueller and Dato-On 2013; Plant and Ren 2010). However, since gender is socially and culturally constructed sex (Ahl 2006; Gupta et al. 2009; Hofstede 1998), and since sex gaps in the prevalence of entrepreneurial traits were found to vary systematically across cultures (Mueller 2004), one can draw attention to a potential interaction effect between sex and culture via gendering. This interaction remains largely unstudied despite its potential in providing at least a partial explanation to the contradictory findings presented earlier, when either sex or culture was considered separately.

Earlier literature has often used the terms sex and gender interchangeably, when essentially referring to biological sex. In this study, a distinction between the terms is drawn, where the term 'sex' refers to the biological sex and the term 'gender' refers to the social construction of sex. The latter capturing the social practices and representations of femininity and masculinity (Ahl 2006).

Hence, the primary goal of this study is to examine the culture–sex interaction and to evaluate its effect on entrepreneurial intentions. For this purpose, we adopt the TPB framework, which is both well established in entrepreneurial intentions research (Krueger 2009) and has been shown to be robust cross-culturally (Engle et al. 2010; Liñán and Chen 2009). Accordingly, data were collected from two social contexts representing different cultural and gender role constellations, namely Norway and Turkey. According to Hofstede (1998, 2001), Norway represents a gender egalitarian society characterized by high individualism, low masculinity, low power distance and low uncertainty avoidance;

while Turkey represents a less gender egalitarian social context characterized by lower levels of individualism, higher masculinity, higher power distance and higher uncertainty avoidance.

This study's main contribution is in identifying an interaction effect between sex and culture, interpreted as gendering effect, on entrepreneurial intentions. It is doing so, by showing that this effect comes in addition to the separate effects of sex and culture, which have been shown in earlier studies. Moreover, it also contributes to the debate on culture's influence on entrepreneurship by providing support to the dissatisfaction approach of cultural profiling for more and less entrepreneurially conducive environments.

In the following sections we first provide a literature overview on the roles of sex/gender and culture in entrepreneurial intentions' formation, which culminates in a list of hypotheses about their individual and interaction effects. Methods and findings sections follow, presenting the results of our analysis of data collected in Norway and Turkey. Later a discussion is presented, while examining our findings in light of existing research. Finally, the study concludes by highlighting its main findings, potential contributions, limitations and avenues for future research.

Literature review

Entrepreneurial activity is widely regarded as intentional planed behaviour (Bird 1988; Krueger and Carsrud 1993; Krueger, Reilly, and Carsrud 2000). Accordingly, intention models represent parsimonious and robust framework for pursuing a better understanding of entrepreneurial processes (Krueger 1993). Although models of entrepreneurial intention come in many variations and levels of detail, they have more similarities than differences (Hindle, Klyver, and Jennings 2009). At the core of these models lie fundamental antecedents of entrepreneurial intention as captured in two dominant frameworks, including Shapero and Sokol's (1982) EE, and Ajzen's (1991) TPB. These fundamentals include the TPB's attitudes and social norms, paralleling perceived desirability in the EE model, and perceived behavioural control, paralleling perceived feasibility in the EE model. However, due its wider applicability, greater coherence and cross-cultural validations (Engle et al. 2010; Moriano et al. 2012), this paper focuses its analysis and discussion on the TPB (Ajzen 1991).

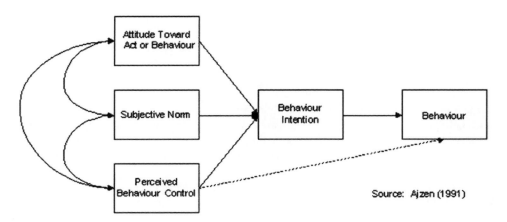

Figure 1. Theory of planned behaviour.

The first component of the TPB (Figure 1) is *attitude towards the behaviour*, which is defined as an individual's overall evaluation of the behaviour by balancing the strength of related behavioural beliefs and their outcomes. The second component is *social norms/subjective norms*, which balances normative beliefs about behaviour and the motivation to comply with them. Finally, the third component is *perceived behavioural control/self-efficacy*, which is defined as an individual's perception about his or her ability to perform certain behaviour. More specifically, when entrepreneurial intentions are concerned, the TPB suggests that attitudes towards entrepreneurial behaviour, social norms related to entrepreneurial behaviour and one's perception about their ability to engage in entrepreneurial behaviour all influence the formation of entrepreneurial intentions. These notions have been repeatedly supported in multiple studies from a variety of national contexts (i.e. Autio et al. 2001; Kolvereid 1996; Krueger, Reilly, and Carsrud 2000; Liñán and Chen 2009; Liñán, Urbano, and Guerrero 2011; Tkachev and Kolvereid 1999; Van Gelderen et al. 2008).

However, Hindle, Klyver, and Jennings (2009) suggest that intentionally models need to be improved by incorporating social factors that inform a person's intention. Their basic claim is that while intentionality is a 'state of mind', it is a contextualized 'state of mind' that requires greater attention to the social environment in which individual thought takes place. Therefore, these authors suggest an 'informed intention model', in which entrepreneurial intentions' formation process is informed by an individual's stock of human and social capital. Both human and social capital are said to provide direction and information that are accounted for in the cognitive process of entrepreneurial intentions' formation. Here, human capital was equated with knowledge and experience, and social capital with benefits and resources that are embedded in social networks.

In this study, while we adopt Hindle, Klyver, and Jenning's (2009) call for social contextualization of entrepreneurial intentions models, we do so by taking a step further back and focusing on culture and sex/gender, as generic social sources of both direction and information. Furthermore, by exploring interaction effects between sex and culture via gendering, we are answering Krueger's (2009) call for testing contingencies in the context of entrepreneurial intentions. Overviews of the way in which both elements influence various aspects of entrepreneurial intentions' formation, both independently and jointly, are detailed in the following sections.

Culture's effects on entrepreneurial intentions

According to Hofstede (1980, 25), culture is defined as 'the collective programming of the mind which distinguishes the members of one human group from another and includes systems and values'. Culture is said to shape the cognitive schema that ascribes meaning and values to motivational variables and guide choices, commitments and standards of behaviour (Erez and Earley 1993). Hence, differences in national culture, in which values and beliefs are embedded, may influence decisions to engage in entrepreneurship (Hofstede et al. 2004). Moreover, as culture reinforces certain characteristics while penalizing others, it is plausible that some cultures will be more entrepreneurially oriented than others (Mueller and Thomas 2001).

Hofstede et al. (2004), in their review of research at the intersection of culture and entrepreneurship at the national level, identify two main streams of thought. One stream, labelled as the 'aggregate psychological traits perspective', assumes that cultures characterized by low power distance, low uncertainty avoidance, high masculinity and high individualism represent social settings in which more individuals have entrepreneurial values, and hence a larger supply of potential entrepreneurs (Davidsson and Wiklund 1997). This approach mostly draws on Shane's (1993) findings showing a fit between such cultural profile (masculinity excluded) and national rates of innovation, as well as on McGrath, MacMillan, and Scheinberg (1992) study showing that entrepreneurs (vs. non-entrepreneurs) are characterized by the same profile with respect to three of the dimensions (power distance excluded). One explanation for differences of results with respect to power distance is that the studies compared different groups (Hofstede et al. 2004) – the first compared countries, while the second compared entrepreneurs versus non-entrepreneurs.

A second stream, labelled as the 'dissatisfaction perspective', which assumes that cultures characterized by high power distance, high uncertainty avoidance, low masculinity and low individualism represent social settings in which entrepreneurial individuals face greater difficulty to do things their way within existing organizations, while forcing them towards self-employment. This approach draws on social legitimation perspectives (i.e. Etzioni 1987), and the theory of the displaced entrepreneur (Shapero 1975; Shapero and Sokol 1982), as well as on the empirical findings of studies by Baum et al. (1993) and Acs, Audretsch, and Evans (1994).

To further support these notions, the analyses of Hofstede et al. (2004) have exhibited that countries in which people are less satisfied with life as a whole have higher levels of entrepreneurship; and, more specifically, dissatisfaction with life and with democracy are both stronger predictors of level of entrepreneurship than economic variables. Other studies' findings, although not explicitly considering the dissatisfaction thesis, also fit this line of argumentation. These include Kristiansen and Indarti (2004), who find higher entrepreneurial intentions in Indonesia than in Norway; Nguyen et al. (2009), who found higher entrepreneurial intentions in Vietnam than in both Taiwan and the USA; and Plant and Ren (2010) who found higher entrepreneurial intentions in China than in the USA.

Overall, Hofstede et al.'s (2004) own analyses found support for this second stream of cultural profiling, while adjusting the expectation concerning masculinity; now predicting higher (rather than lower) levels of entrepreneurship in masculine societies, where dissatisfaction with life can be associated with materialistic well-being. At this stage, the authors choose to follow Hofstede et al.'s (2004) line of argumentation due to its greater proximity and embeddedness in a larger context of culture studies and understanding. This choice affects both our formulations of hypotheses and the choice of our contexts for data collection and analysis.

Building on this refined cultural profile, we have purposefully selected two cultural contexts, each representing the opposite cultural configuration, based on the Hofstede (1980, 2001) study scores, including Norway and Turkey. Norway represents a high individualism, low power distance, low masculinity and low uncertainty avoidance. Turkey represents a context with lower levels of individualism, higher power distance, higher masculinity and higher uncertainty avoidance.

When importing this logic into the TPB, a number of assumptions can be made about entrepreneurial intentions and their core antecedents. First, based on the modified dissatisfaction approach, one can expect Turks to exhibit higher levels of entrepreneurial intentions than Norwegians. Here, by extension of the dissatisfaction thesis, and based on the cross-cultural validity of the TPB (Engle et al. 2010; Moriano et al. 2012), one can also suggest that Turkish people, who are expected to exhibit higher levels of entrepreneurial intentions, should also exhibit higher levels of self-efficacy, social norms and lower levels of risk perceptions (as proxy for attitudes). Such line of argumentation receives support in Liñán and Chen (2009), who claim that cultural particularities may be reflected by the effect of external variables on the antecedents of intention, as well as by the relative strength of links between these cognitive constructs.

Accordingly, we hypothesize the following:

H1:   Turks are expected to exhibit higher levels of entrepreneurial intentions, self-efficacy and perceived social norms, as well as lower levels of risk perceptions than Norwegians.

Sex's effects on entrepreneurial intentions

Although the term gender is used to distinguish between biological sex and socially constructed sex (Ahl 2006), many studies use the terms 'sex' and 'gender' interchangeably for drawing a distinction between men and women, in terms of their biological sex (Hofstede 1998). Interest in differences between sexes in the context of entrepreneurship grew from the observation that women entrepreneurs systematically represent lower proportions of the population (Hindle, Klyver, and Jennings 2009; Shinnar, Giacomin, and Janssen 2012; Wagner 2007; Yordanova and Tarrazon 2010).

Accordingly, numerous studies of entrepreneurial intentions have included the biological sex variable in their analyses. However, the literature findings are split between those finding significant differences between sexes (Kautonen, Luoto, and Tornikoski 2010; Kolvereid and Moen 1997; Kuckertz and Wagner 2010; Lee and Wong 2004; Liñán, Santos, and Fernández 2011; Yordanova 2011), implying higher levels of entrepreneurial intentions among males, and those finding no such effect (Fitzsimmons and Douglas 2011; Kolvereid 1996; Kolvereid and Isaksen 2006; Mueller 2011; Singh and DeNoble 2003; Tkachev and Kolvereid 1999). Other studies suggest indirect effect of sex via its TPB antecedents (Liñán, Urbano, and Guerrero 2011; Zhao, Hills, and Seibert 2005), or a moderator effect between entrepreneurial intentions and their antecedents (BarNir, Watson, and Hutchins 2011; Kickul et al. 2008).

Whether it be a direct, indirect or moderator effect, those suggesting a sex effect base their claims mostly on a historical disadvantage of women in access to human and social capital (Hindle, Klyver, and Jennings 2009; Scherer, Brodzinski, and Wiebe 1990; Shinnar, Giacomin, and Janssen 2012). This manifests itself in a consistent perception of higher barriers to entrepreneurship among females than among males (Shinnar, Giacomin, and Janssen 2012).

First, females tend to both exhibit lower levels of self-efficacy and self-confidence in their own skills and abilities to become entrepreneurs (Kristiansen and Indarti 2004; Scherer, Brodzinski, and Wiebe 1990; Wilson, Kickul, and Marlino 2007; Wilson et al. 2009; Yordanova and Tarrazon 2010), as well as to attribute greater importance to self-efficacy in forming entrepreneurial intentions overall (Kickul et al. 2008). Interestingly, education, which some may view as a gender equalizing factor, was found to have a stronger effect on self-efficacy among females than males (Wilson, Kickul, and Marlino 2007).

Females also tend to be less willing to take risks (Díaz-García and Jiménez-Moreno 2010; Walter, Parboteeah, and Walter 2011), as well as to exhibit higher levels of concern with potential failure (Shinnar, Giacomin, and Janssen 2012; Wagner 2007).

However, when one considers social norms, different studies present us with different results. Some studies suggest that females tend to perceive social norms, as captured by access to social environmental support as more difficult to attain than males (Shinnar, Giacomin, and Janssen 2012; Yordanova and Tarrazon 2010). Others show that environmental hostility is viewed similarly by members of both sexes (Díaz-García and Jiménez-Moreno 2010). However, when brought together with facts indicating that females indeed experience greater challenges in access to finance and credit (Carter and Rosa 1998; Coleman 2000), one can assume that, overall, females experience environmental support less favourably than males.

In accordance with this approach, we hypothesize the following:

H2:   Males will exhibit higher levels of entrepreneurial intentions, self-efficacy and perceived social norms, as well as lower levels of risk perceptions than females.

However, one must acknowledge that a number of cross-cultural studies found that the effects of sex on self-efficacy, attitudes (risk perception included), social norms and entrepreneurial intentions were evident in some cultural contexts, while being absent in others (Liñán and Chen 2009; Plant and Ren 2010; Shinnar, Giacomin, and Janssen 2012). Hence, leading us to suggest effects of a 'gendering' approach, in which an interaction between sex and culture influences entrepreneurial intentions and their antecedents.

'Gendering'/ sex–culture interaction effect on entrepreneurial intentions

Gender, as socially constructed sex, captures the social practices and representations of femininity and masculinity (Ahl 2006). Earlier research shows that those who perceive greater congruence between masculine and entrepreneurial characteristics are more likely to have a firm entrepreneurial intention (Díaz-García and Jiménez-Moreno 2010). Moreover, recent studies (Gupta et al. 2009; Mueller and Dato-On 2008) show that an individual's intention to become an entrepreneur, as well as their perceived levels of its antecedent of self-efficacy, is more likely to be determined by his or her gender perception of self than by biological sex *per se*.

However, one is not free to perform gender in any way one chooses, as each culture's norms restrain proper gender behaviour, and these norms have social effects including the gendering of professions (Ahl 2006; Shinnar, Giacomin, and Janssen 2012). Here, initial steps towards cross-cultural study of gender roles and entrepreneurship provide interesting insights. First, a study by Gupta et al. (2009) showed that respondents with high male gender identification had higher entrepreneurial intentions than those with low male gender identification, across all three countries where data were collected (USA, India and Turkey). Moreover, a later study showed that while the traditional view of the entrepreneur as male in certain cultures, such as the USA, is fading, in others, such as Spain, it persists (Mueller and Dato-On 2013).

According to Hofstede (1998), gender role variations exist across countries, especially when related to the masculinity–femininity dimensions of national culture. These differences arise from different socialization processes, as facilitated via parent–child relations, which instils the value of modesty in feminine cultures, versus the values of assertiveness and ego boosting in masculine cultures. Accordingly, the position of a country on the masculinity–femininity dimension impacts the trade-off between career and family interest. Here, while Japan, Austria, Italy, Venezuela and Mexico are identified as most predominantly masculine cultures, all Nordic countries and the Netherlands are identified as most predominantly feminine cultures. Some of the cultures positioned in the middle between these two extremes include culturally heterogeneous societies such as Israel, Canada, Brazil, Malaysia and Singapore.

In essence, some of the key social norms underlying the masculinity–femininity dilemma revolve around putting premium on sympathy for the big and strong versus the small and weak, stressing importance of money and material things versus the importance of relationship and self-belief, as well as an appreciation of assertiveness and ambition versus modesty and inclusiveness (Hofstede 1998, 2001).

Since, as shown earlier, entrepreneurship is associated with the masculine characteristics of aggressiveness, autonomy, independence, courage as well as being driven to success for the sake of success itself (Ahl 2006; Gupta et al. 2009), it is plausible to assume that entrepreneurship will be more prevalent in masculine rather than feminine social contexts.

In addition, while building on Williams and Best (1990), Hofstede (1998) also highlights that in feminine countries (such as Norway) women present gender stereotypes that differ more from men's than in masculine cultures, where women use more masculine terms to describe themselves. These notions gained further support in a 17-country study by Mueller (2004), who found that gender gap in internal locus of control (paralleling the entrepreneurial intention antecedent of self-efficacy) was negatively correlated with Hofstede's masculinity dimension.

Further support for the sex–culture interaction thesis can be found when viewing Mueller's (2004) findings via the dissatisfied entrepreneur perspective prism. His study shows that greater gender gaps in entrepreneurial traits were highest in advanced economies, where less dissatisfaction with life and material well-being is expected; and least so in less developed economies, where higher dissatisfaction is likely. Overall, these findings suggest that the extent to which males differ from females in terms of their entrepreneurial intentions is contingent on the national cultural context from which they originate.

Hence, building on the above insights, an argument for a gendering effect on entrepreneurial intentions is suggested. Such effect is identified with the tension between assigning gender characteristics to entrepreneurial career paths, and the extent to which these deviate from perceptions of proper gender behaviour, as dictated by cultural values and norms.

One way to tap into the gendering effect is the view that while entrepreneurship is predominantly male gendered in both cultures, its manifestations are coloured by masculine and feminine aspects of each culture. In Turkey, as more masculine culture, entrepreneurship is associated with strong growth ambitions, where both males and females view it as a path to achieve material well-being through aggressive and competitive efforts (Aycan and Fikret-Pasa 2003). However, in such cultures, gender equality has not yet been achieved, and females adopt male stereotyping (Williams and Best 1990; Özkan and Lajunen 2005) in their pursuit of more independent economic well-being, as a way to enter a male gender-biased business world (Karataş-Özkan, Erdoğan, and Nicolopoulou 2011).

On the other hand, in Norway, as a feminine culture, entrepreneurship is associated with moderate growth ambitions (Kolvereid 1992), where males and females view it as an alternative lifestyle which may or may not lead to a significant improvement in material well-being. However, since in such cultures gender equality is the norm, females freely choose whether to adopt male or female stereotyping (Williams and Best 1990) in their pursuit of more independent career paths. More specifically, while Turkish women may view entrepreneurship as a path to resist culturally laden gender discrimination in the work life (Karataş-Özkan, Erdoğan, and Nicolopoulou 2011), Norwegian women do not need to follow entrepreneurial paths for the same purpose due to culturally laden gender equality (Berglan, Golombek, and Rørd 2012).

Therefore, in accordance with a 'gendering' perspective, as captured by the sex–culture interaction, we hypothesize the following:

H3:   The association between sex and students' levels of entrepreneurial intentions, self-efficacy, risk perceptions and perceptions of social norms will be contingent on their national cultural context.

Methodology

For analysing the effects of culture, sex and their interaction on entrepreneurial intentions, we have collected data from members of both sexes in two distinct cultural settings. These settings were purposefully selected so as to fit opposing ends along Hofstede et al.'s (2004) cultural profiling of entrepreneurship-conducive environments. Norway represents a cultural context characterized by relative high individualism, low masculinity, low power distance and low uncertainty avoidance. Turkey, on the other hand, represents a cultural context characterized by relatively lower individualism, higher masculinity, higher power distance and higher uncertainly avoidance.

Data

Data in this study were collected from students. The study of entrepreneurial intentions requires examining entrepreneurial phenomena before they occur, while including non-entrepreneurial intending subjects. Therefore, samples of students are often used in such studies, as they reveal vocational preferences at a time when individuals face real career decisions (Krueger, Reilly, and Carsrud 2000). Indeed, students represent publics that can be characterized by the 'between things' type of displacement, often associated with higher likelihood of starting a new venture (Shapero and Sokol 1982). Accordingly, such samples include subjects with a broad spectrum of intentions and attitudes towards entrepreneurship (Krueger, Reilly, and Carsrud 2000).

Data in Norway were collected during autumn 2009 from students enrolled in programmes under the faculty of economics at the University of Agder. The questionnaire was first pre-tested with 20 students, all of whom showed adequate understanding of all items. The final version of the questionnaire was distributed as a web-based form by e-mail to all 2461 students registered under the faculty. In accordance with Dillman's (2006) recommendations, weekly reminders were sent to those who did not complete it. Overall response rate was 23.2%.

Later, data in Turkey were collected during spring 2011 from students enrolled in programmes under the faculty of economics and administrative sciences at Hacettepe University. A total of 350 printed format surveys were distributed and collected in the class. Overall response rate was 86.5%.

Here, while a 2-year lag between the data collection efforts may pose some challenges, we believe this has not biased the results, as there were no grand macro effects that have dramatically influenced the two economies in this period. Indeed, the two countries have successfully weathered the global financial crisis, and enjoyed relative stability throughout it (IMF 2012; The Financial Crisis Commission 2011).

All surveys were anonymous and did not include individual identification elements. Moreover, respondents were assured of the anonymous nature of the data collection effort in advance. At the end of the process, in Norway, we have received 401 valid questionnaires with complete data, incorporating 45% male and 55% female respondents. In Turkey we have received 292 valid questionnaires with complete data, incorporating 48% male and 52% female respondents.

The original survey was formulated in English and then translated to Norwegian and Turkish in two rounds of back-translations involving three native speakers in each language.

Measures

Self-report measures in this study were adopted from earlier research, with occasional adaptations (Table 1). These measures were deemed suitable as they seek to capture constructs that are defined as an individual's own self-efficacy, attitudes and perceptions.

Table 1. Variable measurements and sources.

Variable	Measurement	Source(s)
Entrepreneurial intentions	Five items: 'My professional goal is to become an entrepreneur' 'I am determined to create a firm in the future' 'I have the firm intention to start a firm someday' 'I intend to start a firm within five years after graduation' 'I prefer to be self-employed' 1 – Strongly disagree, 7 – strongly agree.	First three items from Liñán and Chen (2009), fourth from Kuckertz and Wagner (2010) and fifth from Grilo and Thurik (2005)
Self-efficacy	Five items: 'I am able to deal effectively with unexpected events' 'I can solve problems with my own efforts' 'I have ability to solve and remain calm when facing difficulties' 'I am resourceful and can handle unexpected challenges' 'I can think of solutions if faced by several problems' 1 – Strongly disagree, 7 – strongly agree.	Own instrument Inspired by items under the 'coping with unexpected challenges' factor in DeNoble, Jung, and Ehrlich (1999) and the 'risk taking' factor in Chen, Greene, and Crick (1998) and Kolvereid and Isaksen (2006)
Social norms	Three items 'My closest family members think I should start my own business' 'My friends and classmates think I should start my own business' 'People who are important to me think I should start my own business' 1 – Strongly disagree, 7 – strongly agree.	As used in Kolvereid (1996), Iakovleva and Kolvereid (2009), Liñán and Chen (2009)
Entrepreneurial attitudes/risk perception	Two items: 'Starting a new business is very risky' 'The possibility of a new business doing poorly is very high' 1 – Strongly disagree, 7 – strongly agree.	Own instrument Similar items used by Fitzsimmons and Douglas (2011), Fernandez, Linan, and Santos (2009), Liñán, Rodríguez-Cohard, and Rueda-Cantuche (2011), Liñán, Santos, and Fernández (2011) and Liñán, Urbano, and Guerrero (2011)

Entrepreneurial intentions have been measured in various ways in the literature, using both single (i.e. Fernandez, Linan, and Santos 2009; Lee and Wong 2004) and multiple items (i.e. Kolvereid 1996; Liñán and Chen 2009), while capturing aspects of startup/firm establishment and self-employment. In our study, a construct capturing entrepreneurial intentions has been measured through a 7-point Likert-type scale with five items, which were adopted from Liñán and Chen's (2009), Kuckertz and Wagner (2010) and Grilo and Thurik (2005) as specified in Table 1.

Self-efficacy is a cognitive estimate, which captures a person's belief in their own abilities to perform on the various skill requirements necessary for pursuing a new venture opportunity (Chen, Greene, and Crick 1998; DeNoble, Jung, and Ehrlich 1999). Various authors have used different measures for capturing self-efficacy, both single (i.e. Fernandez, Linan, and Santos 2009; Liñán, Rodríguez-Cohard, and Rueda-Cantuche 2011) and multiple items (i.e. Liñán and Chen 2009; Zhao, Hills, and Seibert 2005). In this study, a construct capturing self-efficacy has been measured through a 7-point Likert-type scale with five items, all reflecting the extent to which respondents believe in their ability to cope with uncertainty, change and risk. All items were re-formulated based on the earlier published items loading on the 'risk-taking' dimension in Chen, Greene, and Crick (1998), Kolvereid and Isaksen (2006) and DeNoble, Jung, and Ehrlich (1999) 'coping with unexpected challenges' dimension.

Social norms is an estimate, which captures normative beliefs about what important people think about an individual's choice to pursue an entrepreneurial career and/or self-employment (Yordanova and Tarrazon 2010), and the social pressures that are associated with them (Carey, Flanagan, and Palmer 2010). In line with earlier studies, we have adopted Kolvereid's (1996) three items for capturing social norms, while relating to whether close family, friends and people important to the individual encourage him or her to establish his or her own business. Here as well, respondents were required to indicate the extent to which they agree with each statement on a 7-point Likert scale.

Risk perception is an estimate, which captures the extent to which individuals associate entrepreneurship and self-employment with risk, and their attitudes towards it.

The use of a narrow proxy for attitudes, only focusing on risk aspects, while non-conventional, is undertaken based on the following. First, earlier studies show that entrepreneurial action is an outcome of more willingness to bear risk (Grilo and Thurik 2005; Kihlstrom and Laffont 1979) and uncertainty (McMullen and Shepherd 2006). Second, some studies have captured entrepreneurial attitudes while including items specifically relating to risk, uncertainty and personal sacrifice (Iakovleva and Kolvereid 2009; Kautonen, Luoto, and Tornikoski 2010; Yordanova and Tarrazon 2010). And third, this aspect was assumed to be of particular relevance to this study, as earlier research indicates lower risk tolerance among females versus males (Buttner and Rosen 1988; Sexton and Bowman-Upton 1990), as well as identifying uncertainty avoidance as a dimension along which cultures significantly differ (Hofstede 1980, 2001). Accordingly, we created the risk perceptions construct, based on two items, for capturing the extent to which respondents associate entrepreneurship with risk. Here, again, respondents were requested to indicate the extent to which they agree with each statement on a 7-point Likert scale, as used earlier.

The above measurements were analysed using confirmatory factor analysis (CFA) using LISREL 8 (Joreskog and Sorbom 1999). We compared the measurement models in two countries with regard to the model fit statistics, convergent and discriminant validities.

Given the sensitivity of χ^2 test to sample size and model complexity, goodness of fit was evaluated through root mean square error of approximation (RMSEA), comparative fit index (CFI), non-normed fit index (NNFI) and standardized root mean square residual (SRMR). Acceptable model fit was defined by the following multiple cut-off values proposed by Hu and Bentler (1999): RMSEA $\leq$ 0.06, CFI $\geq$ 0.95, NNFI $\geq$ 0.95, SRMR $\leq$ 0.08. CFA results indicated a good fit of the model to the data in Norway ($\chi2$ = 131.96, df = 84, p < 0.01, RMSEA = 0.04, CFI = 0.99, NNFI = 0.99, SRMR = 0.03). Similarly, the model fit was also satisfactory in Turkey ($\chi2$ = 146.38, df = 84, p < 0.01, RMSEA = 0.05, CFI = 0.98, NNFI = 0.98, SRMR = 0.05).

Convergent validity refers to the extent to which items related to a construct share a high proportion of variance in common. Following Anderson and Gerbing (1988), convergent validity was examined using average variance extracted (AVE) and composite reliability (CR). All items had standardized loading estimates above the suggested 0.50 level, except one risk item in Turkey. To ensure convergent validity, each dimension should have AVE higher than 50% and CR higher than 0.70. As seen in Tables 2 and 3, only the risk perceptions measure was below the threshold levels in both countries. All other measures illustrated satisfactory levels of convergent validity. Accordingly, we have excluded risk perceptions from further analysis and discussion.

Discriminant validity refers to the extent to which a construct is truly distinct from other constructs. To ensure adequate levels of discriminant validity for each dimension, AVE within factors is compared to the square of the inter-factor correlations as proposed by Fornell and Larcker (1981). In this test, the squared correlations between latent variables should be less than the AVE of each variable. An examination of Tables 4 and 5 reveals that all squared correlations were below AVE values, indicating adequate discriminant validity of the constructs in both countries.

Analysis

Since our data violated the assumptions of normal distribution for all variables included, as made evident by significant values of the Kolmogorov–Smirnov tests at 0.001 levels, we have opted for non-parametric statistics (Field 2005). Entrepreneurial intentions,

Table 2. Convergent validity analysis – Norway.

	Self-efficacy	Entrepreneurial intentions	Risk perceptions	Social norms
E1a	0.77			
E1b	0.80			
E1c	0.70			
E1d	0.84			
E1e	0.81			
E2a		0.80		
E2b		0.89		
E2c		0.95		
E2d		0.92		
E2e		0.83		
E3a			0.75	
E3b			0.65	
E4a				0.90
E4b				0.91
E4c				0.96
AVE (%)	61.7	77.4	49.3	85.3
CR	0.89	0.95	0.66	0.94

Note: Standardized factor loadings, AVE and CR values for items in Norway.

Table 3. Convergent validity analysis –Turkey.

	Self-efficacy	Entrepreneurial intentions	Risk	Norm
E1a	0.87			
E1b	0.76			
E1c	0.69			
E1d	0.68			
E1e	0.68			
E2a		0.69		
E2b		0.88		
E2c		0.92		
E2d		0.84		
E2e		0.71		
E3a			0.43	
E3b			0.63	
E4a				0.80
E4b				0.90
E4c				0.89
AVE (%)	54.7	66.1	29.1	74.7
CR	0.86	0.91	0.44	0.90

Note: Standardized factor loadings, AVE and CR values for items in Turkey.

Table 4. Discriminant validity analysis – Norway.

	Self-efficacy	Entrepreneurial intentions	Risk perceptions	Social norms
Self-efficacy	–	0.05	0.00	0.06
Entrepreneurial intentions	0.22*	–	0.00	0.37
Risk perceptions	0.01	−0.07	–	0.00
Social norms	0.24*	0.61*	0.07*	–
AVE (%)	61.7	77.4	49.3	85.3

Notes: Values below the diagonal are the inter-factor correlations and values in italic above the diagonal are squared correlations. *Significant at $p < 0.05$ level.

$D(556) = 0.074$, $p < 0.001$; self-efficacy, $D(556) = 0.090$, $p < 0.001$, $p < 0.001$; and social norms, $D(556) = 0.185$, $p < 0.001$, were all significantly non-normal.

Conover and Iman (1981) suggest using rank transformation procedures for developing non-parametric tests. Accordingly, we have used Shirley's (1987) procedure for two-way non-parametric ANOVA, which uses rank transformations. The hypotheses

Table 5. Discriminant validity analysis – Turkey.

	Self-efficacy	Entrepreneurial intentions	Risk perceptions	Social norms
Self-efficacy	–	0.05	0.00	0.01
Entrepreneurial intentions	0.22*	–	0.03	0.44
Risk perceptions	−0.07	−0.18*	–	0.01
Social norms	0.12	0.67*	−0.10	–
AVE (%)	54.7	66.1	29.1	74.7

Notes: Values below the diagonal are the inter-factor correlations and values in italic above the diagonal are squared correlations. *Significant at $p < 0.05$ level.

Table 6. Two-way non-parametric ANOVA results.

Effects	Country	Sex	Country × sex
Entrepreneurial intentions	86.834***	15.763***	6.636**
Self-efficacy	4.452*	8.925**	0.704
Risk perceptions	23.990***	9.981**	0.243
Social norms	2.028	6.186*	0.007

Notes: F values significant at $*p < 0.05$, $**p < 0.01$, $***p < 0.001$; degrees of freedom = 555.

were tested via a 2 (culture: Norway vs. Turkey) × 2 (sex: male vs. female) non-parametric ANOVA, as presented in Table 6. For further simplifying the interpretation of the interaction terms, a description of the two-way cell means is provided in Table 7.

Moreover, since ANOVA is fairly robust to violations of the assumption of homogeneity of variance when sample sizes are equal (Field 2005), we have created equal sample sizes for further enhancing the robustness of our test. Since the smallest sub-group was of Turkish males with 139 observations, we have equalized all group sizes to 139 observations (556 observations in total). This was achieved by randomly removing 14 observations from the Turkish female set, 40 observations from the Norwegian male set and 83 observations from the Norwegian female set.

Findings

First, since the main effects reflected in H1 and H2 are contingent on the interaction test in H3, we first present the results for H3.

Table 7. Mann–Whitney tests.

	Male	Female	Total by country
Entrepreneurial intentions			
Norway	118.06[a,b]	101.27[a,b]	220.39[c]
Turkey	160.94[b]	177,73[b]	336.61[c]
Total by gender	303.26[d]	253.74[d]	
Self-efficacy			
Norway	135.68[a]	129.28[a,b]	264.31[c]
Turkey	143.32	149.72[b]	292.69[c]
Total by gender	298.59[d]	259.41[d]	
Risk perceptions			
Norway	157.38[b,e]	153.95[b,e]	310.71[c]
Turkey	121.62[a,b]	125.05[a,b]	246.29[c]
Total by gender	257.72[d]	299.28[d]	
Social norms			
Norway	133.47[e]	135.94[e]	268.98
Turkey	145.53	143.06	288.02
Total by gender	295.13[d]	261.87[d]	

[a] Significant between-cell row difference (at $p < 0.05$ or higher).
[b] Significant between-cell column difference (at $p < 0.05$ or higher).
[c] Significant marginal row difference (at $p < 0.05$ or higher).
[d] Significant marginal column difference (at $p < 0.05$ or higher).
[e] Significant between-cell row difference ($p < 0.1$).

The results confirm H3 only for entrepreneurial intentions, but not for its antecedents. Interaction effects between country and sex are only significant in determining levels of entrepreneurial intentions ($F(2,552) = 6.636$, $p < 0.01$), and non-significant in determining self-efficacy and social norms.

When examining Table 7, we can see that among Norwegian students there were significant differences between sexes in levels of entrepreneurial intentions ($U = 6738$, $p < 0.001$, $r = -0.26$), self-efficacy ($U = 7929$, $p < 0.01$, $r = -0.16$), though only weakly significant in levels of perceived social norms ($U = 8460.5$, $p < 0.1$, $r = -0.11$). Furthermore, in accordance with expectations, among Turkish students there were non-significant differences in levels of entrepreneurial intentions, social norms and self-efficacy.

The results confirm H1 for entrepreneurial intentions ($U = 22487$, $p < 0.001$, $r = -0.36$) and self-efficacy ($U = 34697.5$, $p < 0.05$, $r = -0.20$), by which Turkish students exhibited higher levels of both, relative to their Norwegian peers. However, no significant differences were found between Turkish and Norwegian students in levels of perceived social norms.

The results confirm H2 for all variables studied. Males exhibited significantly higher levels of entrepreneurial intentions ($U = 31759$, $p < 0.001$, $r = -0.15$), self-efficacy ($U = 33057$, $p < 0.01$, $r = -0.13$) and perceived social norms ($U = 34019.5$, $p < 0.05$, $r = -0.11$).

Discussion

The purpose of this study was to explore the effects of sex, culture and their interaction on entrepreneurial intentions. The main findings presented above suggest that levels of individuals' entrepreneurial intentions in different sex groups are contingent upon the culture from which they originate. This finding is explained by the view that while the gendering of entrepreneurship is predominantly male across cultures (Ahl 2006; Gupta et al. 2009), its prevalence across sexes varies in different cultures based on their particular legitimation of gender roles and stereotypes (Ahl 2006). In relatively masculine societies, such as Turkey, members of both sexes put premium on masculine characteristics (Özkan and Lajunen 2005), and since entrepreneurship is associated with masculinity, its appreciation does not differ between males and females. However, in feminine societies, such as Norway, each sex group evaluates the virtues of masculine characteristics differently (Hofstede 1998; Williams and Best 1990), and, again, since entrepreneurship is associated with masculinity, evaluations of its own virtues vary between males and females.

When considering the TPB approach, which was chosen for reflecting the intentional nature of entrepreneurship (Krueger and Carsrud 1993; Krueger, Reilly, and Carsrud 2000), the findings of this study suggest that while entrepreneurial intentions are impacted by gendering (as captured by the sex–culture interaction), its TPB antecedents of self-efficacy and social norms do not. A possible explanation here may be that unlike entrepreneurship, which is perceived as masculine (Ahl 2006; Gupta et al. 2009), self-efficacy and social norms may themselves be gender-neutral concepts. If these antecedents are not perceived as having either masculine or feminine characteristics in particular, then there is no culture-laden evaluation of their congruence with acceptable gender roles and stereotypes.

Moreover, this study shows that entrepreneurial intentions vary across cultures and, hence, in tune with earlier studies exhibiting significant differences across countries

(Giacomin et al. 2011; Lee et al. 2006; Nguyen et al. 2009; Pruett et al. 2009). However, unlike earlier studies, our study provides cultural anchoring for these results by providing support to the dissatisfaction thesis of cultural profiling in the context of entrepreneurship. In this sense, we support Hofstede et al.'s (2004) suggestion that a culture characterized by low individualism, low power distance, high uncertainty avoidance and high masculinity represents a more conducive environment for the rise of entrepreneurs than others.

Here, in addition to levels of entrepreneurial intentions, the antecedent of self-efficacy also was found to differ significantly across cultures. Hence, our study supports earlier documentation of cross-country differences in self-efficacy/confidence (Giacomin et al. 2011; Lee et al. 2006; Nguyen et al. 2009; Pruett et al. 2009). However, perceptions of social norms did not. In this sense, our findings contradict those of Giacomin et al. (2011) who showed that 'lack of support structure and financial and administrative costs' was perceived as much greater barrier to entrepreneurship among Indian students than among Chinese, Spanish and Belgian students; as well as the findings of Pruett et al. (2009) who showed that Chinese were much more concerned with 'lack of support from family and friends' than their American and Spanish counterparts. A possible explanation for the discrepancy may be found in the fact that our study included business students only, versus a general student population in the two earlier studies. Here, one can assume that business students, by definition of their study area, are naturally surrounded by friends, colleagues and educators who are generally more supportive of entrepreneurship.

When sex is concerned, our study joins a long list of earlier studies showing that males exhibit higher levels of entrepreneurial intentions (Kautonen, Luoto, and Tornikoski 2010; Kolvereid and Moen 1997; Kuckertz and Wagner 2010; Lee and Wong 2004; Liñán, Santos, and Fernández 2011; Yordanova 2011). And since our study includes both sex and the gendering aspect of sex, our findings may be considered even stronger, showing that when controlling for culture, both these effects are evident.

Similarly, when the TPB antecedents are concerned, our study also shows that males exhibit higher levels of self-efficacy and social norms than females. Accordingly, our study supports similar findings in earlier research with respect to self-efficacy/confidence (Kristiansen and Indarti 2004; Scherer, Brodzinski, and Wiebe 1990; Wilson, Kickul, and Marlino 2007; Wilson et al. 2009; Yordanova and Tarrazon 2010). Finally, in terms of social norms, our study supports earlier studies that found significant differences between sexes (Shinnar, Giacomin, and Janssen 2012; Yordanova and Tarrazon 2010), rather than none.

Acknowledging limitations

The findings of this study are constrained in terms of their generalizability beyond the two cultural contexts from which they emerged. In this sense, the study presents findings from two case studies, each representing a particular configuration of national cultural profile that is purposefully selected for its fit with divergent theoretical approaches. Here, the quantitative analysis helps us to identify significant differences, and hence allowing us to develop hypotheses that require a larger scope of data collection for achieving wider generalizability. Having that in mind, one must also acknowledge that culture is not measured directly in this study, but rather assumed. Hence, both a direct measurement of culture and a wider scale study, incorporating more cultural settings, are likely to provide stronger evidence for findings presented here.

In addition, since our data were collected from economics and business students, our findings may be biased to this public. Data collection among students in other fields of study such as arts, education, medicine and law may all show different results, based on conventions and career opportunities in each of these domains.

Furthermore, our data collection relies only on self-reported measurements. The main reason for that was that we aimed to tap into individual's self-efficacy, attitudes and perceptions – all of which representing information with limited alternative sources. Nevertheless, we acknowledge that use of mono-method may lend itself to a certain level of method bias. While conscious efforts have been made to alleviate such concerns via CFA, convergent and discriminant validity analyses, as well as by ensuring anonymity of respondents, using alternative forms of questions for capturing same construct, as well as repeating data collection rounds, may have helped to reduce concerns of method bias further.

Finally, our use of risk perceptions as proxy measurement for attitudes, while mainly aiming to amplify differences between sexes and cultures, is conceptually controversial, and may represent too drastic of a departure from the original TPB. Here, alternative measurements, as already used and validated in earlier cross-cultural studies, are likely to be more suitable for capturing attitudes in TPB applications in the context of entrepreneurship studies (i.e. Engle et al. 2010; Liñán and Chen 2009)

Conclusions

Building on an earlier call for the contextualization of entrepreneurial intentions (Hindle, Klyver, and Jennings 2009), this study sought to contribute to such line of research by focusing on the aspects of culture, sex and their interaction via 'gendering'. First, in terms of the effects of culture, our study provides support for the relatively understudied dissatisfaction thesis of cultural profiling of societies that are more conducive to entrepreneurship (Hofstede et al. 2004). These cultural effects are further extended to the TPB's antecedent of self-efficacy, but not to perceptions of social norms.

Second, our study supports the body of literature that finds systematically higher levels of entrepreneurial intentions, self-efficacy and social norms among males versus females across cultures. Since our study includes both sex and the gendering aspect of sex, our findings may be considered even stronger showing that when controlling for culture, both these effects are evident.

Finally, our study's main contribution is in identifying an interaction effect between sex and culture on entrepreneurial intentions, interpreted as a gendering effect. Such effect suggests that the extent to which males differ from females in terms of their entrepreneurial intentions is contingent on the national context from which they originate. Here, the tension between gendering of entrepreneurial career paths and the extent to which it deviates from perceptions of proper gender behaviour, as dictated by cultural values and norms, influences the extent to which members of different sex groups in different cultures develop entrepreneurial intentions.

Implications for research and practice

First, in terms of implications for research, we first acknowledge that our data does not lend itself to process analysis, which can be valuable in qualitative fine grounding of the dynamics behind the statistical associations we are able to show. In particular, qualitative analyses of the association between culture and entrepreneurial intentions, as well as between aspects of gendering and entrepreneurial intentions, are both promising venues for deeper understanding of these phenomena.

Quantitative extensions of the study may examine its generalizability across additional cultural contexts and sample groups. Data from additional contexts that can fit theoretically driven cultural profiles may further enhance and fine tune our understanding of the role of culture in the formation of entrepreneurial intentions and their antecedents. Such insights may also be harnessed from different groups such as different ethnic groups within same country contexts, students of different educational background and specialization, as well as experience levels.

Moreover, studies exploring additional dimensions of contextualization of entrepreneurial intentions should be encouraged. These may include analyses of entrepreneurial intentions under a variety of institutional conditions such as market versus coordination economies, democratic versus autocratic regimes, religiously pious versus secular societies and so on.

A practical implication of our findings may suggest that educational institutions as well entrepreneurship promotions agencies should acknowledge the importance of contextualizing entrepreneurship education and training. For example, such contextualization should not be satisfied with creating special programmes for female entrepreneurs, but taking into account the cultural context in which these females operate, while adapting curriculum and educational activities to these cultural realities. Here, one can argue that uncritical replications of educational programmes created in culturally masculine environments may work well in such societies, but may prove less successful in feminine cultural environments in general, and among females within feminine cultures in particular.

In this sense, the acknowledgement of the 'gendering' effect on the formation of entrepreneurial intentions may also constitute an invitation for research that will examine how to effectively contextualize entrepreneurship training programmes and curriculum in different cultural environments in general, and when creating such programmes for specific gender groups in particular.

Acknowledgements

The authors would like to first thank the anonymous reviewers for their professional, constructive and helpful feedbacks throughout the revision process of this paper. We also wish to thank research fellow Burak Tunca for his contributions and assistance in developing the paper. Final thanks go to many who have helped us with repeated proof-reading, and in particular to research fellow Lisa Whitehead, who has been instrumental in this effort.

References

Acs, Zoltan J., David B. Audretsch, and David S. Evans. 1994. *The Determinants of Variations in Self-Employment Rates Across Countries and over Time*. London: Centre for Economic Policy Research.

Ahl, Helene. 2006. "Why Research on Women Entrepreneurs Needs New Directions." *Entrepreneurship Theory and Practice* 30 (5): 595–621.

Ajzen, Icek. 1991. "The Theory of Planned Behavior." *Organizational Behavior and Human Decision Process* 50 (2): 179–211.

Anderson, James C., and David W. Gerbing. 1988. "Structural Equation Modeling in Practice: A Review and Recommended Two-Step Approach." *Psychological Bulletin* 103 (3): 411–423.

Autio, Erkko, Robert H. Keeley, Magnus Klofsten, George G. C. Parker, and Michael Hay. 2001. "Entrepreneurial Intent Among Students in Scandinavia and in the USA." *Enterprise and Innovation Management Studies* 2 (2): 145–160.

Aycan, Zeynep, and Selda Fikret-Pasa. 2003. "Career Choices, Job Selection Criteria, and Leadership Preferences in a Transitional Nation: The Case of Turkey." *Journal of Career Development* 30 (2): 129–144.

BarNir, Anat, Warren E. Watson, and Holly M. Hutchins. 2011. "Mediation and Moderated Mediation in the Relationship among Role Models, Self-Efficacy, Entrepreneurial Career Intention, and Gender." *Journal of Applied Social Psychology* 41 (2): 270–297.

Baum, J. Robert, Judy D. Olian, Miriam Erez, Eugene R. Schnell, Ken G. Smith, Henry P. Sims, Judith S. Scully, and Ken A. Smith. 1993. "Nationality and Work Role Interactions: A Cultural Contrast of Israeli and U.S. Entrepreneurs' Versus Managers' Needs." *Journal of Business Venturing* 8 (6): 499–512.

Berglan, Helge, Rolf Golombek, and Knut Rørd. 2012. "Entrepreneurship in Norway – Mostly for men?" *Women as Entrepreneurs – Will they not take risks?* Oslo: Norwegian Research Council (in Norwegian).

Bird, Barbara. 1988. "Implementing Entrepreneurial Ideas: The Case for Intention." *Academy of Management Review* 13 (3): 442–453.

Buttner, E. Holly, and Benson Rosen. 1988. "Bank Loan Officers' Perceptions of the Characteristics of Men, Women, and Successful Entrepreneurs." *Journal of Business Venturing* 3 (3): 249–258.

Carey, Thomas A., David J. Flanagan, and Timothy B. Palmer. 2010. "An Examination of University Student Entrepreneurial Intentions by Type of Venture." *Journal of Developmental Entrepreneurship* 15 (4): 503–517.

Carter, Sara, and Peter Rosa. 1998. "The Financing of Male- and Female-Owned Businesses." *Entrepreneurship and Regional Development* 10 (3): 225–242.

Chen, Chao C., Patricia Gene Greene, and Ann Crick. 1998. "Does Entrepreneurial Self-Efficacy Distinguish Entrepreneurs from Managers?" *Journal of Business Venturing* 13 (4): 295–316.

Coleman, Susan. 2000. "Access to Capital and Terms of Credit: A Comparison of Men- and Women-Owned Small Businesses." *Journal of Small Business Management* 38 (3): 37–52.

Conover, William J., and Ronald L. Iman. 1981. "Rank Transformations as a Bridge Between Parametric and Nonparametric Statistics." *The American Statistician* 35 (3): 124–129.

Davidsson, Per, and Johan Wiklund. 1997. "Values, Beliefs and Regional Variations in New Firm Formation Rates." *Journal of Economic Psychology* 18 (2–3): 179–199.

DeNoble, A., D. Jung, and S. B. Ehrlich. 1999. "Entrepreneurial Self-Efficacy: The Development of a Measure and Its Relationship to Entrepreneurial Action." In *Frontiers in Entrepreneurship Research*, edited by P. D. Reynolds, W. D. Bygrave, S. Manigart, C. M. Mason, G. D. Meyer, H. J. Sapienza, and K. G. Shaver, 73–87. Waltham, MA: P&R Publications Inc.

Díaz-García, Maria Cristina, and Juan Jiménez-Moreno. 2010. "Entrepreneurial Intention: The Role of Gender." *International Entrepreneurship and Management Journal* 6 (3): 261–283.

Dillman, Don A. 2006. *Mail and Internet Surveys, the Tailored Designed Method.* 2nd ed. New York: Wiley.

Engle, Robert L., Nikolav Dimitriadi, Jose V. Gavidia, Christophe Schlaegel, Servane Delanoe, Irene Alvarado, Xiaohong He, Samuel Buame, and Birgitta Wolff. 2010. "Entrepreneurial Intent: A Twelve-Country Evaluation of Ajzen's Model of Planned Behavior." *International Journal of Entrepreneurial Behaviour and Research* 16 (1): 36–58.

Erez, Miriam, and Christopher P. Earley. 1993. *Culture, Self-Identity and Work.* New York: Oxford University Press.

Etzioni, Amitai. 1987. "Entrepreneurship, Adaptation and Legitimation: A Macro-Behavioral Perspective." *Journal of Economic Behavior and Organization* 8 (2): 175–189.

Fernandez, Jose, Francisco Linan, and Francisco J. Santos. 2009. "Cognitive Aspects of Potential Entrepreneurs in Southern and Northern Europe: An Analysis Using Gem-Data." *Revista de Economia Mundial* 23: 151–178.

Field, Andy. 2005. *Discovering Statistics Using SPSS.* 2nd ed. London: Sage Publications.

Fitzsimmons, Jason R., and Evan J. Douglas. 2011. "Interaction Between Feasibility and Desirability in the Formation of Entrepreneurial Intentions." *Journal of Business Venturing* 26 (4): 431–440.

Fornell, Claes, and David F. Larcker. 1981. "Structural Equation Models with Unobservable Variables and Measurement Error: Algebra and Statistics." *Journal of Marketing Research* 18 (3): 382–388.

Giacomin, Olivier, Frank Janssen, Mark Pruett, Rachel S. Shinnar, Francisco Llopis, and Bryan Toney. 2011. "Entrepreneurial Intentions, Motivations and Barriers: Differences among American, Asian and European Students." *International Entrepreneurship and Management Journal* 7 (2): 219–238.

Grilo, Isabel, and Roy Thurik. 2005. "Latent and Actual Entrepreneurship in Europe and the Us: Some Recent Developments." *International Entrepreneurship and Management Journal* 1 (4): 441–459.

Gupta, Vishal K., Daniel B. Turban, Arzu S. Wasti, and Arijit Sikdar. 2009. "The Role of Gender Stereotypes in Perceptions of Entrepreneurs and Intentions to Become an Entrepreneur." *Entrepreneurship: Theory and Practice* 33 (2): 397–417.

Hayton, James C., Gerard George, and Shaker A. Zahra. 2002. "National Culture and Entrepreneurship: A Review of Behavioral Research." *Entrepreneurship: Theory and Practice* 26 (4): 33–52.

Hindle, Kevin, Kim Klyver, and Daniel F. Jennings. 2009. "An Informed Intent Model: Incorporating Human Capital, Social Capital, and Gender Variables into the Theoretical Model of Entrepreneurship Intentions." In *Understanding the Entrepreneurial Mind: Opening the Black Box*, edited by Alan L. Carsrud, and Malin Brännback, 35–50. New York: Springer.

Hofstede, Geert. 2001. *Culture's Consequences: Comparing Values, Behaviors, Institutions, and Organizations Across Nations.* 2nd ed. Thousand Oaks, CA: Sage Publications.

Hofstede, Geert. 1980. *Culture's Consequences: International Differences in Work-Related Values.* Beverly Hills, CA: Sage.

Hofstede, G. 1998. "The Cultural Construction of Gender." In *Masculinity and Femininity: The Taboo Dimension of National Culture*, edited by G. Hofstede, 77–102. Thousand Oaks, CA: Sage Publications Inc.

Hofstede, Geert, Niels G. Noorderhaven, Roy A. Thurik, Lorraine M. Uhlaner, Alexander R. M. Wennekers, and Ralph E. Wildeman. 2004. "Culture's Role in Entrepreneurship: Self-Employment out of Dissatisfaction." Chap. 8. In *Innovation, Entrepreneurship and Culture*, edited by Terrence E. Brown, and Jan Ulijn, 162–203. Cheltenham: Edward Elgar.

Hu, Li-Tze, and Peter M. Bentler. 1999. "Cutoff Criteria for Fit Indexes in Covariance Structure Analysis: Conventional Criteria Versus New Alternatives." *Structural Equation Modeling: A Multidisciplinary Journal* 6 (1): 1–55.

Iakovleva, Tatiana, and Lars Kolvereid. 2009. "An Integrated Model of Entrepreneurial Intentions." *International Journal of Business and Globalisation* 3 (1): 66–80.

IMF. 2012. *Turkey: Financial System Stability Assessment.* IMF Country Report Washington, DC: IMF Intrnational Monetary Fund.

Joreskog, K. G., and D. Sorbom. 1999. *LISREL 8: User's Reference Guide.* Lincolnwood, IL: Scientific Software International Inc.

Karataş-Özkan, M., A. Erdoğan, and K. Nicolopoulou. 2011. "Women in Turkish Family Businesses: Drivers, Contributions and Challenges." *International Journal of Cross Cultural Management* 11 (2): 203–219.

Kautonen, Teemu, Seppo Luoto, and Erno T. Tornikoski. 2010. "Influence of Work History on Entrepreneurial Intentions in Prime Age and Third Age: A Preliminary Study." *International Small Business Journal* 28 (6): 583–601.

Kickul, Jill, Fiona Wilson, Deborah Marlino, and Saulo D. Barbosa. 2008. "Are Misalignments of Perceptions and Self-Efficacy Causing Gender Gaps in Entrepreneurial Intentions among Our Nation's Teens?" *Journal of Small Business and Enterprise Development* 15 (2): 321–335.

Kihlstrom, Richard E., and Jean-Jacques Laffont. 1979. "A General Equilibrium Entrepreneurial Theory of Firm Formation Based on Risk Aversion." *Journal of Political Economy* 87 (4): 719–748.

Kolvereid, Lars. 1992. "Growth Aspirations Among Norwegian Entrepreneurs." *Journal of Business Venturing* 7 (3): 209–222.

Kolvereid, Lars. 1996. "Prediction of Employment Status Choice Intentions." *Entrepreneurship: Theory and Practice* 21 (1): 47–57.

Kolvereid, Lars, and Espen Isaksen. 2006. "New Business Start-up and Subsequent Entry into Self-Employment." *Journal of Business Venturing* 21 (6): 866–885.

Kolvereid, Lars, and Oystein Moen. 1997. "Entrepreneurship among Business Graduates: Does a Major in Entrepreneurship Make a Difference?" *Journal of European Industrial Training* 21 (4/5): 154–160.

Kristiansen, Stein, and Nurul Indarti. 2004. "Entrepreneurial Intention among Indonesian and Norwegian Students." *Journal of Enterprising Culture* 12 (1): 55–78.

Krueger, Norris. 2009. "Entrepreneurial Intentions Are Dead: Long Live Entrepreneurial Intentions." In *Understanding the Entrepreneurial Mind: Opening the Black Box*, edited by Alan L. Carsrud, and Malin Brännback, 51–74. New York: Springer.

Krueger, Norris F. 1993. "The Impact of Prior Entrepreneurial Exposure on Perceptions of New Venture Feasibility and Desirability." *Entrepreneurship: Theory and Practice* 18 (1): 5–21.

Krueger, Norris F., and Alan L. Carsrud. 1993. "Entrepreneurial Intentions: Applying the Theory of Planned Behaviour." *Entrepreneurship and Regional Development* 5 (4): 315–330.

Krueger, Norris F., Michael D. Reilly, and Alan L. Carsrud. 2000. "Competing Models of Entrepreneurial Intentions." *Journal of Business Venturing* 15 (5): 411–432.

Kuckertz, Andreas, and Marcus Wagner. 2010. "The Influence of Sustainability Orientation on Entrepreneurial Intentions – Investigating the Role of Business Experience." *Journal of Business Venturing* 25 (5): 524–539.

Lee, Soo Hoon, and Poh Kam Wong. 2004. "An Exploratory Study of Technopreneurial Intentions: A Career Anchor Perspective." *Journal of Business Venturing* 19 (1): 7–28.

Lee, S. M., S. B. Lim, R. D. Pathak, D. Chang, and W. Li. 2006. "Influences on Students Attitudes Toward Entrepreneurship: A Multi-Country Study." *International Entrepreneurship and Management Journal* 3 (2): 351–366.

Liñán, Francisco, and Yi-Wen Chen. 2009. "Development and Cross-Cultural Application of a Specific Instrument to Measure Entrepreneurial Intentions." *Entrepreneurship: Theory and Practice* 33 (3): 593–617.

Liñán, Francisco, Juan Carlos Rodríguez-Cohard, and José M. Rueda-Cantuche. 2011. "Factors Affecting Entrepreneurial Intention Levels: A Role for Education." *International Entrepreneurship and Management Journal* 7 (2): 195–218.

Liñán, Francisco, Francisco J. Santos, and Jose Fernández. 2011. "The Influence of Perceptions on Potential Entrepreneurs." *International Entrepreneurship and Management Journal* 7 (3): 373–390.

Liñán, Francisco, David Urbano, and Maribel Guerrero. 2011. "Regional Variations in Entrepreneurial Cognitions: Start-up Intentions of University Students in Spain." *Entrepreneurship and Regional Development* 23 (3/4): 187–215.

McGrath, R. G., I. C. MacMillan, and S. Scheinberg. 1992. "Elitists, Risk-Takers, and Rugged Individualists? An Exploratory Analysis of Cultural Differences between Entrepreneurs and Non-Entrepreneurs." *Journal of Business Venturing* 7: 115–135.

McMullen, Jeffery S., and Dean A. Shepherd. 2006. "Entrepreneurial Action and the Role of Uncertainty in the Theory of the Entrepreneur." *Academy of Management Review* 31 (1): 132–152.

Moriano, Juan A., Marjan Gorgievski, Mariola Laguna, Ute Stephan, and Kiumars Zarafshani. 2012. "A Cross-Cultural Approach to Understanding Entrepreneurial Intention." *Journal of Career Development* 39 (2): 162–185.

Mueller, S. L., and Conway Dato-on, M. 2013. "A Cross Cultural Study of Gender-Role Orientation and Entrepreneurial Self-Efficacy." *International Entrepreneurship and Management Journal* 9: 1–20.

Mueller, Stephen L. 2004. "Gender Gaps in Potential for Entrepreneurship Across Countries and Cultures." *Journal of Developmental Entrepreneurship* 9 (3): 199–220.

Mueller, Stephen L., and Mary Conway Dato-On. 2008. "Gender-Role Orientation as a Determinant of Entrepreneurial Self-Efficacy." *Journal of Developmental Entrepreneurship* 13 (1): 3–20.

Mueller, Stephen L., and Anisya S. Thomas. 2001. "Culture and Entrepreneurial Potential: A Nine Country Study of Locus of Control and Innovativeness." *Journal of Business Venturing* 16 (1): 51–75.

Mueller, Susan. 2011. "Increasing Entrepreneurial Intention: Effective Entrepreneurship Course Characteristics." *International Journal of Entrepreneurship and Small Business* 13 (1): 55–74.

Nguyen, Thang V., Scott E. Bryant, Jerman Rose, Chiung-Hui Tseng, and Supara Kapasuwan. 2009. "Cultural Values, Market Institutions, and Entrepreneurship Potential: A Comparative Study of the United States, Taiwan, and Vietnam." *Journal of Developmental Entrepreneurship* 14 (1): 21–37.

Özkan, Türker, and Timo Lajunen. 2005. "Masculinity, Femininity, and the Bem Sex Role Inventory in Turkey." *Sex Roles* 52 (1–2): 103–110.

Plant, Robert, and Jen Ren. 2010. "A Comparative Study of Motivation and Entrepreneurial Intentionality: Chinese and American Perspectives." *Journal of Developmental Entrepreneurship* 15 (2): 187–204.

Pruett, Mark, Rachel S. Shinnar, Bryan Toney, Francisco Llopis, and Jerry Fox. 2009. "Explaining Entrepreneurial Intentions of University Students: A Cross-Cultural Study." *International Journal of Entrepreneurial Behaviour and Research* 15 (6): 571–594.

Scherer, Robert F., James D. Brodzinski, and Frank A. Wiebe. 1990. "Entrepreneur Career Selection and Gender: A Socialization Approach." *Journal of Small Business Management* 28 (2): 37–44.

Sexton, Donald L., and Nancy Bowman-Upton. 1990. "Female and Male Entrepreneurs: Psychological Characteristics and Their Role in Gender-Related Discrimination." *Journal of Business Venturing* 5 (1): 29–36.

Shane, Scott. 1993. "Cultural Influences on National Rates of Innovation." *Journal of Business Venturing* 8 (1): 59–73.

Shapero, Albert. 1975. "The Displaced, Uncomfortable Entrepreneur." *Psychology Today* 9 (6): 83–88.

Shapero, Albert, and Lisa Sokol. 1982. "The Social Dimensions of Entrepreneurship." In *Encyclopedia of Entrepreneurship*, edited by C. Kent, D. Sexton, and K. Vesper, 72–90. Englewood Cliffs, NJ: Prentice-Hall.

Shinnar, Rachel S., Olivier Giacomin, and Frank Janssen. 2012. "Entrepreneurial Perceptions and Intentions: The Role of Gender and Culture." *Entrepreneurship: Theory and Practice* 36 (3): 465–493.

Shirley, Eryl A. C. 1987. "Applications of Ranking Methods of Multiple Comparison Procedures and Factorial Experiments." *Journal of the Royal Statistical Society. Series C (Applied Statistics)* 36 (2): 205–213.

Singh, Gangaram, and Alex DeNoble. 2003. "Views on Self-Employment and Personality: An Exploratory Study." *Journal of Developmental Entrepreneurship* 8 (3): 265–281.

The Financial Crisis Commission. 2011. *Better Positioned against Financial Crises*. Oslo: Norwegian Ministry of Finance.

Tkachev, Alexei, and Lars Kolvereid. 1999. "Self-Employment Intentions among Russian Students." *Entrepreneurship and Regional Development* 11 (3): 269–280.

Van Gelderen, Marco, Maryse Brand, Mirjam van Praag, Wynand Bodewes, Erik Poutsma, and Anita van Gils. 2008. "Explaining Entrepreneurial Intentions by Means of the Theory of Planned Behaviour." *Career Development International* 13 (6): 538–559.

Wagner, Joachim. 2007. "What a Difference a Y Makes-Female and Male Nascent Entrepreneurs in Germany." *Small Business Economics* 28 (1): 1–21.

Walter, Sascha G., Praveen K. Parboteeah, and Achim Walter. 2011. "University Departments and Self-Employment Intentions of Business Students: A Cross-Level Analysis." *Entrepreneurship: Theory and Practice* 37 (2): 175–200.

Williams, John E., and Deborah L. Best. 1990. *Sex and Psyche: Gender and Self Viewed Cross-Culturally.* Newbury Park, CA: Sage.

Wilson, Fiona, Jill Kickul, and Deborah Marlino. 2007. "Gender, Entrepreneurial Self-Efficacy, and Entrepreneurial Career Intentions: Implications for Entrepreneurship Education." *Entrepreneurship: Theory and Practice* 31 (3): 387–406.

Wilson, Fiona, Jill Kickul, Deborah Marlino, Saulo D. Barbosa, and Mark D. Griffiths. 2009. "An Analysis of the Role of Gender and Self-Efficacy in Developing Female Entrepreneurial Interest and Behavior." *Journal of Developmental Entrepreneurship* 14 (2): 105–119.

Yordanova, Desislava I. 2011. "The Effects of Gender on Entrepreneurship in Bulgaria: An Empirical Study." *International Journal of Management* 28 (1): 289–305.

Yordanova, Desislava I., and Maria-Antonia Tarrazon. 2010. "Gender Differences in Entrepreneurial Intentions: Evidence from Bulgaria." *Journal of Developmental Entrepreneurship* 15 (3): 245–261.

Zhao, Hao, Gerald E. Hills, and Scott E. Seibert. 2005. "The Mediating Role of Self-Efficacy in the Development of Entrepreneurial Intentions." *Journal of Applied Psychology* 90 (6): 1265–1272.

Bourdieuian approaches to the geography of entrepreneurial cultures

Ben Spigel

University of Edinburgh Business School, Scotland, UK

Culture has emerged as an important concept within the entrepreneurship literature to help explain differences in the nature of the entrepreneurship process observed between regions, industries and socio-cultural groups. Despite voluminous research on the topic, theories about how culture affects the entrepreneurship process remain underdeveloped. Without a framework to connect culture with everyday entrepreneurial practices and strategies, it is difficult to critically compare the role of culture between multiple contexts. Such a framework is necessary when examining the influence of local cultures on entrepreneurship, given the diverse ways they can influence economic activities. This paper introduces a Bourdieuian perspective on entrepreneurial culture that can be used to explain how particular entrepreneurial cultures emerge within regions, influence the local entrepreneurship process and evolve in the face of internal and external developments. Building on existing work on Bourdieu and entrepreneurship, this paper argues that entrepreneurship research must carefully consider how the concept of culture is used if it is to be a useful factor in explaining the heterogeneous geography of entrepreneurship we observe in the modern economy.

1. Introduction

Culture is critical to the study of entrepreneurship. Far from being a solitary economic activity, entrepreneurship is a social endeavour embedded in multiple cultural and economic contexts. This is particularly true of the geography of entrepreneurship, where researchers have long agreed that variations in the nature of entrepreneurship between regions or nations are the result of complex interactions between economic and social institutions, histories and cultures (Audretsch et al. 2011). Although culture is generally accepted as a useful concept within entrepreneurship research, it remains under-theorized. It is difficult to understand the processes through which culture affects the entrepreneurship process (the course of the entrepreneurship phenomenon from idea generation, firm formation, growth, to final exit) without a suitable theoretical framework. This results in either overly generalized views of culture based on simplistic proxies or descriptive case studies of particular cultures that provide few generalizable findings. As a result, it is difficult for researchers to identify the salient attributes of a culture which affect entrepreneurship as well as to describe how this influence occurs. There is a need for a framework that can help explain how these cultures affect both economic practices and their origin and evolution.

The sociology of Pierre Bourdieu offers such a framework. This paper discusses how Bourdieuian approaches can help understand how local entrepreneurial cultures influence the practices entrepreneurs employ as they start and grow their firms. Local entrepreneurial culture refers to the collective worldviews common to a place that affects how the act of entrepreneurship is understood and experienced. Drawing on recent work on Bourdieuian perspectives on entrepreneurship (de Clerq and Voronov 2009a, 2009b, 2009c, 2011; Terjesen and Elam 2009; Karataş-Özkan and Chell 2010; de Clerq and Hoing 2011; Spigel 2013), this paper argues that Bourdieu's sociology of practice is a useful way to understand the processes through which culture affects the entrepreneurship process. A Bourdieuian approach sees entrepreneurial practices as emerging from actors' understanding of the social rules surrounding them, particularly the 'values' of the different forms of capitals (economic, cultural or social) they possess and which they want to acquire. This paper builds upon existing Bourdieuian approaches to entrepreneurship by placing them within a geographic context and by developing a conceptual model to explain the emergence, evolution and influence of entrepreneurial cultures within regions.

Section 2 provides an overview of the use of culture in the study of entrepreneurial geographies and discusses some of the problems that result from the lack of a rigorous theory connecting culture and entrepreneurial practices. Section 3 introduces the overarching themes of Bourdieu's work and recent research that has applied this work to the study of entrepreneurship. Section 4 develops on this work to place culture within a Bourdieuian framework and discusses how this new understanding can be used to understand how regionally based cultures emerge and influence the entrepreneurship process in particular communities. Section 5 concludes by discussing the usefulness of this perspective and how it can be operationalized in future research.

2. Entrepreneurial culture and geography

2.1. *Culture and entrepreneurship*

An examination of the role of culture in the entrepreneurship process begins with a rejection of the Schumpeterian view of the entrepreneur as a 'heroic economic superman' who creates a firm in isolation (Schumpeter 1934, 85). Instead, entrepreneurship is both an economic and a social process embedded in complex networks of resources, power relations and institutions (Nijkamp 2003). Culture is one of many social factors influencing the entrepreneurship process. Culture is defined here as the collective ways of understanding the world common to a group of people, such as an ethnic group, employees in the same organization or those living in the same region or nation. From this perspective, entrepreneurial cultures are those outlooks that shape the actions of actors connected with the entrepreneurial phenomenon, including the entrepreneur herself as well as other entrepreneurial actors such as investors, advisors, employees and customers. Although there is always a great deal of difference within the worldviews of a community, a cohesive culture is defined by exhibiting less overall variation within the community than between communities.

Beginning with Weber's (1930) work on the Protestant Ethic, there has been a sustained research focus on the relationship between cultural attributes and entrepreneurial ability and desire. This body of work has examined how both external labour market discrimination and internal cultural preferences contribute to patterns of entrepreneurial practices within ethnic communities, such as the use of co-ethnic or family labour

(Sanders and Nee 1996) or particular financing choices (Bates 1997). However, this research has been criticized for over-homogenizing ethnic groups, such as when researchers assign an entrepreneur the label of 'Chinese' when they identify as Hakka (Basu and Altinay 2002) or because it assumes the existence of trust and social capital within an ethnic community where none exists (Hsu and Saxenian 2000).

The importance of culture is well understood in spite of these issues. Davidsson and Wiklund (1997, 2) argue that cultural differences can be 'a powerful determinate of regional or national variation in the "supply" of entrepreneurship'. However, researchers are still grappling with how to conceptually understand and empirically study its role. This is not surprising: definitions range from particular forms of art to certain industries such as fashion or music as well as ethnicity, race or class. The proliferation of meanings makes it difficult for researchers to communicate effectively with each other, leading to more confusion in understanding how culture affects economic activities (Castree 2004).

There are two broad approaches to studying the relationship between culture and entrepreneurship. The first is quantitative analysis of cultural attributes and their association with different levels of entrepreneurial activity. This steam of work relies on the quantification of culture through surveys in order to identify a group's salient cultural attributes and provide hypotheses about how these attributes might either encourage or discourage entrepreneurial activities. However, such approaches are difficult to operationalize, with complex cultural attributes frequently modelled through simple proxies (e.g. Chrisman, Chua, and Steier 2002 or Brons 2006). This has the unintended consequence of ignoring regional variations of cultural attributes across heterogeneous populations and reducing the complicated interplay of multiple overlapping cultural values into membership in an ethnic group, region or nation.

In light of such challenges, a second approach has emerged which investigates the social and discursive aspects of entrepreneurship. As Steyaert and Katz (2004, 186) argue, 'entrepreneurship, like everything else people "know", is a socially constructed reality or concept', meaning that researchers must critically examine how the social, cultural and political milieux in which entrepreneurship takes place construct the entrepreneurship process. These views of entrepreneurship can be broadly termed a 'contextual approach', because it seeks to study the influence of social and cultural contexts in the entrepreneurship process. This builds on earlier work on the role of context within firms as well as shows the increasing influence of other disciplines such as geography, sociology and psychology in the domain of entrepreneurship research (Licht and Siegel 2006). While previous research has '...underappreciated [or] controlled away' context, this new wave of work has sought to highlight the role of social context within what have previously been seen as solely economic activities (Welter 2011, 173–174). Context surrounds economic phenomenon, providing a source of variation and difference that cannot necessarily be detected through quantitative means (Johns 2001).

2.2. *Entrepreneurial geographies and environments*

Culture plays an important role in explaining the geography of entrepreneurial activities. While economic factors such as economic growth, unemployment and human capital explain a great deal of the variation in economic activity between the regions, social and cultural factors remain important sources of differentiation (Davidsson and Wiklund 1997). Given the role of entrepreneurship in generating resilient regional economies, research on the local cultural factors that encourage or discourage the creation of innovative start-ups has become a point of paramount importance (Fritsch and Schindele

2011). The relational connections between local cultures and entrepreneurship are complex and difficult to untangle, but difficult to ignore. Audretsch et al. (2011, 380) argue that 'the fortunes of regions and entrepreneurs are intertwined: regional endowments provide opportunity and resources for entrepreneurs, while entrepreneurs simultaneously shape the local environment'. As the work of Saxenian (1994) and Feldman (2001) among others shows, understanding how the cultural forces within a region affect the entrepreneurship process is necessary in understanding those regions' economic history and future economic potential.

This work also suggests that the region, rather than the nation, is the most appropriate scale to examine the interactions between culture and entrepreneurship. Within this literature, 'regional' or 'local' is frequently defined as a metropolitan area: a contiguous labour shed with a cohesive economy. Entrepreneurs largely draw on local resources as they start and grow their firms, be it venture capital (Sorenson and Steuart 2001), mentorship (Lafuente, Yancy, and Rialp 2007) or knowledge and support obtained through their social networks (Westlund and Bolton 2003). Therefore, the provision of all these resources will be affected by local cultural norms, such as how 'respectable' entrepreneurship is compared to traditional employment or the social consequences of business failure (Vaillant and Lafuente 2007). Thus, entrepreneurial practices and aspirations 'are shaped by regionally distinctive opportunity costs, and are also formed relative to established regional norms' (Aoyama 2009, 507).

Malecki's work (1997, 2009) on entrepreneurial environments is a useful way to conceptualize the role of culture within regions. The right combination of formal and informal institutions, networks and economic structures creates what Malecki (2009) describes as local entrepreneurial environments (known elsewhere as ecosystems). These beneficial institutional, economic and historical forces combine to create a virtuous cycle that supports and strengthens entrepreneurial endeavours. Part of this environment is made up of formal institutions such as government policies and networks of support firms such as specialized lawyers and financiers (Kenney and Patton 2005) along with informal institutions such as networks of role models and advisors. While culture is only one of many social forces at play within a region, it underlies other formal and informal institutions, helping to encourage actors to engage in or support entrepreneurial endeavours.

Despite culture's importance to entrepreneurial environments, its role is not fully understood. Granovetter's (1985) theory of embeddedness has been a popular way to explain how the cultural forces surrounding actors affect them. Here, the choices actors can make are constrained by the institutions and networks they are embedded in due to the threat of sanction or expulsion. However, this does little to explain the processes connecting culture and action nor how actors perceive the cultural and institutional environments in which they are embedded. As James (2007, 395) argues:

> ... while 'cultural embeddedness' has quickly become established as a conceptual lynchpin of the regional development literature, our understanding of the causal mechanisms and everyday practices through which spatially variable sets of socio-cultural conventions, norms, attitudes, values and beliefs shape and condition firms' economic performance remains under-specified.

This criticism is more than a conceptual quibble. Without a way to explain how and why entrepreneurial actors are affected by the cultures that surround them, we risk using culture as an all-encompassing, deterministic force to account for otherwise unexplained variations. That is, we cannot say that an actor desires to build a fast-growing firm because he is in a region known for its entrepreneurship or because he is a member of an ethnic group with high rates of entrepreneurial activity. This removes all individual agency from the analysis and over-simplifies complex cultural outlooks to the point of absurdity. Rather, we should seek to explain why a particular set of entrepreneurial practices makes sense given the cultural and social contexts in which they occur. We must rigorously specify how to understand both culture and the causal mechanisms through which it influences economic and social actions. These mechanisms should specify not only how cultural structures and outlooks affect actors, but also how feedback from those actors' practices reciprocally affects culture itself.

Research on entrepreneurial cultures suffers from a lack of a conceptual framework to connect actors' practices with larger social influences. Without a strong theoretical grounding, it is impossible to specify how culture matters. At the heart of this issue is the question of structure versus agency: how much influence do social and economic structures have on the choices humans make versus their own free will? Are economic and social structures or individual choices and agency more important in producing certain economic outcomes? The answer, as Martin and Sunley (2003) argue, is often a very unsatisfying 'both'. The challenge is to develop a framework that can balance structural and individualistic explanations for entrepreneurial behaviour while still allowing for a rigorous examination of the elements affecting both social structure and human agency.

3. Bourdieu and culture

The work of Pierre Bourdieu offers such a framework. A Bourdieuian analysis examines practices: the actions performed by actors in pursuit of their goals. In the context of entrepreneurship, practices are the material actions entrepreneurs and other associated actors carry out as they start, grow and eventually leave the firm. These include daily, mundane activities such as manners of dress and interaction as well as long-term strategic decisions such as the creation of a business plan, taking on external capital or entering new markets. Practices are not determined by social structures such as culture; rather, they are carried out within a social context that makes certain actions seem more sensible (Bourdieu and Wacquant 1992). To understand the emergence of practices, Bourdieu's work employs three main conceptual tools: field, habitus and capital.

Practices take place within fields, which Bourdieu (1977) defined as historically produced social spaces of rules, traditions and power relations. Fields represent the 'rules of the game' that participants implicitly agree to follow; social interaction is impossible without this agreement. Many of a field's rules are so embedded in everyday life that they become invisible. Such rules and traditions are termed *doxa* because they are not only unquestioned by those who follow them, but they also appear to be so natural and unremarkable that they are unquestionable. However, fields are not simple lists of what is allowed or banned. They are spaces for strategic decision-making in which an infinite variety of practices can play out (Bourdieu 1990).

Although fields may have real and objective rules and structures, actors do not understand them identically. Rather, actors interpret the field through a set of internalized intentions and dispositions, referred to as the habitus (Bourdieu 1990). Through their habitus, actors not only generate an understanding of the rules of the field they also develop an implicit knowledge of how those rules apply to them given their status or position within the field. The habitus is best understood as the internalization of the rules, structures and hierarchies of a field as well as a simultaneous knowledge of one's position within the field (Swartz 1997). These understandings help actors determine what their goals are as well as the practices they will use to achieve them.

The relationship between field and habitus provides a way to understand practices without reverting to deterministic structural explanations or individualistic rational-actor approaches. While fields have objective rules, actors understand those rules in different ways and can exploit indeterminacies within those rules by experimenting with new practices (Bourdieu 1989). Through their habitus, actors understand the rules of a field as well as how those rules apply to them. Based on this knowledge, actors may choose to closely follow the rules of the field by imitating the practices they observe, try to invent new practices that they think will be successful within the field or violate the rules of the field. Breaching the rules of the field may be a result of not knowing about those rules or it may be a conscious choice based on the belief that the rewards of such a violation outweigh the possible sanctions. The field does not ordain that actors select certain practices in response to a given situation, but rather it creates a context for habitus-informed practices to play out.

The position and power of actors within a field are determined by their stocks of capital. Bourdieu (1986) argued that capital takes many forms: its traditional economic form, social capital (the value of resources accessible through one's social network), cultural capital (knowledge of particular social rules and norms), symbolic capital (the respect accorded to different professions) and many others. The value of these forms of capital depends on the nature and structure of the field. For technology entrepreneurs, technical skills (human capital) are only valuable if they have the savings and investments (economic capital) and ability to sell their vision to customers and investors (cultural capital), which is helped by previous entrepreneurial successes or degrees from particular universities (symbolic capital).

Power is the ability to control the value of different forms of capital in a field. Established players will use the resources they control to ensure the continued value of the forms of capital they possess while those without these valuable forms of capital will try to influence the field to the advantage of the forms of capital they do control. Within established industries, prominent firms use their economic capital as well as their symbolic capital (brand name and historical trust) to maintain their position and power while entrepreneurs try to disrupt the value of these capitals through their own social and technological capital (new innovations or strategies). If they are successful, the entrepreneurs will have the ability to create new power hierarchies within the field in order to accumulate economic, social and symbolic capital to solidify their position.

Actors choose the practices they think will increase their stocks of the capitals that they believe are valuable and which will therefore raise their social position within the field. These practices are strategic and, within the context of the field, rational. Critically, the definition of 'rational' shifts between fields, depending on each field's individual rules and valuation of different forms of capital. Actors perform those practices they believe that they are the best choice given the present situation, not because tradition or culture compels them. For Bourdieu, an actor is 'a virtuoso with a perfect command of his "art of living" [who] can play on all resources inherent in the ambiguities and uncertainties of behavior and situation in order to produce the actions appropriate to each case' (Bourdieu 1977, 8).

What scholars call culture is better understood as the dominant understandings of a particular field which emerge within a group or region. Even if an individual actor does not understand these cultural views (for instance, a new migrant to a region), she is affected by the field because successful interaction with others requires adherence to the field-specific norms and rules. While entrepreneurs may try to purposefully break these rules in order to open up new market niches, too much deviation from accepted cultural norms will make it difficult for them to get the resources they require to start and grow their firm. This adherence might only emerge after a period of failed social interactions due to misunderstandings of the rules, but it must occur eventually. Culture then is not a disembodied force but rather the way in which actors understand the social world around them and which helps create a context in which different types of practices appear more sensible or rational.

4. Bourdieuian approaches to regional entrepreneurial cultures

4.1. *Bourdieuian approaches to entrepreneurship*

There is a bourgeoning interest in the application of Bourdieuian analysis in the study of entrepreneurship. This interest is related to a larger movement towards the study of social context among management scholars and builds on previous work integrating Bourdieu into organizational and management studies (e.g. Gorton 2000; Emirbayer and Johnson 2008; Swartz 2008; Vaughan 2008). This literature has two major themes: a practice-based approach (Terjesen and Elam 2009) and an interest in how legitimacy is constructed within fields (Elam 2008; de Clercq and Voronov 2009a, 2011; de Clerq and Hoing 2011). The practice-based approach draws on an increasing awareness that entrepreneurs' decisions are embedded in larger social contexts (Licht and Siegel 2006). Instead of a normative focus on what entrepreneurs should do given a certain set of economic conditions, a practice approach seeks to understand why entrepreneurs employ particular practices and how these practices emerge from their habitus.

The second stream of Bourdieuian research examines how entrepreneurial legitimacy is constructed within fields and how entrepreneurs employ specific practices to appear legitimate in order to access the resources they need. To access the resources they need, entrepreneurs must appear legitimate to investors and other actors. This legitimacy comes through the performance of certain practices, such as creating a business plan or how they dress and present their ideas (de Clerq and Voronov 2009a). The ability to choose the right practices depends on an entrepreneur's knowledge of the field. Even though these practices may be so common as to be unspoken, entrepreneurs need a habitus attuned to the particularities of the field in order to be able to successfully perform them (de Clerq and Voronov 2009c). Entrepreneurs must adhere to these unwritten rules about legitimacy while they simultaneously signal their independence by violating some of them (de Clerq and Voronov 2009b). This requires them to ' . . . artfully navigate the tensions among the attributes of their potentially novel activities, the dominant field arrangements and broader field-level templates of change' (de Clerq and Voronov 2009c, 813). However, this work has not yet considered the development and evolution of entrepreneurial fields or their material geography. As a result, it is difficult to use Bourdieuian approaches to entrepreneurship as part of larger empirical projects that examine the causes and consequences of entrepreneurial practices.

Power within entrepreneurial fields can be seen as the ability to define the practices that are seen as legitimate forms of entrepreneurship and therefore deserving of support. This power comes not just from control of economic capital but also through the symbolic capital of being associated with previous successful entrepreneurial endeavours, either as the founder, as an early investor or as an advisor. These are not strict rules but rather a set of dispositions, outlooks and miens that through the structures of the field signal entrepreneurial legitimacy (de Clercq and Hoing 2011).

The rules of the field, and how entrepreneurs and other actors understand these rules, affect the practices at all stages of a start-up's life cycle. An entrepreneur's willingness to leave the traditional labour market to start a firm, and the willingness of her friends and family to support this decision, depends on how the symbolic capital of creating a start-up is valued compared with the economic capital of waged work. Similarly, the inclination to embrace the risks of fast growth catalyzed by angel or venture investment is not a rational economic calculation but instead depends on how these risks are normalized within the field; that is, if the loss of control associated with taking on outside investors is outweighed by the symbolic and economic capital of their investment. Both the large strategic decisions and mundane daily practices of entrepreneurs are made within the context of their field and the cultural outlooks it produces.

4.2. *Relational geographies of fields*

Bourdieu's field-based framework provides a way to understand the relationship between culture and entrepreneurship. Collective understandings of a field produce a culture, which in turn becomes the context surrounding entrepreneurs' choice of practices. Such cultures do not cause practices to occur. Instead, they provide an environment in which certain types of practices make sense. Understanding how norms of 'common-sense' practices emerge involves the complex interplay of a variety of fields operating at several different geographic scales. How entrepreneurial actors choose their practices relative to multiple fields is key to understanding the development of unique, local entrepreneurial cultures. We can envision a series of fields influencing the practices of entrepreneurial actors. First, the local field is the rules, structures and positions tied to a particular place or region. This field is of paramount importance because entrepreneurs draw most of their resources from their local community, meaning that many of the actors involved in the creation and growth of a small firm are based in this field. But there are also non-local fields that can affect the entrepreneurship process: industrial fields represent the rules, norms and social structures of particular industrial sectors such as Internet technologies, banking or publishing; national fields, which are the economic, social and political rules of specific countries, and ethnic fields or the social norms of ethnic, religious or cultural groups. These non-local fields may exert influence in a region due to the presence of a cohesive ethnic group or a major firm or industry the presence of which gives it the power to influence the value of forms of capital and the types of practices seen as normal.

The rules and norms of local fields have an outsized influence on the entrepreneurship process because most of the resources entrepreneurs draw on as they start and grow their firms come from actors embedded in it. Entrepreneurs must constantly react to local beliefs about the purpose of creating a start-up (such as maximizing profitability, ensuring financial stability or sustaining a particular lifestyle) if others are to see them as legitimate entrepreneurs deserving of investment and support. However, local fields do not exist in isolation and non-local fields also influence entrepreneurial actors. The focus, therefore, should not be whether entrepreneurs are 'inside' of a local field, but rather the extent to which they operate within unique sets of norms and rationalities found within a region. Revealing how entrepreneurial practices develop around the rules of multiple fields is one of the key aspects of a Bourdieuian analysis of entrepreneurship.

It is not enough to say that each region has its own field; to do so would only reintroduce the existing oversimplification of culture under a new name. Rather, there is a complex geography to fields. Local and non-local fields have different, often contradictory, rules and norms, meaning that choices that make sense in one field are often seen as illegitimate in others. For instance, the choice to employ a cousin might help an entrepreneur increase his social capital within his family in order to obtain informal capital (investments from family and friends or other non-institutional sources), but such a practice might be seen as nepotism by an angel investor who is outside of the family's ethnic field. Similarly, the high-growth norms of an industry such as social media start-ups might conflict with a risk-adverse culture of a rural community. In order to be successful, entrepreneurs must be able to navigate these conflicting rules and norms. They must be able to select practices that either simultaneously appear legitimate to people occupying different fields or at least choose practices that minimize harm in other fields. The ability to do this successfully rests in the entrepreneur's habitus: her internalized knowledge about the rules of these multiple fields and their position within all of them.

Although non-local fields play a role in actors' choice of entrepreneurial practices, their influence is experienced through the local field. The influence of non-local fields materializes locally as actors understand the rules and structures through their habitus, which are in turn heavily influenced by the local field they are constantly embedded in. That is, actors depend on their habitus to understand the rules of a non-local field, a habitus developed within a local field that the actor is constantly exposed to. The structures and rules of non-local fields are 'filtered' through each local field. This is due to the overwhelming influence of the local field, which actors are continuously exposed to as they carry out their daily activities. The local field provides the context through which non-local fields are understood.

As a result, the rules of a non-local field (e.g. the importance of informal knowledge sharing within the technology start-up field) are experienced differently based on the nature of the local fields these rules are interpreted in. For example, Aoyoma (2009) points to how informal norms of risk-taking and inter-firm communication were understood differently by entrepreneurs in Hamamatsu and Kyoto, Japan, leading to the development of distinct entrepreneurial cultures. The interaction between local and non-local fields is therefore not static or hierarchical, but is rather a reflexive, relational connection between a local field and the non-local fields materializing within it.

This points to the need for a relational approach to the multi-scalar geography of fields. Instead of seeing space as a causal force for economic or social activity, a relational approach sees space as a lens through which economic activity and social activity are studied and interpreted (Bathelt and Glücker 2011). From a Bourdieuian perspective, this means going beyond seeing local fields in isolation, but rather examining how actors balance the competing demands of local fields against other outside fields, such as ethnic, economic or business fields. That is, how do entrepreneurs choose practices that can maintain their legitimacy in multiple fields, such as the local field they live in, the industrial field their firm and investors exist in and the ethnic field their family inhabits?

It follows that regional culture is more than the rules of the local field. Rather, regional cultures are the collective views of the multiple fields that operate in the region that emerge over time. Such fields include both local and non-local fields that influence the region. As actors carry out their day-to-day lives within this overlapping assemblage of fields, they create an internalized knowledge of them as their habitus develops. Over time, collective understandings of these fields emerge within a region, creating what can be referred to as a regional culture. A relational perspective of fields emphasizes the interconnected nature of fields on multiple scales and emphasizes a holistic analysis which includes the effects of the diverse array of fields that operate within a region, be they based on institutional forces working at a local, national or global level.

The analysis of local entrepreneurial cultures involves examining not only the influence on non-local fields but also how actors understand these fields through the locally based habitus. Non-local fields influence the practices of entrepreneurs, but that influence is channelled through the already established rules, norms and outlooks associated with the local field. The local field, and actor's habitus-based knowledge of it, helps determine how the rules of non-local fields are understood and acted upon (or ignored). The key to understanding the emergence of entrepreneurial cultures is unravelling the interplay between an array of local and non-local fields and rationalities.

4.3. *The emergence and evolution of regional fields*

Fields do not arise from nothing nor are they immune from change. New fields emerge from pre-existing fields after a period of struggle (Bourdieu and Wacquant 1992). New developments, such as the creation of a new disruptive technology or the change in political regimes, shift control of power in a field away from incumbents to new players and open up new strategies and change the values of different forms of capital. In most cases, the change occurs internally within an existing field. However, within modern economic systems, new fields can potentially emerge along with new industries. For instance, the modern information technology industry emerged out of the telecommunications industry of the 1970s and 1980s. New players, armed with new types of capital – specific technical knowledge and expertise – were able to establish a new field with rules and conventions different from the pre-existing field. In such situations, new rules emerge organically from the new players' prior experience and new technical and economic realities (Aldrich and Fiol 1994).

Social rules are not kept because they are traditional but because they play some role in maintaining the social order and distribution of power in a field. In many modern economic fields with diffuse hierarchies of power and well-distributed capital – including entrepreneurial fields – norms and conventions can be very fluid. Within such fields, entrepreneurs have a great deal of freedom to improvise new practices based on their immediate needs. This improvization is a result of the diverse array of habitus exposed to the rules of the fields in which they reside and the different interpretations entrepreneurs make of them based on their goals, knowledge of the fields and their current situation. Entrepreneurs are able to observe the practices of other firms and copy those that appear to be successful. The definition of success depends on the lens of their individual habitus and the contexts of their local and industrial fields. As these new practices continue to be effective, they become a natural part of actors' habitus. These successful practices are now performed not because they necessarily lead to success but because they have now become common sense. Over time, successful practices coalesce into new traditions or institutions: they have become part of the field's *doxa*, its unquestionable logic (see Figure 1). This process shows that rules within a field are not static entities, but rather dynamic social processes that are continuously being reproduced and modified according to the present needs of the actors in the field. The constant churn of new practices and practitioners in entrepreneurial and business fields creates a system of constant renewal and reinvention. This model does not imply that change will always occur within fields, but it creates a space for evolution through purposeful or accidental experimentation with new forms of practice.

This model helps differentiate between local and non-local entrepreneurial fields. The local field is defined by the fact that its rules, norms and structures are reproduced through fundamentally *local* processes and entities. These can be powerful players in the region, such as dominant firms or industry or local communal beliefs. For instance, the high status of entrepreneurship in a region might be reproduced through institutions such as schools, universities or networks of successful entrepreneurs, which celebrate successful start-ups

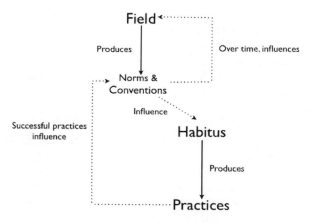

Figure 1. The dynamic nature of norms and conventions within a field.

and instil a respect for the risks of entrepreneurship. This is opposed to non-local fields, of which the structures are formed and reproduced outside of the region, such as through the national media or national government policy. Local cultures are therefore the dominant understandings of a field shaped through fundamentally local social systems as opposed to cultures created by fields operating at different scales.

There is a material geography to the development and evolution of fields. The act of observing successes and failures is easier within a local field than in a global industrial or an ethnic field. Because social networks are densest locally, stories of new practices spread quickly within communities. This is particularly true for entrepreneurs who tend to know many other proximate entrepreneurs and discuss business issues with them (Westlund and Bolton 2003). Entrepreneurs who are constantly scanning their local environment for new opportunities are primed to observe changes in the local field and experiment with new practices that they think will now be successful. Local fields are therefore more open to change than their non-local counterparts.

Interactions between local and non-local fields are not static or hierarchical but are rather a dynamic, relational connection between a local field and the non-local fields materializing within it. Actors who are embedded in the local field will understand these non-local rules through the structures of the local field, which has deeply affected their habitus. Neither local nor non-local fields are necessarily dominant or immune to change or influence. The nature of the local field does not control those who operate within its boundaries; fields only set up a social space in which practices play out. Rather, through their habitus, actors create an internal understanding about the relationships between local and non-local fields and their positions within them, and then enact the practices that make the most sense given those relationships and their current circumstances.

As such, this dynamic process operates all stages of entrepreneurial activity. The decision to launch a start-up firm is not made based on objective financial analysis, but rather depends on how they balance the potential economic and symbolic rewards of starting a business with the perceived financial and social risks. This is rarely a conscious, strategic decision but rather an internalized determination generated through their habitus-based understanding of how entrepreneurship is valued within their local field. This understanding is developed by observing the world around them and learning which types of start-up practices appear legitimate and accepted and which are seen as illegitimate and have to be justified. Similarly, other critical stages of the entrepreneurial endeavour, such as hiring employees, entering new markets, taking on investment or the decision to exit the firm, are not disinterested economic choices but decisions made within the context of multiple overlapping fields interpreted through an entrepreneur's habitus. Entrepreneurs choose their practices based on which appear to make sense given their understanding of these complex considerations. While scholars have long acknowledged the social and cultural contours of entrepreneurship, this model demonstrates how these types of contexts influence entrepreneurial activity through how entrepreneurs understand the social rules and hierarchies surrounding them.

5. Conclusion – Bourdieu and regional entrepreneurial cultures

Why bring in a complex theory to an already confused debate about culture? Bourdieuian approaches are necessary because culture is too often cast as a deterministic force within entrepreneurship research. Consequently, discussions about the role of culture in entrepreneurship frequently either over-simplify culture as a dummy variable or are dependent on descriptive case studies of particular cultural attributes that do not probe the connections between culture and action. These issues result from the absence of a theoretical mechanism connecting culture with entrepreneurial practices. Without such a mechanism, it is difficult to go beyond simply describing a local culture and to fully analyse the culture's origin and how it affects actors' daily and long-term practices and strategies.

As concepts such as enterprise culture and entrepreneurial ecosystems gain currency within the academic, policy and popular literature, researchers are increasingly confronted by questions about what makes a place 'entrepreneurial'. Often, the root answer appears to be a local culture enabling practices such as risk taking or information sharing (e.g. Saxenian 1994; Lafuente, Yancy, and Rialp 2007) or conversely, a culture discouraging them (e.g. James 2005). The importance of these questions to regional development means that the study of entrepreneurial cultures must go beyond associating cultural outlooks with practices. We must instead examine how cultural outlooks create social contexts where particular kinds of practices make sense to entrepreneurial actors. Furthermore, we must be able to demonstrate that the culture in question is truly local by identifying the local processes that create and reproduce it. This paper introduces a dynamic model that demonstrates how the cultural outlooks created by the structure of a local field influence entrepreneurial actors while at the same time how these cultural outlooks evolve through actors' experimentations with new types of practices. This allows a more nuanced examination of the role of culture in the development of entrepreneurial communities, regions and ecosystems without falling into the trap of seeing culture as the *sole* cause.

The purpose of a Bourdieuian approach to entrepreneurship is therefore to provide a critical framework to analyse the role of social influences and constraints in such a way that neither reduces the agency of actors nor restricts pathways for change. Conceptualizing the role of culture within such a framework reduces problems of *ad-hoc* cultural analysis and atheoretical description. Through the Bourdieuian focus on how entrepreneurial actors understand the fields they operate within, it is possible to examine how practices emerge relative to cultural outlooks and values rather than simply describing those outlooks and values. Culture is therefore no longer a disembodied force applied to entrepreneurs but rather forms the context in which the entrepreneurship process unfolds.

This approach opens up several new avenues for empirical research. The first is identifying the rules and structures of different entrepreneurial fields and their relationship to entrepreneurship-led economic growth. What types of structures tend to encourage or discourage entrepreneurial innovation and risk taking? This research should also examine how such rules evolved and their relationship to fields at other scales as well as contingent historical events. Second, research can examine how entrepreneurs become embedded in such fields and the learning processes which take place as their habitus adjusts to the specificities of the fields they are engaging with. Finally, more research is needed to understand the complex power relationships between entrepreneurial actors and how they are able to develop and control the types of capital most important to them.

The most critical area for future theoretical development in Bourdieuian approaches to entrepreneurship is the emergence of cultural outlooks and practices relative to multiple, overlapping fields. Case studies are needed to better understand how entrepreneurs balance the competing demands of these fields and how local entrepreneurial cultures are influenced by the presence of non-local fields. Further, the influence of individual entrepreneurs, firms or regions on larger-scale fields must be acknowledged in order to understand how even these global social structures can change over time. The ways in which entrepreneurs navigate the conflicting rules of these fields is an area ripe for conceptual and empirical research. Finally, empirical research should look how individual entrepreneurial practices, such as the use of a business plan or taking on venture capital, are viewed by actors in different local fields as well those in different positions within the same field. This will further illuminate the relationship between entrepreneurial practices and culture.

Given the increasing focus on the cultural underpinnings of entrepreneurship within disciplines as diverse as economic geography, management science, economics and psychology, the development of a theoretical framework for culture is critical. Without a framework to describe the connections between culture and entrepreneurial practice, research on the topic risks descending into static determinism or descriptivism that ignores the reflexive relationship between entrepreneurs' agency and their social and economic contexts. This framework is key to linking the macro-level social processes that make up culture with the micro-level daily practices and decisions that make up entrepreneurship. The Bourdieuian approach discussed here offers one such framework to describe not only why particular local cultures can affect the entrepreneurship process, but also how these cultures develop and why different kinds of actors are affected by the culture in different ways.

Acknowledgements

The author is grateful for the recommendations and suggestions of both the anonymous reviewers and the editors of the special issue. In addition, this manuscript benefited from the guidance of advice of Harald Bathelt, Meric Gertler, Pierre Desrochers and Olav Sorenson. This paper was previously presented at the 2012 Babson Entrepreneurship Research Conference and the 2013 Association of American Geographers Annual Conference.

References

Aldrich, Howard E., and Marlene Fiol. 1994. "Fools Rush in? The Institutional Context of Industry Creation." *Academy of Management Review* 19 (4): 645–670.

Aoyama, Yuko. 2009. "Entrepreneurship and Regional Culture: The Case of Hamamtsu and Kyoto, Japan." *Regional Studies* 43 (3): 495–512.

Audretsch, David B., Oliver Flack, Maryann P. Feldman, and Stephan Heblich. 2011. "Local Entrepreneurship in Context." *Regional Studies* 46 (3): 379–389.

Basu, Anuradha, and Eser Altinay. 2002. "The Interaction Between Culture and Entrepreneurship in London's Immigrant Businesses." *International Small Business Journal* 20 (4): 371–393.

Bates, Timothy. 1997. "Financing Small Business Creation: The Case of Chinese and Korean Immigrant Entrepreneurs." *Journal of Business Venturing* 12 (2): 109–124.

Bathelt, Harald, and Johannes Glücker. 2011. *The Relational Economy: Geographies of Knowing and Learning.* Oxford: Oxford University Press.

Bourdieu, Pierre. 1977. *Outline of A Theory of Practice.* Cambridge: Cambridge University Press.

Bourdieu, Pierre. 1986. "The Forms of Capital." In *Handbook of Theory and Research for the Sociology of Education,* edited by JG Richardson, 241–258. New York: Greenwood.

Bourdieu, Pierre. 1989. "Social Space and Symbolic Power." *Sociological Theory* 7 (1): 14–25.

Bourdieu, Pierre. 1990. *The Logic of Practice.* Stanford: Stanford University Press.

Bourdieu, Pierre, and Loic J. D. Wacquant. 1992. *An Invitation to Reflexive Sociology.* Chicago, IL: University of Chicago Press.

Brons, Lajos L. 2006. "Indirect Measurement of Regional Culture in the Netherlands." *Tijdschrift Voor Economische En Sociale Geografie* 7 (5): 547–566.

Castree, Noel. 2004. "Economy and Culture Are Dead! Long Live Economy and Culture!" *Progress in Human Geography* 28 (2): 204–226.

Chrisman, James J., Jess H. Chua, and Llyod P. Steier. 2002. "The Influence of National Culture and Family Involvement on Entrepreneurial Perceptions and the Performance at the State Level." *Entrepreneurship Theory and Practice* 26 (4): 113–130.

de Clercq, Dirk, and Benson Hoing. 2011. "Entrepreneurship as an Integrating Mechanism for Disadvantaged Persons." *Entrepreneurship and Regional Development* 23 (5–6): 353–372.

de Clercq, Dirk, and Maxim Voronov. 2009a. "The Role of Domination in Newcomers' Legitimation as Entrepreneurs." *Organization* 16 (6): 799–827.

de Clercq, Dirk, and Maxim Voronov. 2009b. "Towards a Practice Perspective of Entrepreneurship: Entrepreneurial Legitimacy as Habitus." *International Small Business Journal* 27 (4): 395–419.

de Clercq, Dirk, and Maxim Voronov. 2009c. "The Role of Cultural and Symbolic Capital in Entrepreneurs' Ability to Meet Expectations About Conformity and Innovation." *Journal of Small Business Management* 47 (3): 398–420.

de Clercq, Dirk, and Maxim Voronov. 2011. "Sustainability in Entrepreneurship: A Tale of Two Logics." *International Small Business Journal* 29 (4): 322–344.

Davidsson, Per, and Johan Wiklund. 1997. "Values, Beliefs and Regional Variations in New Firm Formation." *Journal of Economic Psychology* 18: 179–199.

Elam, Amanda Brickman. 2008. *Gender and Entrepreneurship: A Multilevel Theory and Analysis.* Cheltenham: Edward Elgar.

Emirbayer, Mustafa, and Victoria Johnson. 2008. "Bourdieu and Organizational Analysis." *Sociological Theory* 37 (1): 1–44.

Feldman, Maryann. 2001. "The Entrepreneurial Event Revisited: Firm Formation in a Regional Context." *Industrial and Corporate Change* 10 (4): 861–891.

Fritsch, Michael, and Yvonne Schindele. 2011. "The Contribution of New Businesses to Regional Employment – An Empirical Analysis." *Economic Geography* 87 (2): 153–180.

Gorton, Matthew. 2000. "Overcoming the Structure-Agency Divide in Small Business Research." *International Journal of Entrepreneurial Behavior and Research* 6 (5): 276–292.

Granovetter, M. S. 1985. "Economic Action and the Economic Structure: The Problem of Embeddedness." *American Journal of Sociology* 91: 481–510.

Hsu, Jinn-Yuh, and Anna Lee Saxenian. 2000. "The Limits of *Guanxi* Capitalism: Transnational Collaboration Between Taiwan and the USA." *Environment and Planning A* 32–2005.

James, Al. 2005. "Demystifying the Role of Culture in Innovative Regional Economies." *Regional Studies* 39 (9): 1197–1216.

James, Al. 2007. "Everyday Effects, Practices and Casual Mechanisms of 'Cultural Embeddedness': Learning from Utah's High Tech Regional Economy." *Geoforum* 38 (2): 393–413.

Johns, Gary. 2001. "In Praise of Context." *Journal of Organizational Behavior* 22 (1): 31–42.

Karataş-Özkan, Mine, and Elizabeth Chell. 2010. *Nascent Entrepreneurship and Learning.* Cheltenham: Edward Elgar.

Kenney, Martin, and Donald Patton. 2005. "Entrepreneurial Geographies: Support Networks in Three High-Technology Industries." *Economic Geography* 81 (2): 201–228.

Lafuente, Esteban, Vaillant Yancy, and Josep Rialp. 2007. "Regional Differences in the Influence of Role Models: Comparing the Entrepreneurial Process of Rural Catalonia." *Regional Studies* 41 (6): 779–795.

Licht, Amir N., and Jordan I. Siegel. 2006. "The Social Dimension of Entrepreneurship." In *The Oxford Handbook of Entrepreneurship*, edited by Mark Casson, Bernard Yeung, Anuradha Basu, and Niegel Wadeson, 511–539. Oxford, UK: Oxford University Press.

Malecki, Edward J. 1997. "Entrepreneurs, Networks, and Economic Development: A Review of Recent Research." In *Advances in Entrepreneurship, Firm Emergence, and Growth*, edited by J. A. Katz. Vol. 3, 57–118. Greenwich, CT: JAI Press.

Malecki, Edward J. 2009. "Geographical Environments for Entrepreneurship." *International Journal of Entrepreneurship and Small Business* 7 (2): 175–190.

Martin, Ron, and Peter Sunley. 2003. "Deconstructing Clusters: Chaotic Concept or Policy Panacea." *Journal of Economic Geography* 3 (1): 5–35.

Nijkamp, Peter. 2003. "Entrepreneurship in a Modern Network Economy." *Regional Studies* 37 (4): 395–405.

Sanders, Jimy M., and Victor Nee. 1996. "Immigrant Self-Employment: The Family as Social Capital and the Value of Human Capital." *American Sociological Review* 61 (2): 231–249.

Saxenian, AnnaLee. 1994. *Regional Advantage: Culture and Competition in Silicon Valley and Route 128.* Cambridge, MA: Harvard University Press.

Schumpeter, J. A. 1934. *The Theory of Economic Development.* Translated by R. Opie. Boston: Harvard University Press.

Sorenson, Olav, and Toby Stuart. 2001. "Syndication Networks and the Spatial Distribution of Venture Capital Investments." *The American Journal of Sociology* 106 (6): 1546–1588.

Spigel, Ben. 2013. "The Emergence of Regional Cultures and Practices: A Comparative Study of Canadian Software Entrepreneurship." PhD diss., University of Toronto.

Steyaert, Chris, and Jerome Katz. 2004. "Reclaiming the Space of Entrepreneurship in Society: Geographical, Discursive and Social Dimensions." *Entrepreneurship and Regional Development* 16: 179–196.

Swartz, David. 1997. *Culture and Power: The Sociology of Pierre Bourdieu.* Chicago, IL: University of Chicago Press.

Swartz, David. 2008. "Bringing Bourdieu's Master Concepts into Organizational Analysis." *Theory and Society* 37 (1): 45–52.

Terjesen, Siri, and Amanda Elam. 2009. "Transnational Entrepreneurs' Venture Internationalization Strategies: A Practice Theory Approach." *Entrepreneurship Theory and Practice* 33 (5): 1093–1120.

Vaillant, Yancy, and Esteban Lafuente. 2007. "Do Different Institutional Frameworks Condition The Influence of Local Fear of Failure and Entrepreneurial Examples Over Entrepreneurial Activity?" *Entrepreneurship and Regional Development* 19: 313–337.

Vaughan, Diane. 2008. "Bourdieu and Organizations: The Empirical Challenge." *Theory and Society* 37 (1): 61–81.

Weber, Max. 1930. *The Protestant Ethic and the Spirit of Capitalism.* New York: Scribner.

Welter, Friederike. 2011. "Contextualizing Entrepreneurship — Conceptual Challenges and Ways Forward." *Entrepreneurship Theory and Practice* 35 (1): 165–184.

Westlund, Hans, and Roger Bolton. 2003. "Local Social Capital and Entrepreneurship." *Small Business Economics* 21 (1): 77–113.

Index

Note: Page numbers in *italics* represent tables
Page numbers in **bold** represent figures
Page numbers followed by 'n' refer to notes

achievement motivation theory 18
actors 106; position and power 107
age 63
aggregate psychological traits 80; perspective 82
Ajzen, T.: theory of planned behaviour 19–20, 79–81, **81**
Aoyama, Y. 18, 110
assertiveness 63; innovation-growth relationship 32, 36, *45*, **45–6**; UK 46
attitude: behaviour 82; can-do 59
Audretsch, D.: *et al.* 105
Autio, E.: *et al.* 2, 54–78

Baum, J.R.: *et al.* 21, 23
Bausch, A.: *et al.* 32, 33, 36, 38, 45, 46, 48
behaviour: attitude 82; entrepreneurial 59; fear of failure 57; planned behaviour theory 19–20, 79–81, **81**, 93; value-driven 2
behavioural control: perceived 82
bias: regional 47
bonuses 59
Brinckmann, J.: *et al.* 32, 33, 36, 38, 45, 46, 48
Busenitz, L.W.: and Lau, C.M. 24, 25

Cacciotti, G.: and Hayton, J.C. 6–29
Camgöz, S.M.: *et al.* 2, 79–101
can-do attitude 59
Cape Verde 19
capital: forms 107; human 82, 84, 107; power 107; social 82, 84, 107; symbolic 107
career: entrepreneurial 1
causality: reversed 48
China 37; motives 18
Chinese Americans 20–1
Chinese entrepreneurs 20–1
CLOP analysis: innovation-growth relationship 39, *41*
cognition 25–6; entrepreneurial 8, 20–1, 23–6

cognitive venture creation model: cross-cultural 24, **25**
collectivism 19; in-group 54; innovation-growth relationship 32, 35–6, *43*, **44**; institutional 57–9, 68, **69**, 73; societal 57–9; UK/US 46
common sense: norms 109
communities: ethnic 103–4
competitive advantage 32
contextual approaches 104
control: internal locus of 18–19; perceived behavioural 82
conventions: and norms within a field 111, **112**
convergent validity analysis: Norway *90*; Turkey *91*
cross-culture: cognitive model of venture creation 24, **25**; entrepreneurial mindset 21; entrepreneurship research 31
cultural dimensions 2, 19
cultural embeddedness 105
cultural practices 33; definition 56; GLOBE study 74n
culture: definition 1, 7; measuring 8, 38, *see also* national culture

Davidsson, P.: and Wiklund, J. 8, 104
deviance 8
discriminant validity analysis: Norway 90–2, *91*; Turkey 90–2, *91*
dissatisfaction 83; hypothesis 80; Norway 83; perspective 83; Turkey 83
dissatisfied entrepreneur 86

economies: regional 104–5
ecosystems 105
education 63
embeddedness: cultural 105
embeddedness theory (Granovetter) 105
empirical research 6–20
entrepreneurial behaviours: uncertainty avoidance 59

117